TRAINING
AND RACING
WITH A
POWER METER

TRAINING AND RACING

WITH A

POWER METER

HUNTER ALLEN AND

ANDREW COGGAN, PH.D.

BOULDER, COLORADO

VeloPress®, a division of Inside Communications, Inc.
1830 North 55th Street
Boulder, Colorado 80301–2700 USA
303/440-0601; fax 303/444-6788; e-mail velopress@insideinc.com

To purchase additional copies of this book or other VeloPress books,
call 800/234-8356 or visit us at www.velopress.com.

Distributed in the United States and Canada by Publishers Group West.

Cover design by Michael Quanci
Cover photo by Don Karle
Interior design by Judith Stagnitto Abbate / Abbate Design
Frontispiece courtesy of Getty Images

Library of Congress Cataloging-in-Publication Data

    Allen, Hunter.
      Racing and training with a power meter / Hunter Allen and Andrew Coggan.
        p. cm.
      Includes index.
      ISBN-13: 978-1-931382-79-3 (pbk. : alk. paper)
      ISBN-10: 1-931382-79-4 (pbk. : alk. paper)
      1. Cycling--Training. 2. Triathlon--Training. I. Coggan, Andrew. II. Title.
    GV1048.A55 2005
    796.6'2--dc22

                                         2005035540

Printed in the United States of America
10 9 8 7 6 5 4

For Kevin Williams,
thank you for opening a whole new world to us.

It's been exciting to actually see my progress quantitatively
for the first time in thirty years of racing.

—PHIL WHITMAN

CONTENTS

FOREWORD

IN 1995, Uli Schoberer loaned me an SRM power meter so I could play with it. At the time I was writing a book called *The Cyclist's Training Bible*, and I wanted to include information on power-based training. I had heard that Greg LeMond was using a power meter in training, but I wasn't sure what it was all about. I rode with the SRM for three months, but I had barely scratched the surface in coming to understand how to use it when it was time to return the unit. With a limited amount of experience, I devoted only three pages in my book to the topic.

In the book's epilogue, however, I suggested that some day there would be a less expensive tool available for measuring power (the SRM, the only power meter available in 1995, retailed at that time for about $4,000). In 1998, two engineers who were also cyclists and had read my book contacted me to ask if we could meet so I could see their new invention—a power meter that would be less than half the price of the SRM. That summer I saw the first prototype of the PowerTap. They gave me one to try out, and I once again began to consider how to train and race with power.

To try to flatten the learning curve a bit, I searched the Internet and all the training books I could find on how to use a power meter—to no avail. There was absolutely nothing on the subject. So in 1999 I decided to put on paper what little I had learned. The resulting 32-page manual explained all I knew about training with power at the time. In the introduction, I commented that readers should view the manual as nothing more than an introduction to the subject, and that they should expect more elaborate and detailed discussions in the near future. Remarkably, it has been six years since I wrote that booklet, and nothing more has been written. Until now.

In your hands you hold the ultimate guide to training with power. It is what I sought several years ago—a thorough examination of training and racing with a power meter. Our knowledge on the subject has come a long way since my first encounter with a power meter ten years ago. *Training and Racing with a Power Meter* presents this wealth of information to you in a clear and concise manner. Finally!

You are in good hands with the authors, Hunter Allen and Andrew Coggan. They are, without a doubt, among the most knowledgeable people on the planet when it comes to power meters. I have read their draft of the book and am impressed with how far they take the same topic that I devoted three pages to in 1995. I haven't come across anything else that even comes close to what you will find on the following pages.

Once you have read this book, I think you will agree with what I wrote ten years ago after playing with an SRM for three months: "[Power meters] are the wave of the future and will change the way cyclists train." The future is now.

Joe Friel
Founder and president of Ultrafit Associates and Training Peaks

ACKNOWLEDGMENTS

W E WOULD LIKE TO THANK the many people that have helped our book become a reality. First and foremost, our respective spouses, Kate and Angie, without whose support and help on the home front this book would still be on the drawing board. Our parents deserve a big thank-you as well for supporting our dreams in cycling and beyond.

Many thanks to: Kevin Williams, Gear Fisher, Donovan Guyot, Dirk Friel, Joe Friel, Jeb Stewart, Todd Roberts, and Jeffrey Hovorka, who all have played a large role in the creation, support, and help with Cycling-Peaks software, which really started it all for us.

Thanks to Leslie Klein and Uli Schoberer at SRM, Siegfried Gerlitzki, Gabi Allard, Matthias Gartner at ergomo, Alan Cote for his help with the Polar power meter, Jesse Bartholomew at PowerTap, and Paul Smeulders for his help and hard work with the Intellicoach software.

A huge round of applause goes out to Sam Callan of USA Cycling, who has supported us from the beginning and played a large role in helping to get the knowledge of training with a power meter out to all the coaches in USA Cycling. Thanks to all the members of the topica.com wattage forum, who have inspired us to think more critically about training with power and without a doubt have contributed greatly to this book. Richard Wharton gets a big pat on the back for his undying support and great help with all the requests we asked of him. Thanks to Richard Sawiris of Wheelbuilder.com for the many hours spent of fiddling, machining, and customizing the PowerTap BMX wheel. Charles Howe also deserves a great big thank-you, for all of his work on the Wattage FAQ, the amazing things he can do in Excel, and for letting us use his variability index and comparison table of the power meters. Thanks to Steve Karpik, Gavin Atkins, Jeremiah Bishop, Dean Golich, James Mattis, Frank Overton, Pam Maino, Sam Krieg, Dave Jordaan, Dave Harris, Dr. David Costill, Dr. Dennis Ryll, Dr. Sami Srour, Joey D'Antoni, Jeff Labauve, Jim Martin, John Verheul, Bill Black, and Dave Martin and Bernie Sanders, who kindly let us incorporate some of their data into our analysis.

Thanks to everyone who helped us along the way, from those who supported us in the feed zones of our races to those who challenged us in the lab to those who helped us develop new ways of implementing our training ideas and theories. Without a doubt, this book is the sum of many contributions, and we thank all of our friends.

Finally, thanks to the team at VeloPress: Renee Jardine, Iris Llewellyn, Dave Trendler, Kathy Streckfus, and Paula Megenhardt. They truly work behind the scenes in the production of every book and deserve a big thank-you!

Hunter Allen and
Andrew Coggan

INTRODUCTION

THIS BOOK is designed to help you learn the step-by-step process of using a power meter for performance improvement. Power meters have been around a relatively long time—indoor power meters, or ergometers, as exercise physiologists call them, first appeared in the late 1800s. The most significant advances in power meter technology have come about in the past ten years, but even today few cyclists know how to use them effectively, and information about them has not been widely available. Up until this point, knowledge about training with power meters has been a closely guarded secret held by top coaches around the world and a few select, elite athletes. This book was written to demystify the tools and techniques used by those people "in the know" and to help a wide range of cyclists tap into cycling's top technology. It is geared toward everyone from the recreational enthusiast all the way to the serious professional cyclist or multisport athlete.

Coauthor Andrew Coggan, an exercise physiologist, first began working with ergometers in the early 1980s in his exercise physiology lab. Creating testing protocols using specific workloads (wattage), he learned about how carbohydrates work in the body and how blood-lactate levels affect an athlete's performance. He eventually authored more than fifty scientific papers that related to the subject. As a very talented cyclist himself, Andrew often took advantage of indoor ergometers to improve his own training and racing—with great success. With the introduction of a less expensive mobile power meter in the late 1990s, he began to collect even more data while racing and training outdoors. From what he had learned in the lab, he knew that this tool would benefit cyclists in training outdoors in the "real world," in quantifying the demands of racing, in improving their pacing, and even in tracking fitness changes. Soon, however, it became clear that this tool would provide many cyclists with more information than they could handle, and so he set out to create a schema of training with a power meter and began teaching the coaches at USA Cycling how to use this schema. Much of that schema is presented here.

Coauthor Hunter Allen, an elite-level cycling coach and a former professional cyclist, is the owner of the Peaks Coaching Group. He has been coaching endurance athletes since 1995. Once his "early adopter" athletes began to question him on how to effectively use a power meter in the late 1990s, he realized he needed to buy one and start training on it so that he could begin to apply his own training principles and philosophy to using wattage. In 2003, he codeveloped CyclingPeaks software with Andrew Coggan and Kevin Williams. Their goal was to help cyclists with a power meter to easily gain access to the information downloaded from it. Hunter Allen is now known as one of the world's experts in training and coaching with a power meter, having analyzed thousands of power meter files and successfully coached hundreds of athletes using power meters.

From this experience, it can be said with confidence that power meters are here to stay. The number of serious cyclists using them is bound to increase with every racing season. Professional cyclists are beginning to see the value of using them not only in training but also in races as big as the Tour de France. As they gain experience with the technology, they are realizing that a power meter can make the difference between a mediocre season and a successful one. In Chapter 1, you will discover the advantages of using a power meter in order to help you determine whether training with this new tool is right for you. There are many reasons to use a power meter, and taking this step may be just what you need to reach the next level of training and fitness.

Chapter 2 considers the power meter equipment and software itself. What is a power meter, and how does it work? What are the main features to look for in purchasing a power meter? There are several types of power meters on the market today, along with software to interpret the data that they collect. Chapter 2 provides an overview of these products and reviews the pros and cons of each one. If you haven't already purchased a power meter, this analysis should help you to select the one that is best for you.

Chapter 3 will teach you how to find your functional threshold power and discuss the different training levels that you can reach with the aid of a power meter, and Chapter 4 will show you how to use a power meter to identify your cycling strengths and weaknesses.

Some sample workouts are provided in Chapter 5, based on wattage, to get you started with using your power meter in time trials, hill climbs, interval training, and so on, and in Chapter 6 you will learn how to interpret the data from your power meter. There are plenty of sample graphs here to show you exactly what you can learn from using your power meter software. Chapter 7 continues this theme, explaining how to use analysis tools to look deeper into your data. Chapter 8 will help you to set up a training plan, and in Chapter 9, we explain what the data will mean over a longer period of time. For example, you can use the power meter data to track long-term changes. Again, ample illustrations offer concrete examples of how to use your power meter software in reaching your goals. Chapter 10 goes into the specifics of using the power meter in racing to reach your peak performance. Finally, Chapter 11 summarizes the main points to help you to put it all together and inspire you to reach your goals.

A power meter is probably the best tool ever developed for a cyclist looking to reach new thresholds of achievement.

At the end of the book there is a Glossary to will help you to keep track of new terms, and the appendixes provide more sample workouts and additional resources.

This book is not a training manual—it will not explain the nuances of peaking or go into the details of exercise physiology. There are already many great books on the market today that go over these concepts in detail. The goal of this book is to teach cyclists at every level of ability that training and racing with a power meter is not hard to do. You do not need a Ph.D. in exercise physiology to understand what the data mean. For that matter, you do not have to be an elite racer to benefit from the technology the power meter offers. If you are a cyclist with an interest in improving your cycling, this book is for you, whether you have a power meter already or you are just considering purchasing one. Any athlete can benefit from being challenged to think critically about training and coming to a better understanding of the essential components that comprise peak performance.

A power meter is probably the best tool ever developed for a cyclist looking to reach new thresholds of achievement. By recording a second-by-second diary of your ride, a power meter can help you uncover hidden areas for improvement that never would have come to light through the use of a heart rate monitor or simple cyclometer. The ability to record your ride and save that information for later download and analysis on your computer is the key to the power meter's usefulness. Far from being just another gadget on your bike, the power meter is a tool that can track your improvements over any period of time. Would you like to compare this week's hill repeats to last week's? How does your best twenty minutes of effort from this year compare to your best twenty minutes from two years ago? Do you want to see if your average cadence has changed over the past three years? With a power meter and a few clicks of the mouse, you will be able to begin answering questions like these. We have entered the age of computer-aided scientific training, with microcomputers attached to our bicycles to record every second of every ride, and with this technology we are able to learn more than ever about what "makes us tick."

AT CYCLING EVENTS and triathlons, bike shops, velodromes, and anywhere else cyclists and multisport athletes gather, the power meter has become the topic that everyone wants to discuss. The consensus is the same: For cyclists, training with power is the next big step in achieving peak performance.

Through coaching and exercise physiology, we have seen the benefits of training with a power meter firsthand. Using a power meter can take your training to a new level and allow you to fine-tune your training program. Simply put, the power meter allows you to quantitatively track your fitness changes, more easily define your weaknesses, and then refocus your training based on those weak areas. It can be an impetus for change in your training program.

Even riders who have been racing for many years and think they have little left to learn are likely to benefit from a power meter, and this includes masters riders who have been cycling for twenty or thirty years. Phil Whitman, for example, a masters 60+ rider, had seen many advances in cycling over the years and was hesitant to adopt the power meter, thinking it unlikely that it could help him improve further. However, he gave it a try and found that his power meter did help him improve. "I have seen all the little 'gadgets' that have promised improvement, and most have come and gone," he said, "so it took some convincing to purchase a power meter." Phil has used it for a full season and says he doesn't need anymore convincing. "I know it really helped me this year in focusing my training for specific intervals, pacing in breakaways, and also in time trials, plus it's been exciting to actually see my progress quantitatively for the first time in thirty years of racing."

By installing a power meter on your bicycle, you will gain access to more data than you can now imagine. True, the benefits accrue only when you know what to do with all that data and how to interpret it using the power meter software. This has been a problem for many power meter users: Seeing the graphs of all the data from your ride may seem daunting at first. Chapters 6 and 7 are devoted to explaining how to extract the information necessary to focus your training and track improvements. And you also will need to understand how to implement new wattage-based workouts in your training regimen and when and how to make changes in your training. Chapters 3, 4, 5, and 8 will teach you how to train effectively with a power meter and use this new technology to achieve your performance goals. By learning some simple steps, you will be well on your way to training with a power meter effectively and expertly. You take this fancy bike computer and turn it from an expensive toy into a tool to be utilized completely. Truly, this is what a power meter is: a tool to be used to improve performance.

Here is an overview of the benefits that you can look forward to realizing when you take the simple steps to improvement that are presented in this book. The benefits are many, but they generally fall into four main categories. These can be expressed in four brief phrases that sum up what you can do when you know how to use the power meter technology properly:

Know Thyself: A power meter supplies a great deal of information about your ride, and this data will enable you to identify your strengths and weaknesses.

Work Together: A power meter communicates this detailed information to your coach and teammates in a way that will enable everyone to work together more efficiently.

Focus Your Training: With this information at your fingertips, and better coaching and teamwork, you can better identify training goals and methods.

Achieve Peak Performance: With better information, better communication, and better training, you will be positioned to do your best in cycling.

As you can see, these four areas are interconnected. They build on each other. Without the data that the power meter provides, analysis of your ride, communication with your coach and teammates, and development of a training plan all remain limited to guesswork. With the data as a basis, you can move to a whole new level in all these areas.

However, let the old-timers be warned: If you do not use a cyclo-computer or heart rate monitor now, or if you are unwilling to change the way you train, then training with a power meter might not be for you. It will take some time and effort on your part, using your computer and adjusting your training program, but in the end, if you are serious about training and going faster, then a power meter will help you reach your peak performance.

Know Thyself

Record Your Effort

Power meters record massive amounts of data that you can download after your ride. By literally creating a second-by-second diary of your ride, you will be able to see exactly how strong you were as you "stomped" up that hill, whether you should have eaten more snacks or rehydrated yourself better along the way, whether you had the right gearing on your bicycle when you hit that "wall" 50 miles into the ride, and so on.

A power meter records your effort from both a cardiovascular viewpoint (heart rate) and a muscular viewpoint (watts). The watts that you are able to produce are what drive the bicycle forward. Your heart rate is your body's response to the pressure you are exerting on the pedals, and by being able to quantify the exact training "dose," you will be able to better understand all the other aspects of your training and racing. You will know exactly how much time you've spent in your wattage training zone while riding. You will be able to highlight the areas of your ride where you need the most practice—concentrating, for example, on intervals, hills, sprints, or attacks during a race. By reviewing your data after the fact, you will know with certainty whether you completed your training goals or need to revise your training methods.

Add Meaning to Heart Rate Monitoring

Solely monitoring your heart rate does not tell you how much you are improving on your bicycle; it just tells you how fast your heart is pumping. Your heart rate may be affected by factors that have little to do with actual performance, however, and using only a heart monitor could easily trick you into believing a false conclusion about your fitness, mislead you about your performance, or even undermine your confidence.

Your heart rate is influenced by your level of hydration, by the air temperature, by your core temperature, by how well you slept the night before, by the level of stress in your life, and other factors. The rate at which your heart can pump depends on so many factors that sometimes you really are better off not knowing your heart rate when training or competing, and going on your perceived exertion instead. Although heart rate monitors can be valid and useful tools—athletes have been training with them now for more than twenty years, and certainly this has improved the level of fitness of many athletes—heart rate is just one small piece of the puzzle. How fast your heart is pumping is a response to a stimulus, whether that is you being chased by a bear in the woods, your level of anxiety before a big presentation at work, or the exertion required to push harder on the pedals as you try to latch onto the tail end of that winning breakaway. Think of your heart rate as being similar to the rpm dial (tachometer) in your car. The more you step on the gas pedal, the higher the rpms go.

How does a power meter add more meaning to heart rate data and thus allow you to improve your performance? A power meter measures your true rate of work (power); that is, how hard you are pushing on the pedals. Power is the amount of horsepower your car engine uses to cruise at 60 mph. You are the engine for your bike, and a power meter tells you how much power you are exerting in the form of watts. By comparing your heart rate response to the power output, you may find there are days when your heart rate is telling you to slow down, but your power meter is telling you to speed up because you are not making those muscles work hard enough to really create a training stimulus. Your heart is a muscle, just like any other muscle in the body, and it gets tired too. This means that if, for example, you've been training hard for seven days, your heart rate may be lower than normal for a given wattage while you are riding. If your heart rate is normally 165 bpm when you are riding at 280 watts, then after seven days of hard training it may only be 158 bpm at 280 watts. This does not necessarily mean that you should not train that day, however, because clearly you are still getting training benefits. It's highly probable that you would still be able to do the same amount of watts, or nearly the same amount, as when you were fresh at the beginning of the block. Your wattage will be the key to knowing when you truly need a rest day.

Track Fitness Changes

Gaining the ability to track change in performance is possibly one of the most exciting reasons to train with a power meter: Over time, you will know with certainty whether your fitness is improving and by exactly how much. Is all this hard work really worth it? Are you really getting faster? Will doing all those blasted intervals really help you get over that last hill in the Tuesday night group ride with the leaders?

Since you will be able to download your information directly after your ride, you will easily be able to see the differences between today's effort and the same ride last week, and the week before, and so on. Since your fitness changes continually, and you will have different strengths and weaknesses from one month to the next, it's essential to see on a regular basis exactly where you are in the bigger picture of the season. With power data, you will be able to find out whether your lactate threshold is improving, for example, or whether you are making improvements in your anaerobic capacity, and then make appropriate changes to your training regime. You will be able to look back on previous data and see how long it has taken for you to achieve a new level of fitness, which will enable you to set realistic goals. On the other side of the coin, it is also important to know when to take a rest to avoid overtraining, and this is also one of the great uses of a power meter. By tracking the overall training stress, using a method such as Training Stress Score (TSS), which will be discussed in more detail in Chapter 10, you will be able to make more accurate decisions about your training load.

Analyze Your Race

Using your power meter during a race and analyzing the data later is a great way to gain an objective view of your race performance. You can use the data to examine the demands of the racecourse and to determine what would have been needed to finish well. In fact, often your best data will come from races, as you always go harder in races than in routine training.

Sometimes the most interesting data you can gather will come from a race in which you were "dropped." You can review the power meter file, much in the same way that a football coach would review a videotape of a game, to see what changes are necessary to avoid similar problems in the future. During a very hard stage in the Gila Stage Race, for example, one of Hunter's athletes was dropped on a particularly hard part of the climb. In reviewing the post-race data, Hunter was able to pinpoint other races in which Steve had been dropped from the lead pack and then compare these very critical times to each other. Whenever Steve had to pedal at a slower cadence than 70 rpm while producing watts at his threshold for more than five minutes, he was dropped. There were also many cases in which Steve was able to stay with the same athletes at and above his threshold wattage as long as his cadence was over 95 rpm. As a result, they changed the gearing on his bike so that the largest cog had twenty-seven teeth instead of the standard twenty-three. This allowed him to spin at a cadence of over 100 rpm on the steepest climbs, thus maximizing his ability to produce watts based on his body's physiology. Steve benefited immensely from this change, and for the rest of the year he was able to stay in the front group of riders.

> *Often your best data will come from races, as you always go harder in races than in routine training.*

A power meter can also help you determine when you are using too much energy in a race. Could it be that you are pedaling too much? From the thousands of power meter files that Hunter has analyzed, he has found that the racers who consistently win are also the ones who do not pedal as much as the rest of the peloton. How can this be? Well, the best racers usually just sit in the pack, watch, wait, and hide from the wind, conserving their energy. These aren't the guys who are sitting out front driving the peloton down the road for hours on end. The winners are the ones who pedal less than the rest, but when they do pedal, watch out, because they pedal harder than the rest of the pack.

In this same vein, a power meter can tell you when you "burned a match"—that is, performed a very hard effort (you only have so many matches in your "matchbook" to burn)—or whether you used too much energy in parts of the race that were not decisive. Maybe you made a tactical error in a race but didn't realize it. By analyzing the data, you can replay the race in your head, while viewing your power meter file, and understand exactly what it would have taken to make the winning break or the decisive split. If you fell apart, then this information can be used to better focus your training.

Pinpoint Your Strengths and Weaknesses

Ultimately, armed with this new information, some simple testing protocols, and experience with your power meter in a variety of races and training rides, you will begin to get a clearer picture of your specific strengths and weaknesses. Before the advent of power meters, cyclists had to guess at their strengths and weaknesses, and many times these guesses were wrong. Guessing can hurt your ability to improve. With a power meter, you will be able to find out whether you need to work on changing the gearing for your bike or on building your muscular strength.

Learning what your weaknesses are may not always be pleasant. Finding out that you are a Category I racer in your best 5-minute power, but a Category IV racer in your best 20-minute power, may be exciting for a track racer, but it would be a bit of a disappointment for a road racer desperately trying to improve. However, you cannot improve until you know what your weaknesses are. Each racer is different, and each racer has different goals. Just knowing your strengths and weaknesses will make a big difference in the focus of your training. What will happen if you have to do 105 percent of your threshold power for more than three minutes? Will your lungs feel like they're about to explode, or will this be easy for you? With a power meter, you can analyze your performance and training to find out what your natural talents are and where you need improvement.

Work Together

Improve Interaction with Your Coach

Coaches love power meters and the information that they provide. Once a coach starts using a power meter to work with athletes, he or she will almost never go back to the old way of doing things. The information from the power meter is clear and concise, and it is right there on the computer screen—an objective set of facts that can't be denied. That is why most coaches who have worked with power meters will work hard to persuade all their cyclists to use them. Plain and simple, using a power meter brings you and your coach closer together.

Jeb Stewart, head coach for the Peaks Coaching Group, put it this way: "Coaching with a power meter allows me to know for certain if my athletes are doing their training schedules correctly, and then I can immediately see their response to the training. It gives me and the athlete the opportunity to talk more in depth about how each training session went and how we can improve, and also to clearly see the results of our hard work."

With the data that you collect with your power meter, your coach will discover things about you and your riding abilities, both positive and negative, that he or she would not otherwise have been able to figure out even by racing with you. Your coach can then use this data to improve your training plan. He or she will be able to react more quickly to changes in your fitness and will be able to make adjustments to your plan accordingly.

One of the primary ways a power meter aids the coach/athlete relationship is that it improves communication between the two parties. With a power meter, there can be no dispute over what is going on with your fitness or whether you are on the right path. Instead, where you are with your training, and whether you are doing the workouts correctly or not, will be fairly clearcut. Your coach will be able to see instantly what you are doing in races and training rides, and he or she will be able to make more useful suggestions for further improvements.

A power meter also should increase your accountability—that feeling you get of having to be "responsible" to someone for your training. You will know that your coach is going to see that you only did five out

> *"Coaching with a power meter allows me to know for certain if my athletes are doing their training schedules correctly, and then I can immediately see their response to the training. It gives me and the athlete the opportunity to talk more in depth about how each training session went and how we can improve, and also to clearly see the results of our hard work."*
>
> *Jeb Stewart, head coach for the Peaks Coaching Group*

of the ten prescribed efforts as soon as you download and e-mail your weekly data. This can also be a reason not to have a power meter: It's the equivalent of having your coach with you on every ride. A power meter doesn't lie, and sometimes, the truth can be tough to face!

When Sam Krieg started using a power meter, he found the added accountability made a real difference. He started working with a coach in his second season of training with power. Later, he said, "Combining both [coaching and power] made my training super focused and my racing the perfect test to see if what we were training created results. Several times during my pre-season training, I would see my workouts on my e-mail and think, 'I can't finish that.' I would start the workout saying to myself, 'When I blow up, I'll just e-mail my coach the power file and let him know I tried but just couldn't pull it off.'" However, most of the time the opposite would happen: "Minute by minute the intervals would come and go and somehow I would still be turning the pedals," Sam said. "More times than not I survived all the intervals in complete disbelief of what I had just accomplished."

One workout in particular stood out. "My coach prescribed doing 50 minutes at my threshold power, with several cadence changes and power spikes," Sam said. "I didn't think I could survive 20 minutes of this workout, much less 50. Slowly the seconds on the computer just ticked away. In the back of my mind, I knew I would have to e-mail this power file to my coach, so I figured that as long as I could sustain the prescribed wattage, I would continue. Several times during the interval I didn't think I could make it another minute, but my power and heart rate were stable so I pedaled on. Fifty minutes later I finished. I had a new 50-minute peak power, and I had mentally grown more in one workout than I had over the past three months."

This mental and physical strength translated into racing strengths throughout the season. "In one early-season race, I made the selection early on, only to get dropped out the back door of an echelon 20 minutes later. I just wanted to kick myself. Struggling to regain some composure, I was able to regroup mentally and reframe the remainder of the race into a 30-minute time trial with threshold wattage as my goal. As demented as it sounds, I was racing for a great power file, not against the racers who were up the road. I struggled for the next half hour just like I did in my winter workouts, racing my power meter minute to minute." As it turned out, Sam caught the break and managed to finish at the front of the remaining riders. "Without having to e-mail that file I would have stopped at my car and called it a day," he said. Sam carried this new level of persistence into the rest of the season: "My placing in races was not half as telling as the power files I had created during those efforts," he said. "I had won on days when I was actually weak and struggled on my strongest days of the year. It's pretty cool to have bad days that are actually great days."

Improve Interaction with Teammates

The use of a power meter can have a profound impact on how well a cycling team works together. Many times in teams, it is not always clear who should be the leader; sometimes, it's hard to know exactly who is riding the best. When all the team members use a power meter, and with regular testing, coach and riders alike will know exactly who is riding well enough to be a protected leader and who ought to be a "worker bee" for the race.

While in a race, a very good rider will be able to teach by example exactly where to ride in the peloton to save the most energy. With a power meter, the leader will know just how many watts were needed to make it over the climb in the lead group. In addition, power meters can build confidence in the team when the data show that team members have the physical ability to win. It's right there on the graph if, say, three out of five riders have the necessary fitness to win the race, and having that level of certainty can really help a team to success.

Focus Your Training

Gain Motivation to Work Harder

As a motivator, a power meter can be very effective. For example, if you are doing a five-minute effort, and you see your average watts drop near the end of the effort, you'll pick it up just another notch in order to achieve your five-minute wattage goal. As long as the goals are set realistically—that is, they are challenging yet achievable—when you are out there training hard and pushing it to the absolute max, seeing those wattage numbers on your power meter can help you dig for just a tiny bit extra. And in the world of a sport that can be won or lost by less than a fraction of a second, that tiny bit extra is significant.

Every athlete strives to eliminate guesswork and wasted time, and in this day and age, it seems that most athletes are too busy to train as much as they'd like. That's why every training minute must be optimized. If you are strapped for time, having a power meter and sticking to the letter of your workout will help you gain a higher fitness level more rapidly, with fewer wasted junk miles and less of your precious time.

Improve Your Position and Aerodynamics

Your body position is the single greatest factor determining your speed while riding at a specific power output. Why risk the disadvantage of riding with a poor position when you can measure your aerodynamics and discover your fastest position? With some simple tests using a power meter, you can figure out how your current position on the bike is impacting your overall speed, and exactly how to change it in order to produce the most watts and the least amount of aerodynamic drag. With the most recent wind tunnel testing of bicycle frames, wheels, rider positioning, and other factors, it has been found that with improvements in positioning and equipment a rider should be able to pedal at approximately 30 watts less to maintain a given speed. In other words, just by optimizing your position and equipment, you may be able to gain 30 watts of power. This represents a more significant gain than most cyclists see in an entire year of training.

Pace Your Efforts

When you are out training, racing, or just riding around enjoying the countryside, a power meter allows you to pace your effort better in order to achieve your goal for that ride. Whether that's simply to finish the ride or to achieve a particular physiological stimulus, using a power meter as a pacing tool can help you to conserve and to expend energy when necessary.

You can use a power meter on all of your long rides—on ultra-endurance rides, in interval workouts, on hill climbs and time trials (TTs), and so on—in order to get the most out of your effort and avoid overdoing it. Once you know your functional threshold wattage (which you'll learn how to determine in Chapter 3), you can hold to it like glue in a time trial or hill climb so that you will know that you went as hard as you could possibly go. Using a power meter for pacing in time trials is an especially good use of the technology. It can give you a "ceiling" to stay beneath to prevent you from overexerting yourself in the first five minutes of the race. During a race, knowing your wattage helps you to focus, providing a "carrot" when the going gets tough and you are pushing right on the edge of your ability. In mass-start races, pacing is equally important. You can use it in the field in order to conserve your energy until later in the race, and you can use it to judge whether the pace is right for you to attempt a breakaway or to figure out what it will take to win the race.

Randy Weintraub, a highly competitive triathlete, was concerned about the lack of hills near his home and training grounds. His goal was to complete the Ironman Lake Placid in less than ten hours. The Lake Placid race is one of the toughest of the Ironman distance races. The bike course is very hilly and includes a substantial two-mile climb. Randy needed to figure out exactly how many hills he would have to ride up, and how long each one was, and then go back and train for those race-course demands at home in Long Island, New York.

Randy went up to Lake Placid and rode the entire bike course at very close to his goal wattage and recorded it with his power meter. First, he wanted to assess whether his goal wattage was actually correct. He had never done this triathlon before and was unsure whether he could maintain that wattage for the entire 112 miles and then still have something left for the 26.2-mile run. After his ride, he downloaded the information and found that he indeed had averaged his target wattage. Based on his level of fatigue at the end of the bike leg, he surmised that he had enough energy left over for his run. Then, using old-fashioned pencil and paper, Randy simply counted the number of hills that took more than two minutes to complete along the course. With this information, he began to seek out new training routes near his home that would mimic that course as closely as possible. When he did not have a long enough hill, he would simply ride into the wind to simulate a longer climb. He also programmed the number of hill repeats, along with the wattages he would need to reach in order to achieve a peak performance, into his indoor trainer.

Create a Mobile Testing Lab

A power meter allows you to test your fitness on a monthly basis so you can quantitatively see where you have made improvements and where you still need work. For serious racers, using a power meter in this way can even eliminate some of the costly testing that formerly was possible only at a lab, since they now have the mobile equipment installed right on their bikes.

A power meter measures changes in your ability to move the bicycle down the road. It tells you how much force you are putting into the pedals, not just how hard your cardiovascular system is working. By testing your skills regularly, you will better understand your potential for improvement, and you can avoid overtraining. We all undergo changes in our fitness in different areas. Some athletes improve more quickly with shorter efforts, whereas others improve more quickly with longer efforts. With proper periodic testing, you can see exactly which physiological systems are improving and then determine whether it is the right time to focus on a particular area of training.

As Andrew often tells the athletes he consults: Training is testing; testing is training. Make every training session a peak performance.

Enhance Indoor Training

With a power meter, you can use your indoor trainer to the fullest extent. One of the first things you will learn about using a power meter on the road is that your wattage will have a high degree of variability. Your wattage fluctuates on a moment-by-moment basis depending on the conditions, and sometimes this is not the best way to train. On an indoor trainer, without the outside influences of wind, hills, dogs, and so on, you can focus your intervals in exact wattage zones for optimal improvement.

In addition, indoor training gains new meaning when you can compare your intensity to road efforts. Indoor training also becomes more interesting, as now you have a new goal and focus to your workout. With the advent of the latest computerized indoor trainers, a cyclist with a power meter can even go out and ride a particular racecourse, come back, and download this data into the trainer to re-create this exact ride indoors. Power meter data from indoor training sessions are also "cleaner" than road efforts, as the massive wattage fluctuations caused by changes in terrain, riding with others, and the variable nature of pedaling frequency are gone from the power file, making it easier to analyze the periods of effort.

Coordinate Your Sports
Nutrition for Best Performance

The entire time you are riding your bike, you are expending energy based upon how much work you are doing. Knowing how much work (in kilojoules) you are doing while riding is important. If you know your kilojoule expenditure, you can easily estimate your kilocalorie usage (almost a one-to-one ratio), and this can help you determine when you need to consume additional calories or cut back.

Your production of watts will be drastically reduced if you allow your energy stores to become depleted, so making sure that you are eating often enough, and getting the right number of calories, can be a very important factor in the quality of your workout or race. By knowing your energy expenditure on the bike, you can more accurately plan your postexercise meals to the exact kilocalorie. This especially helps if you are trying to balance your energy intake with your energy expenditure to maintain bodyweight during heavy training.

By eating to replenish your expended glycogen fuel stores and possibly packing in more, you should be able to recover faster from training sessions and be ready to train harder, sooner. Take, for example, Sami Srour. A highly competitive recreational cyclist, he had been planning for many months to ride a local metric century with his club. However, in each of his practice runs, he ran out of energy toward the end of the ride and had to stop at a convenience store to refuel. This routine impacted his energy levels for the next two days, and consequently, the quality of his training for those days suffered. Using his two practice runs, however, his total expenditure of energy in kilojoules for the entire ride could be calculated. Then, dividing the ride into segments and determining the number of kilojoules used in each segment, made it possible to set goals for caloric intake in each segment. Sami was able to determine when to eat, and how much to eat, during each section of the ride, and also how much electrolyte replacement drink to use. With this new information, a post-ride recovery protocol could be created, giving him the correct levels of carbohydrates, proteins, and fats to maximize his recovery, so he would be ready and able to complete his next day of training.

Achieve Peak Performance

With all of the benefits that a power meter offers—greater knowledge about your riding, improved communication with your coach and teammates, and better focus for your training efforts—there is no reason why you should not be able to reach your fitness goals and achieve your peak performance at events.

Every top cycling performance in recent years has been aided by the use of power meter training technology. In everything from the Tour de France to hour records, track records, human-powered vehicle (HPV)

What Is a Kilojoule?

Almost all current power meters report the amount of work you have performed in joules, in addition to measuring and recording your power in watts. Joules (J) and kilojoules (kJ) are therefore a measure of energy expenditure, or work performed. In the United States, however, this is usually measured in kilocalories, or Calories (1 kilocalorie, or large Calorie [with a capital "C"] is equal to 1,000 small calories [lowercase]).

By definition, there are 4.184 kJ per Calorie, so at first glance it would seem that to determine your energy expenditure using power meter data, you would simply divide your total work in kJ by 4.184. However, this is not correct because power meters measure external work production, not the amount of energy needed to perform that work. Most of the energy expended during cycling is actually converted into "waste" heat that must be dissipated to the environment, with only a portion available to actually turn the pedals. The relationship between work performed and energy expended depends upon your thermodynamic efficiency (i.e., your ability to process food and convert it into energy) when cycling, which, for most trained cyclists, is on the order of 20–25 percent.

Thus, using a power meter to estimate your energy expenditure (in Calories, or kilocalories) from the amount of work performed, you would need to first divide your total work in kilojoules by 4.184, but then multiply this result by either 4 (if efficiency is at 25 percent) or 5 (if efficiency is at 20 percent). These conversion factors tend to simply cancel one another out, such that you can also take the value for the total work performed in kJ as an estimate of your energy expenditure in kilocalories (or Calories). Although the exact relationship between kJ and kcal is not one to one, it probably is not worth worrying about any error this assumption creates, since an individual's efficiency can only be readily determined in a laboratory setting, and can vary depending upon the intensity and duration of training, environmental conditions, and other factors.

records, mountain bike racing, and even BMX racing, the best cyclists have used power meters not only to determine the exact physiological demands of hard races but also to determine exactly how powerful they are as cyclists and how they stack up against their peers. Controlling training with the latest in computer-aided scientific training tools used to be achievable only by the top cyclists in the world with the biggest budgets. Now almost any serious cyclist can gain access to the same data that the pros have and execute their workouts to the same exacting precision.

Training with a power meter is about results. Simply training with a power meter is not going to bring you success. It's not the power meter that does the work: You must do the work. If you want to go faster on your bike by just throwing money at your bike, then go get a nicer set of aero wheels, a lighter frame, or the latest carbon-fiber widget. But eventually, you are going to have to push harder on those pedals if you are going to ride faster. Training with a power meter is worthwhile only if you are willing to work at it.

> *The best cyclists have used power meters not only to determine the exact physiological demands of hard races but also to determine exactly how powerful they are as cyclists and how they stack up against their peers.*

If the information you have about your training is limited, then you are limiting your ability to improve, and you are ultimately limiting your success. Using a power meter may seem intimidating at first, and learning the details of testing and training with it may entail some frustration, but give yourself some time, and soon you'll be on the way to training more effectively and efficiently using a power meter. If your training and cycling are to change (that is, improve), then you must be willing to change first. This book is about how to change your thinking about training and racing and how to gain a clear understanding of what needs to be done in order to achieve your goals.

2

POWER TOOLS

O NCE THEY HEAR about the power meter and its benefits—and see their competitors racing and training with power meters on their bikes—the first thing that most cyclists and triathletes ask is this: Which one is right for me? Other questions quickly follow:

- Which type of power meter technology is the best?
- What about price? Which model is most cost-effective?
- Do all the models have the same features and ease of use?
- Which type has the fewest problems?
- Does the athlete have to have a degree in computer science or exercise physiology to understand what all those graphs mean?

Let's briefly explore the power meters on the market today and the pros and cons of each. For a checklist of features by company, see Table 2.1 later in the chapter.

The Hardware: Four Different Approaches

The power meter hardware is currently very different from one company to the next. That is because the four companies currently offering power meters all take very different approaches to the technology. Basically, the four methods have resulted in: (1) a crank-based integrated system; (2) a hub-based integrated system; (3) a chainstay-mounted sensor; and (4) a bottom bracket sensor.

SRM

SRM Crank

The first commercial power meter—and the one that started this technological revolution in cycling—was made by the SRM company (Schoberer Rad Messtechnik) in Germany. Ulrich Schoberer, a medical engineer, brought the measurement of wattage to the world in a product that can be used by the masses.

Schoberer developed his first prototype in the 1980s by taking old cranks, cutting off the "spyder" portion (the part between the right crank arm and the chainrings themselves), and then replacing it with a power meter, about the size of a small saucer plate, that consisted of a series of embedded strain gages. The front chainrings were then mounted onto this plate to allow for the measurement of power as the rider applied force to the pedals. As this force is transmitted, there is a twisting, or torsion, within the plate; the strain gauges measure the amount of twisting from normal. This torsion information is then sent to a microprocessor in the bicycle computer and converted into wattage. Uli Schoberer spent the ensuing years working on his ideas and building newer, more advanced models. The first models that he put on the market were incredibly pricey, reaching upward of $10,000 per unit. Greg LeMond was one of the first Americans to use a power meter. Already known for forging his cycling successes partly through the adoption of new technology, he again paved the way here.

The SRM crank power meter, called the SRM Training System, which includes a crank and chainrings, has become the "gold standard" by which all other power meters are measured. It certainly has been around the longest, has been updated and improved the most, and tends to be one of the most reliable of the power meters. Measuring wattage in the spyder of the crank is both convenient and logical, as the data incorporate the force from both legs and measures it in the place where it occurs, right at the crank. Since the power meter is built as one unit with the crank itself, it is integrated into the bike, becoming just part of the equipment. It is also very weatherproof. SRM has models for road riders, track riders, and mountain bikers and also offers a scientific version for the lab. The company also produces indoor spin bikes for use in fitness and performance centers. The computer controller, called the power control, is rechargeable and mounts in front of the handlebar at handlebar height. The rider can view all the necessary data while riding, including wattage, heart rate, cadence, elapsed time, and clock time, all on the same screen. This allows the rider to keep track of his or her effort while riding and pace the effort accordingly. The power control can be customized to a certain degree—for example, you set your own recording rates for later download, with intervals of up to 60 seconds between saved data points, and you can choose among different options for the display.

Each time the rider uses the SRM, he must create a "zero-offset," or "zero-point," to assure that the wattage will be zero when there is no load on the power meter. This is a five-second procedure and can be done throughout the ride with no detrimental effects to your data. Since the SRM uses a strain gauge to measure torsion, the readings can be susceptible to changes in temperature, so if you are riding and all of a sudden the temperature changes drastically and your watts appear to be different from what you would normally expect, then the SRM might need to be "re-zeroed." Since the metal of the crank will change in size with changes in temperature, it is important that you achieve a zero-offset when the crank is at the same temperature as the ambient outside temperature. This only tends to be a problem when a bike goes from 70 degrees Fahrenheit while parked inside a house to a much colder 40–50 degrees outside. It is a good idea to park your bike outside for ten or fifteen minutes before beginning your ride so that the metal of the crank and the strain gauges can adjust to the correct temperature.

The SRM crank power has been around the longest, has been updated and improved the most, and tends to be one of the most reliable of the power meters.

The SRM computer is one of the best-designed models available, in large part due to twenty years of development. The ability to set your own intervals increases the amount of data that can be recorded, and the SRM has a very user-friendly method of marking these intervals while riding. (When you start [and stop] an interval, you press the "set" button on the power control, and this creates a small "time stamp" in the data, so that when you download the data to your PC, you will see immediately where the interval started and stopped). The handlebar mount of the SRM is one of the best and most secure; the screen is easy to read but unobtrusive, and because it is positioned flush and just in front of the handlebar, it is somewhat protected from damage in crashes. The rider can also easily review data while riding and thus determine when it is time to head home and when it is time to do one more hill repeat.

One of the disadvantages to the SRM is its cost. It is currently the most expensive of the power meters. Another drawback is that the battery inside the power meter itself must be replaced by the factory when it is dead, and this requires some downtime for the user while you mail it in and wait for it to be returned. SRM has opened a U.S. service center in Colorado Springs, so the turnaround time has improved.

Another problem that occurs with the SRM is that over time, as the strain gauges age, the watt measurements are susceptible to "drift." If this occurs, the SRM may need to be recalibrated to ensure its accuracy. The user can do this at home by following the recalibration procedure laid out in the SRM manual, but this can be confusing for the first timer. The SRM also does not output torque in the controller for download. This is unfortunate because the meter has the best ability to receive the correct torque of any model on the market. With torque for download, cyclists and coaches could analyze how torque loads might be affected by different types of cycling efforts.

PowerTap

The PowerTap is a complete rear hub for the back wheel of a bicycle that houses a power meter. The hub contains a "torque tube" with strain gauges similar to those used by the SRM. These strain gauges measure the torsion inside the hub as it twists from the load that is applied to the pedals by the rider. The bicycle chain wraps around the cogs on the hub and, as it moves, causes small twists in the hub itself. This torque is measured and then converted into wattage at the PowerTap computer.

The wattage that is measured in the PowerTap is the wattage that is actually getting to the road, as it has to go through the drivetrain from the crank. This causes the wattage to be about 5–10 watts lower than what would be measured by the SRM at the crank. The PowerTap takes measurements sixty times per second, averages these figures over a 1-second time period, and then records the data at intervals as short as 1.26 seconds.

The PowerTap was created back in 1997 by a company called Etune, which consisted of a group of four hardworking partners with a vision for the future of cycling technology. Unfortunately, like so many visionaries who start small companies, they were not able to keep the cash flow going while they dealt with the normal issues that come up when developing hardware of this nature. Graber Products Group, now known as the Saris Cycling Group, bought the company in 2001 and has since poured thousands of development dollars into improving the unit. The computer that mounts on the handlebar (PowerTap Pro model) has been redesigned with more memory, more functions, and upgradable firmware. The harness also has been upgraded in order to include real cadence (the older harness only allowed the computer to estimate cadence based on the pattern of torque pulses within the hub). The release of the new SL hub in 2004 brought PowerTap into a leading role in the marketplace in a big way. Previous complaints about weight and durability in weather are now a thing of the past, and bike geeks will surely like the appearance of the PowerTap units, which incorporate carbon-fiber bits.

One disadvantage of using the PowerTap is that you are locked into the wheel that the hub is laced to. If you want to use your super trick wheels for racing, you'll need to get an additional hub for racing and then keep your standard wheel for training. PowerTap has yet to come out with a disc-wheel solution for time trialing, although many riders use CH Aero Wheel covers over their PowerTap wheel to achieve aerodynamics similar to that of a disc wheel. Though mountain bikers can use a hub to gather important data, the PowerTap is not yet compatible with disc brakes. Track riders are also out of luck at this point; although some prototype track hubs are in use, it is unlikely they will see production because the market for them is limited.

PowerTap SL Hub

There is also a slight problem with the way that the PowerTap computer records the data for download after your ride. Since the computer records at 1.26-second time intervals, the power reading may fluctuate up to 40 watts (20 watts above and below the true wattage level) from second to second. Though it is possible for such fluctuations to reflect actual changes in power output, when this occurs with the PowerTap it is more likely to be the computer that is creating the problem. Once the data are downloaded, the fluctuations are reflected in the graphs by a very jagged wattage line. This problem is called "precession" or "beat frequency" and can be demonstrated by a simple test that entails riding at different rpms: If you attempt to ride at a very smooth perceived wattage using a PowerTap for 2 minutes at 85 rpm, then at 95 rpm, and again at 105 rpm, you will find that at 95 rpm, the problem cancels itself out—the wattage display at that point becomes very smooth on the computer and also in the download. The company came up with a way to work around this issue in the computer display by allowing the owners of the PowerTap Pro to "smooth" the display at 5-, 10-, 15-, 30-, and 60-second intervals. This has the effect of canceling out the precession issue on the display, but it still can be observed in the downloads of the data.

The future of the PowerTap is bright. Saris continues to make strides in hub innovations and also with its software. In 2004, the company released a spin bike with the PowerTap technology integrated into the flywheel, allowing participants in indoor spin class to have the benefits of using wattage data. This is a new market for Saris and certainly is a large one if the firm can break into the fitness world. It would be great to have power measurement in clubs and gyms all over the country, bringing power measurement to hardcore spinners, busy moms, and gym rats. Although the pricing on PowerTap power meters is very competitive, the PowerTap is still a sizable investment, especially considering the fact that you may still have to build a wheel around the hub.

Polar Electro

The lightest and the least expensive unit on the market, the Polar Electro power meter features a unique and interesting measuring system. The technology was developed out of New England by J. J. Cote, Alan Cote, and John Croy, who then sold their patent to Polar. The Polar systems measure chain tension via a chainstay-mounted sensor that detects vibrational frequency; just like a guitar string, a chain vibrates faster as its tension increases. This frequency is translated into an amount of force, which is then multiplied by chain speed, as measured by a magnetic sensor mounted on the rear derailleur, to derive power output:

**Power (in watts, or W) =
chain tension (N) x chain velocity
(in meters per second, or m/s)**

Although there have been reports of inaccuracies with the Polar system on the road, the system's good accuracy and consistency have been demonstrated in numerous tests against the SRM and PowerTap systems. On an indoor trainer, the Polar system may or may not be accurate in all gears. Reports of inaccuracies with the Polar system are often related to improper installation of the system's chainstay-mounted sensor, which some riders feel is difficult to install correctly. Accuracy issues with the Polar system are not due to bumps in the road, but to an interference signal that occurs with some combinations of gear ratio, power, and cadence. The Polar unit also has many little wires that can easily be broken and wrapped around the drivetrain, as one sensor must be mounted onto the derailleur.

The Polar system does have many advantages, however. One is that the computer portion of the unit also doubles as a wrist-mounted heart rate monitor. Polar is best known for its heart rate monitors, and this top-of-the-line monitor has so many features that many riders will buy the Polar power meter just for these alone. Most owners of the Polar unit were owners of the heart rate monitors first and bought the power option later. This makes the Polar unit the least expensive of the four units reviewed here and

Polar Electro Bike Mount

also the most attractive to the triathlon market. A multisport athlete can use the unit for measuring and recording heart rate during a swim, have wattage measurement for cycling, and then use the heart rate data again when running, thereby having a steady supply of data throughout a race or training session and for review afterward. The Polar watch is weatherproof and durable, though unfortunately the power unit has had some problems with these two essential features.

The Polar power meter also contains an altimeter and is one of only two meters on the market with the ability to record altitude changes along with power data (the other is the ergomo model). Although this information does not help coaches and athletes improve their training methods, it does help them to gain an understanding of how wattage and altitude relate to each other, and this can be of great importance to cyclists living or racing at higher altitudes. It also comes in handy to have altitude readings when reviewing downloaded data because it makes it easier to track where you were in a ride or race when the other data were recorded.

The Polar model measures power at forty samples per second (i.e., it samples vibrational frequency several hundred times per second, chain speed slightly less often, and calculates power values forty times per second) and then averages these measurements over a complete pedal revolution for display to the user. The Polar display is updated every 2 seconds, with a displayed number captured and stored every 5 seconds. This timing can be problematic because the power data produced on a bicycle are highly variable. By not averaging the 2-second samples, the unit can create some imprecise data in the information that is saved for later download. Since the cadence-based averaging interval works out to close to 5 seconds, the data results are not ideal, and the stored numbers tend to have short power peaks that are rounded off to whole seconds.

If Polar Electro can correct these problems, it stands a chance of becoming the industry leader with a small, accurate, and inexpensive unit. For those who are interested in power-measuring technology, it is definitely a company to watch.

ergomo

The newest power meter on the market is the ergomo, also made in Germany. The ergomo was invented by Siegfried Gerlitzki as a way to measure the twisting of any spindle or axle. An avid cyclist, Gerlitzki set out to create the unit when he realized that wattage could easily be measured by a sensor placed on a bicycle's bottom bracket. The ergomo has been in production since 2001 in very limited quantities. The company has only recently been able to break out of the small business mold to begin offering a large number of high-quality units for sale to the general public. With the introduction of a smaller, more robust computer, the ergomo stands poised to become a major player in the power meter market. In many ways, its model has the simplest design of all the power meters, and because of this the company may be able to take advantage of economies of scale that no other manufacturer can realize.

The ergomo measures power differently from the units reviewed above in that it measures the torsion, or twisting, of the bottom bracket spindle. Every time you pedal, there is a small amount of twisting that occurs on the spindle, similar to the twisting that might occur with a wet towel if you twisted it into a whip. The ergomo contains an optical sensor that allows it to measure the distance the axle twists, and from this distance it calculates the torque and the corresponding watts that are being applied in order to make that caliber of a twist. A small wire coming out of the bottom bracket shell sends the signal to the handlebar-mounted computer for calculation and display to the rider.

One of the benefits of this system is that it allows the rider to use any square taper (ISO), Octalink, or ISIS crank and any wheel set. For Shimano customers using the new two-piece design or the older octalink spindle, ergomo offers a carbon-fiber crank set as an option that was specifically designed for the ergomo bottom bracket. By placing the power-measuring device essentially inside the bicycle frame, the designers came up with a way to protect the sensor itself from the elements and simultaneously created the potential for a future mountain bike unit. This innovation also could very well position ergomo to retrofit the many indoor spin bicycles that exist and enable the company to bring power training to the masses in every gym and fitness club in the country.

Cut-away of the ergomo bottom bracket

In winter 2005, ergomo released the Pro computer, a major revision to their first model. The original model was quite large, and the handlebar mount was problematic. The new computer features the ability to view the power data in watts per kilogram once the user enters his or her weight into the computer. The company has also incorporated the ability to see Training Stress Score and Intensity Factor while riding (concepts discussed in depth in Chapter 6). Also new to the ergomo Pro computer are a coded heart rate capability and an altimeter. One feature that will be appreciated by every veteran of intervals is the ability to view watts in real time and average watts on the same screen while in interval mode.

The most obvious disadvantage of this system is that because the sensor measures power at the bottom bracket spindle, it only measures the side that twists—the left side. Since the right side of the spindle is attached to the drivetrain, there is no significant twist on the right side. As a result, the ergomo can only measure the rider's left leg power accurately. The computer takes the power output from the left leg and doubles it in order to get the wattage. Although initially this may seem to be a problem, in reality it has not proven to be a significant one for the majority of users. Only riders with a large discrepancy in the strength of their legs would have inaccurate readings from the unit. Every rider has a small discrepancy in leg strength, but for the majority of people, this discrepancy is less than 5 percent; when on the bicycle, this would result in a difference of less than 10 watts between what an ergomo unit would report and what the SRM or PowerTap would report. If a rider does have a large discrepancy in leg strength—from an injury, for example—then the ergomo can be adjusted to provide the rider with a very accurate picture of his or her wattage.

A feature of the original ergomo—the fact that it records the power produced by the rider once every 5 seconds—could be considered either an advantage or a disadvantage. Initially, it seems to be a disadvantage because the Sport cannot capture the very short, intense bursts of energy produced in maximal sprints, and that is indeed the case, as peak power numbers are rounded off in the downloaded data. However, this model captures from 72 to 144 samples per second and then averages those numbers before saving the result. The unit does this for 5 seconds, and then averages those five numbers for download to your computer, hence the 5-second sampling. In reality, this proves to be one of the better ways of measuring power because it eliminates a large amount of noise that is inherent in the way that the other three manufacturers record the data. It turns out that it is important to know your "best 5 seconds" (you'll learn why in Chapter 4). The latest ergomo Pro, however, gives a rider the ability to change the recording intervals, which is a well-designed upgrade. For example, the rider can choose record intervals at 1, 2, 5, 10, 15, or 30 seconds. The wattage can also be "smoothed" on the display so that it updates over a rolling average, quickly (1 pedal revolution) or slowly (8 pedal revolutions), a feature that is especially helpful when trying to maintain a small range of wattage during training.

Some concerns with the ergomo have been the longevity of the bearings inside the sensor, how easily they can be replaced, and the cost of replacement. ergomo includes a warranty on the unit for up to 10,000 miles and states in its literature that the bearings may last longer than 15,000 miles. Whether this will be the case with all owners remains to be seen.

The future of ergomo also looks very bright. With a new computer and a refined design of the sensor, the company looks to take over a large sector of the market. Giving the user the ability to choose from a wide range of wheel sets is definitely a plus, and the unit also currently comes in at a lower price than the SRM, making it a great choice for many riders.

Table 2.1 provides both a break down and a comparison of power meters on the market today.

The Software: How a Bike Geek's Toy Becomes a Tool

The true usefulness of a power meter comes from post-ride analysis of the data. Understanding the data presented on the display while racing or training certainly has benefits and is worthwhile; however, you will be taking advantage of the power meter's true strength only when you can download the recorded data and sift through the graphs to gain meaningful insights that will help you improve in cycling. Because a power meter records data at sampling rates of possibly many times per second, the sheer volume of information from even a one-hour ride can be overwhelming. The question then becomes: What does it all mean? That's where the software comes in. The software that comes with the product should present the facts in an easily digestible manner that allows even the novice computer user to make decisions about training.

Power Software

Each power meter comes with its own software, and each type has its own strengths and weaknesses. These pros and cons are outlined in Table 2.1; in later chapters we will look at specific charts and graphs and discuss what they mean.

TABLE 2.1	A COMPARISON OF POWER METERS		
	ergomo Sport	**ergomo Pro**	**Polar S-720i/710i**
Measurement location	Bottom bracket (Campagnolo or Shimano OctaLink)	Same as Sport	Chainstay and rear deraileur
Method	Photointerrupter circuit	Same as Sport	Chain speed and vibration frequency
Claimed accuracy	± 2%	1.5%	± 10% at any one instant, but 2–5% or less on average
Recording interval	Averaged values recorded every 5 sec.	Current values recorded every 1, 5, 10, or 30 sec.	Current values recorded every 5, 15, or 60 sec.
Memory capacity	11 hr. 1 workout file	12–342 hr. Unlimited files can be recorded before download	4:57–76:37 hr. Up to 99 workout files
Calibration	By manufacturer only	Same as Sport	No; but accuracy can be checked on hill of known grade
Mass (grams)	BB w/bolts & wires = 344g Computer & mount = 168g	BB w/bolts & wires = 304g Computer & mount = 100g	Sensors = 118*g Computer = 53*g Mount/wiring = 71* g
Advantages	**1.** Outstanding software (CyclingPeaks) with many useful analysis tools **2.** Third-generation design **3.** Fully hard-wired system is not affected by electronic or radio interference **4.** Easy installation **5.** Rechargeable computer battery lasts 5,000 hr., is good for ~30 hr., recharges in 2–3 hr. **6.** Almost no limit on component choice	**1.** Same as Sport **2.** Fourth-generation design, major improvements to computer with altitude and coded HR; available in five languages **3.** Same as Sport; allows use of any wheel; up to 30 intervals can be marked. **4.** Same as Sport, Back-light display for night rides, infrared download along with cable download **5.** Rechargeable battery, with 27 hours of time, good for 21,000 hr.	**1.** Least expensive of all options **2.** Feature-rich software, and extra hardware features like altitude **3.** Allows use of any wheel or crank that you want **4.** Large memory capacity, stores many workouts **5.** Incurs the smallest weight penalty **6.** Not affected by temperature **7.** Does not require calibration

PowerTap Standard	PowerTap Pro	PowerTap Pro SL	SRM Professional/ Amateur
Rear hub (130 or 135 mm; 24, 28, and 32 hole drillings)	Same as Standard	Same as Standard	Crank (Shimano OctaLink or Campagnolo; 167– 182 mm lengths in 2.5 mm increments)
4 strain gauges	Same as Standard	Same as Standard	4 strain gauges for Pro, 2 for Amateur, 8 for Dura-Ace
± 1.5%	Same as Standard	Same as Standard	± 2.5% for Pro, ± 5% for Amateur
Current values recorded every 1.26 or 2.52 sec.	Current values recorded 1.26, 2.52, 5.04, 10.08, or 30.24 sec.	Same as Pro	Averaged values recorded 0.1–30 sec.
4 or 8 hr. depending on recording interval 1 workout file	7.5–180 hr. depending on recording interval 1 workout file	Same as Pro	0:45–225 hr. depending on recording interval Numerous workout files
No; accuracy can be checked via static "stomp test" described below	Same as Standard	Same as Standard	Slope setting is user adjustable; manufacturer calibration now avail- able in U.S.
Hub = 579*g (w/o skewer) Computer =39.5* g Mount/wiring = 36*g	Same as Standard, plus slight added mass due to crank-mounted cadence sensor."	Hub = 416g (w/o skewer) Remaining component masses are same as Pro	Pro = 560g Amateur = 640g Computer = 120g Mount bracket/wire = 30g
1. Easiest to move from one bike to another 2. Affordable and accurate 3. Compact, readable, easy-to-use display 4. Most hub internals (axle, freehub, and drive side bearings) are all user- serviceable without disturbing strain gauges and electronics 5. Easiest to install and easiest to remove for racing — just swap rear wheels	Same as Std., plus: 1. Expanded memory (up to 180 hr.); can store only one file but can create unlimited number of intervals 2. Display has time of day and rolling average capability for power, speed, and cadence data; can be custom- ized for these functions 3. Can display "pedaling power" (excludes 0; i.e., coasting values) 4. Can be used with fixed gear	Same as Pro, plus: 1. Improved hub internals (4 sets of sealed cartridge bearings), but not user-serviceable 2. Hub is 162 g lighter than Pro or Std. 3. Available in fixed gear and Campagnolo freehub versions 4. Improved software is also Java-based and Mac-compatible	1. Excellent software 2. Time-tested, reliable design 3. Can display rolling average for current wattage 4. Large memory capacity, can store multiple workouts 5. No limit on wheel choice

(continues)

TABLE 2.1	A COMPARISON OF POWER METERS *(continued)*		
	ergomo Sport	*ergomo Pro*	*Polar S-720i/710i*
Advantages (cont.)		**6.** Same as Sport; computer can be programmed for multiple bikes **7.** Computer setup can be done from software **8.** Contains TSS/IF/NP inside the computer head. Altitude and coded HR **9.** Might be the best solution for MTB	
Drawbacks	**1.** Large/heavy computer **2.** Bearings must be factory serviced ($300) every 15–20,000 mi. **3.** Not easily moved from bike to bike **4.** Cannot accept 2004 Dura-Ace cranks **5.** Not useful on tandems with cooridinated gearing **6.** Averaged data can be accessed only by download (cannot be viewed during interval)	Same as 2–5 for Sport, plus: **1.** Currently must use square taper cranks only **2.** Only left leg power is measured due to measurement in the BB axle	**1.** Most difficult to set up properly **2.** Difficult to move from bike to bike (to the point that it will likely never happen) **3.** Small display is hard for some to navigate **4.** The least "clean" installation (multiple sensors and cables) **5.** Averaged data cannot be viewed during intervals (or "laps"), only at the end of the ride" **6.** Accuracy questionable on stationary trainers, possibly from harmonic vibrations effects **7.** Not practical on MTB, and cannot be used with fixed gear
Pedal analysis	No	No	Yes

PowerTap Standard	PowerTap Pro	PowerTap Pro SL	SRM Professional/ Amateur
	5. Measures actual cadence (more accurate than the Standard model's "virtual" cadence) 6. Easier operation of interval feature 7. Mileage is programmable 8. Faster downloading with Link software v. 1.04		
1. Mediocre software interface (also not Mac-compatible) 2. Limits wheel choice 3. Wheel-based system (not hub itself) is more likely to be damaged in crash 4. No disc version; requires a cover (not USCF-legal after 2006) to be used as a disc 5. No disc brake version for MTB 6. Not available with Campagnolo freehub 7. Drive-side bearings and cone are substandard quality 8. Cannot be used with fixed gear 9. "Virtual" cadence only (limited to 40–140 rpm) 10. Reliability problems in wet weather with original version; Graber version has better seals and coated circuitry 11. Limited memory (7.5 hr.) 12. No rolling average or "pedaling power" capability	Same as 1–7 for Std., plus: 1. Hub requires modification to be used with fixed gear	Same as 1–5 for Std.	1. Expensive 2. Not made to be moved from one bike to another 3. Some find display more difficult to read 4. Daily calibration (takes ~30 sec.) recommended 5. User-serviceable, but factory service recommended every 1500 hr., and replacement interval for cranks (not including power measuring unit) is once yearly 6. Crank is slightly more flexible than other models; Dura-Ace version available at significant extra cost 7. Not useful on tandems 8. Accuracy of Amateur deteriorates outside a ~100W range, and may drift significantly over the course of a season
No	No	No	Extra option

(continues)

TABLE 2.1	A COMPARISON OF POWER METERS (continued)		
	ergomo Sport	ergomo Pro	Polar S-720i/710i
MSRP	$1,200	$1,600	720i, $575; add-on kit only, $315
Other	Due to method of measuring, only left leg power is measured	Major improvements in features, including very robust interval function, and ability to view avg and current power in interval mode, along with TSS/IF/NP	Display and software give average power for pedaling time only

*Actual mass; all others are manufacturer's claims.
**For comparison, the mass of a Shimano Dura-Ace FC-7700 rear hub is 312 g, while Campagnolo lists the Chorus at 260 g, and Record as 248 g (all masses without skewer). A Dura-Ace FC-7700

SRMWin

SRMWin, the software supplied with every SRM power meter and freely downloadable on the Web, is a well-designed program that allows the user to easily view the downloaded data, create a range around any period of interest, and track fitness changes over time (see Figure 2.5). One of the unique features of the software is that each user must know how to use it in order to program the SRM power control and delete old data from the power control. Although the SRM power control can largely be programmed from the computer head itself, a few functions need to be programmed with the software.

The true usefulness of a power meter comes from post-ride analysis of the data.

One of the more perplexing graphs provided in the SRM software is found by clicking on the "Analysis" button. Although it looks like something a three-year-old could draw, it is actually a complex graph showing changes in the relationship between heart rate and power throughout any given workout. Once you learn how to use it, however, it can be useful. Another feature not to be overlooked in the software is the "Periodic Chart," which allows the user to track fitness changes over time.

SRMWin's main weaknesses are that it is very "grid-like" in appear-

PowerTap Standard	PowerTap Pro	PowerTap Pro SL	SRM Professional/ Amateur
$700 without rim and wheel build	$900 without rim and wheel build; $1,000 with built wheel	$840, hub only; $1,200 without rim and wheel build; $1,300 with built wheel	Pro, $2,650; Amateur, $1,770
Display and software give only average power for with 0 (coasting) values; original grey case changed to yellow in 2004		Data transmission is through carbon fiber "windows" in hub shell. Electronics are completely contained inside hub; only batteries are access-ible from cap	Average power display obtained only from pedaling time, but non-zero values (i.e., when coasting) included by SRM software

bottom bracket is 201 g; an FC-7410 right crank and chainrings are 395 g; an Avocet 45 com-puter and mounting bracket are 20 g and 16 g; and a Polar Coach heart rate monitor (HRM) and mounting bracket are 40 g and 26 g, respectively.

FIGURE 2.1: SRMWin

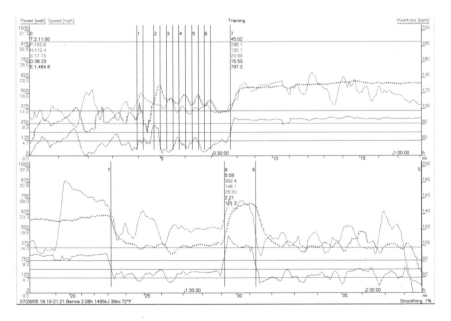

ance and that it does not allow for the creation of custom charts. It also has a less than satisfactory diary function because it does not provide enough space to write in more than brief comments.

PowerTap PowerLink

PowerTap released an updated version of its Link software in late 2004. The original Link software lacked many features that other programs had, such as providing the opportunity to view fitness changes over time, so the new software was created to correct these shortfalls. PowerTap consulted with Dr. Allen Lim in the development of the program, and as a result, many aspects of his coaching and scientific philosophies are reflected in the product.

The new software does a much better job of helping the user to understand the intricacies of tracking fitness changes. It also offers a greater ability to enter and track personal information, such as weight and perceived exertion. Unfortunately, it uses Java as its programming language, and though this has some advantages, ultimately it makes the program run more slowly than competitor's software.

Polar Precision Performance

Polar Electro had an advantage in its software development efforts because it is a large enough company to have in-house programmers. This enabled Polar to produce a very polished product. The Precision Performance software has been updated several times and has improved with each new version.

Polar's product line emphasizes heart rate data, and this is reflected in its software. Although this is a great strength for athletes who are primarily interested in heart rate, it is a weakness in the Polar system for power meter users, and one that such users will find critical.

The most robust areas of the Precision Performance software are its highly detailed calendar functions and its advanced diary tools. However, for detailed power analysis, the Polar software needs some further development.

CyclingPeaks/ErgoRacer

The CyclingPeaks software is one of three programs offered as stand-alone, after-market products. The OEM version of CyclingPeaks is included with the ergomo power meter, where it is called ErgoRacer.

The authors codeveloped CyclingPeaks in 2002–2003 along with Kevin Williams. The power meter software programs available at that time lacked some useful features, and we developed the software to fill this gap. Since CyclingPeaks was introduced in 2003, it has proven to be popular among power meter users for tracking fitness changes and conducting detailed analyses.

One of the most popular features of the program is that it allows users to change and create custom charts on the "Athlete Home Page." By doing this, and by tracking fitness progression with the "Mean Maximal Power Periodic Chart," a rider can very quickly decide whether to make changes in his or her training program or continue with a current plan of action. The development of the CyclingPeaks also incorporated some new concepts, namely "Normalized Power" and "Training Stress Score," which we will discuss in depth in Chapter 7.

By allowing the user to easily "create a range" around important time periods, CyclingPeaks makes it possible for a cyclist to see how well his or her workout goals were achieved over a selected period of time. Through its "Fast Find" feature, the software also allows users to quickly find their best efforts, thereby helping them to understand the exact demands of each race or training ride.

"Fast Find" Feature

CyclingPeaks is platform neutral: Data from any power meter can be downloaded directly into the software, and it can also import all of the file formats produced by the other companies. Thus, old data from a different power meter software application can be quickly imported. This makes CyclingPeaks a user-friendly and robust system. One area in which CyclingPeaks falls short is that it lacks detailed diary features. This can easily be reconciled through the use of the online service provided at www.TrainingPeaks.com. Having an interactive component with the Web is one of the strengths of this software: This is one aspect that is missing from all of the other programs, and in the future the need for this feature will continue to grow.

Intellicoach Erg+

Developed in 2004 by Paul Smeulders, Intellicoach offers some excellent tools for building ergometer or power versus time training sessions on a CompuTrainer. To do so, the user can draw a series of shapes ("Hat,"

"Sawtooth," "Sharkfin," or "Wedges") and lines representing the desired target power profile for the workout, using an absolute watts scale, a percentage of threshold power, or any other standard test quantity.

Intellicoach can also read on-bike power meter files to automatically find, measure, and categorize intervals. It then displays the average power, the power trend, and the duration of each "effort" and "rest" phase. This unique feature shows the user whether he or she executed the interval correctly and notes the amount of time spent over or under a targeted goal. This is a useful feature for coach and athlete alike.

The connection between this feature and the creation of a customized workout for a CompuTrainer is where the product really shines. Intellicoach will take your power meter file from the road and convert it into an erg file, thus easily replicating your favorite ride or race so that you can practice it indoors. You can even "scale" the workout to be harder as your fitness progresses. With the release of version 2.0 in March 2005, Intellicoach added the ability to support MultiRider Compu-Trainer studio sessions and the ability to build workouts based on specific Training Stress Scores (TSS) and Intensity Factors (IF) that you might want to achieve during a workout.

Since Intellicoach was not designed as a complete power meter analysis tool, it's not fair to compare it with CyclingPeaks or Power-Coach (described below). Intellicoach does not provide a way to view fitness changes over time; it also lacks a diary function and some other key ingredients that would make it a complete package. However, it does perfectly what it was designed to do, and if you own a CompuTrainer, then it's an essential piece of software for you to own and use.

PowerCoach

Unfortunately, the authors were unable to obtain a copy of this program to evaluate it in detail. According to the information presented at the PowerCoach Web site, however, this program was originally designed for the Mac, and it appears to be quite detailed and graphics oriented. It enables the user to create 3D graphs that can, for example, show cadence in relation to different time periods and wattages.

POWER-BASED TRAINING: WHERE TO BEGIN?

3

RAINING WITH A POWER METER is not difficult, and certainly
anyone can install one on a bike. But actually using the equipment, and especially the software, in the way that they were intended to be used will take some work on your part. One of the most
common questions athletes ask is, How do I use this thing? As with any
new tool, it will take time for each rider to learn the intricacies of the
power meter and to take the steps that are needed to achieve success.
Look at it this way: If you were the proud owner of a new Ferrari sports
car, would you have to take lessons at the local racecar driving school to
enjoy it? No, of course not. But doing so would certainly enhance the
experience of owning the car. In the same way, you'll get the most out
of owning a power meter when you learn how to take advantage of all
the features that it offers. By following the first three steps presented in
this chapter, you will be able to take the plunge in training with power.

The ultimate reason for having a power meter is to reach your goals
and achieve your potential in cycling. Surely, the scientist in all of us
wants to experiment with new toys and gear, but that same scientist recognizes that, as cyclists or multisport athletes, using a power meter is
quite possibly one of the best ways to get to know ourselves at an even
deeper level. The power meter has brought a very complex tool to the
layperson, and this complexity has created much confusion and caused

many potential users to have reservations about using the technology. Such cutting-edge tools have traditionally been reserved for exercise physiologists in the lab studying the biomechanics of movement and human physiological limits to the nth degree. Until now, what they have has not been common knowledge. But with power meters becoming more accessible and more popular, all that is about to change.

This chapter describes how you can take your first steps in training and racing with a power meter; after reading it you should have a clear understanding of what to do next.

Step 1:
Data Collection and
Functional Threshold Power

The very first thing that you should do, once you have installed the hardware on your bike, is to start riding with your power meter and just downloading the data to get a sense of what, say, 300 watts means in relation to your heart rate, cadence, speed, and so on. You will begin to understand what different wattage numbers mean in the real world, and then to associate those numbers with your ride. A downloaded power meter file is, quite literally, a second-by-second re-creation, or diary, of your ride in graph format. You will begin to see what happened to your power output when you were riding in a crosswind, on a particularly long climb, on a set of short, butt-kicking hills, or before and after you stopped for a drink at the convenience store, and all those associations will help you to better understand your cycling. But it is when you go on to the next step that you will be able to get the biggest bang for your training buck, so to speak.

Once you have some rides under your belt, and a sense of how to operate the computer display attached to your handlebar while riding, you should schedule your first testing session. Running the test described below will enable you to begin to determine your training zones and thus allow you to give the correct focus to your efforts. With this first test, you will find out how many watts you can currently produce at your functional threshold power (FTP), establishing a fitness baseline.

It would be a good idea to repeat this threshold test once a month in order to assess your fitness, track changes, and decide whether to make changes to your training program based on the results. There are two important things to remember: (1) You should always test on the same stretch of road or on an indoor trainer, and at close to the same time of day and with similar weather conditions; and (2) You should minimize any external influences that would affect your performance, such as stress levels or the amount of sleep you got the night before, so that you can be confident in comparing the results from different tests.

But what is functional threshold power, and why is it important for you to test for it?

What Is Functional Threshold Power (FTP)?

The term "threshold" has become synonymous with the word "confusion" in the minds of many athletes. There are many different words for essentially the same concept: anaerobic threshold (AT), lactate threshold (LT), maximal lactate steady state (MLSS), onset of blood lactate (OBLA), and just plain old "threshold." It seems that there are just as many possible quantitative definitions, with different versions of the concept based on heart rate, blood lactate, wattage, and so on. As a result, even in many scientific articles the authors have to present their own definition to clarify what they are talking about.

For more than thirty years, exercise physiologists have known that the exercise intensity at which lactate begins to accumulate in a person's blood—that is, his or her LT—is a powerful predictor of that person's endurance performance ability. This is because although an individual's cardiovascular fitness—that is, his or her maximal oxygen uptake (VO_2max)—sets the upper limit to his or her rate of aerobic energy production, it is the individual's metabolic fitness—that is, their LT—that determines the percentage or fraction of this VO_2max that he or she can utilize for any given period of time.

The physiological factors determining LT are complex, but essentially, blood lactate levels serve as an indirect marker for biochemical events within exercising muscle. More specifically, a person's LT reflects the ability of his or her muscles to match energy supply to energy demand, which in turn determines the fuel "mix" (i.e., carbohydrate versus fat) used and the development of muscle fatigue. Consequently, LT—especially when expressed in terms of power output, which also takes into account cycling efficiency—is the single most important physiological determinant of performance in events ranging from something as short as a 3 km pursuit to a stage race lasting as long as three weeks. Just as important, because the effort that is experienced by an athlete when exercising at any given intensity is dependent upon his or her power output relative to power at LT, this parameter provides a physiologically sound basis around which to design any power meter–based training program. However, few athletes have ready access to lactate testing on a regular basis. What's more, even those who do are still generally dependent on the person performing the test to first design an appropriate protocol, and then to correctly interpret the results. This is actually more difficult than many realize, and the data obtained are rarely more accurate or precise than that obtained using much simpler field tests (since the best predictor of performance is performance itself). Thus, while blood lactate testing does have a role to play in the preparation and training of cyclists, for routine purposes we prefer to rely on a far more pragmatic approach, which is to simply use a power meter to determine a rider's functional threshold power (FTP). FTP is the highest power that a rider can maintain in a quasi–steady state without fatiguing for approximately one hour. When power exceeds FTP, fatigue will occur much sooner, whereas power just below FTP can be maintained considerably longer.

Determining Functional Threshold Power

So, how do you go about determining your functional threshold power using a power meter? There are a number of different ways to do this, each of which has its advantages and disadvantages, but all of which provide very similar estimates of threshold power. In order of increasing complexity, these are:

1. **A good estimate** of your FTP can often be obtained by simply uploading all of your training data into your power meter software and then examining the power frequency distribution chart. Because exercising above threshold power is quite strenuous and there is a limit to how long you can do so, there will often be a rather noticeable drop-off above this point in this graph. (This same approach works even better for identifying an individual's spontaneously achieved maximal heart rate—thus reducing or

even eliminating the need for formal testing.) Of course, this method works best if the time period being examined includes some high-intensity training and/or racing, which serves to make the distinction between sub-threshold and supra-threshold efforts more distinct. Also, sometimes the drop-off in time spent above threshold power is more apparent when the width of each power "bin" is reduced from the default of 20 watts to a smaller value, such as 5 or 10 watts.

FIGURE 3.1: POWER DISTRIBUTION CHART

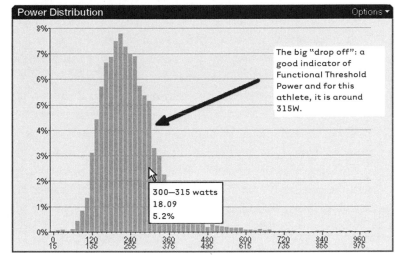

2. Another way to estimate your threshold power without performing any formal testing is to simply evaluate the steady power that you can routinely produce in training during longer hard efforts, such as intervals or repeats aimed at raising LT, or during longer climbs. In most power meter software, perhaps the easiest way of doing this is to add a horizontal gridline to a "stacked" graph of an appropriately chosen workout (or race), and then look for places where your power is quasi-constant for some minutes at a time. You can then adjust the gridline up or down as needed to hone in on the best estimate of your functional threshold power.

3. Perhaps an even more precise way of determining your threshold power, yet one which still does not require formal testing, is to examine your Normalized Power (a concept explained

FIGURE 3.2: ESTIMATE OF 20-MINUTE POWER

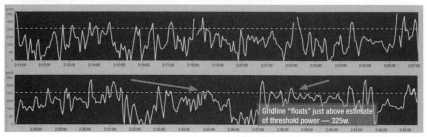

in greater detail in Chapter 7) during hard mass-start races, of approximately one hour, using CyclingPeaks software. Since CyclingPeaks software automatically calculates Normalized Power even if you haven't yet entered a value for your threshold power, using the program to first analyze several race files may be the quickest way to derive a good estimate of your threshold power.

4. Since, by definition, the best measure of performance is performance itself, the most direct estimate of your FTP will be obtained by simply doing a one-hour time trial. By examining the horizontal graph of the data from such a trial in your power meter software (perhaps with a little smoothing applied), you will be able to quickly tell whether your effort was well-paced, or whether you started out too hard and then later faded. In the latter situation, the data for average power will somewhat underestimate your true threshold power.

5. Finally, those who are more mathematically inclined may wish to perform formal testing to determine their "critical power" as described in the scientific literature. Briefly, this approach consists of plotting the total work performed (in joules) during a series of relatively short (i.e., between 3 and 30 minutes), all-out efforts against their duration (in seconds), then fitting a straight line to the data points. The slope of this line is critical power, which corresponds quite closely with FTP as determined by using any of the previously described methods. See the sidebar on "Critical Power" for more detail.

With all these different ways to test your FTP, you may wonder which one to start with. We believe that the best way to begin is to just

Critical Power

There have been a number of equations presented in the scientific literature describing human power output as a function of time, some derived from modeling based on the underlying physiology, and some simply derived empirically. One of the simplest and most robust, though, is the original "critical power" concept first proposed by H. Monod around 1960. Various formulations of this idea have been presented, but the original equation is a hyperbolic of the form:

$$t = AWC/(P - CP)$$

where t = time to exhaustion, P is the current power, CP is the work rate (i.e., power) asymptote, and AWC represents the degree of curvature of the relationship.

In this form, time to exhaustion is the dependent variable and it is determined by power output (P) in relation to the individual's critical power (CP). In other words, how long you can go is determined by how hard you are exercising relative to your own ability. Although this is logical, actually fitting data to such a curvilinear relationship isn't especially convenient. Hence, it is common to rearrange this equation to yield a linear equivalent. That is:

$$Wlim = AWC + (CP \times t)$$

In this expression, Wlim is the total amount of work that can be accomplished during a maximal exercise bout continued to fatigue, and it is the product of power and time (since power = work/time, work = power × time), plus a fixed contribution from anaerobic work capacity, that is, AWC.

The above equation is of the form y = mx + b, with the slope of the line (that is, CP) being a person's "critical power." Conceptually, CP is a power that can be sustained "for a very long time without fatigue," and is "an inherent characteristic of the aerobic energy supply system." On a practical basis, CP has been shown to be closely correlated with (albeit somewhat higher than) power *(continues)*

(continued)

at lactate threshold. On the other hand, the y-intercept of this relationship, AWC, represents a fixed amount of work that can be accomplished during an exercise task to fatigue, but it is nonrenewable. Conceptually, this parameter reflects anaerobic capacity (not power)—that is, the total amount of energy that can be liberated from nonaerobic energy sources, or the breakdown of high-energy phosphate stores (adenosine triphosphate [ATP] and phosphate creatine [PCr]), and via production and accumulation of lactate. Support for this interpretation comes from experiments showing a close correlation between AWC and total work performed during an all-out 30-second exercise test (that is, a Wingate test), or, even more convincingly, between AWC and maximal accumulated oxygen deficit. Moreover, CP may be influenced by interventions that would be expected to affect aerobic energy production, such as hypoxia, whereas AWC is not. Conversely, interventions expected to influence anaerobic capacity, such as creatine loading or resistance training (in untrained persons), have been shown to alter AWC without changing CP.

The critical power concept is not without its limitations. In particular, it tends to greatly overestimate the maximal power that can be generated for only a few seconds, and it predicts that there should be a power output below which fatigue will never occur. In addition, the exact values obtained for AWC and CP depend in part on the testing protocol—for example, the exact combination of powers and durations used to define the curve, how fatigue is defined, and the like. Nonetheless, despite its simplicity, this equation describes the power versus duration curve quite well over a fairly wide range of exercise intensities and durations, from efforts lasting for just a couple of minutes to efforts of a couple of hours (although again, since the relationship between work and time isn't truly linear, extrapolating beyond the range upon which the calculations are based will result in overestimation).

Understanding the original critical power concept can be very helpful if you own a power meter because it provides a means of quantifying changes in fitness beyond just "I was able to sustain *x* watts for *y* seconds!" Specifically, the critical power paradigm allows you to determine whether changes in anaerobic or aerobic function (or both) are responsible for any such improvements in performance, and thus to plan future training based on this insight. Furthermore, if you know your CP and AWC, it is possible to predict your maximal power at intermediate, unmeasured durations with considerable accuracy—which can be quite useful, for example, when preparing for a time trial contested over a distance and duration that you have not raced before (or recently). Finally, because CP corresponds very closely to functional threshold power, determining your CP provides yet another means of determining this parameter.

If you decide to pursue this approach, there are two ways of obtaining the necessary data points: (1) by conducting specific, formal tests to determine the maximal power that you can sustain for various periods of time (or the maximal time that you can maintain a certain power), or (2) by using a software program such as CyclingPeaks or SRM to "cherry pick" your best performances for those same periods out of, for example, race files. In either case, it is important that the data you use in the analysis truly represents your best effort, or your CP and/or AWC may be significantly under- or overestimated. Also, you should avoid using data from efforts that are so short (e.g., less than 3 minutes) that full utilization of AWC may not be assured, or so long (e.g., more than 20 minutes) that the assumption of linearity of the work–time relationship is seriously violated.

Finally, it is important to realize that, as with any regression analysis, the slope (i.e., CP) is estimated with greater certainty than the intercept (i.e., AWC). In other words, whereas the value derived for CP using this method is generally rather robust—that is, quite reproducible from one occasion to the next and relatively insensitive to the particular combination of data points used—the value obtained for AWC will tend to be more variable. You should therefore be a bit more cautious when interpreting changes in AWC and making adjustments in your training based on such measurements than when making decisions based on measured changes in your CP.

go out and do a ride specifically designed to find your threshold, such as the one described in the next section. This is without a doubt the first big step in your new adventure in training with power.

The Threshold Test

The purpose of this initial test is to do a ride where you can average the highest watts possible for a substantial period of time. When you get to the effort, make sure to pace yourself so that you do not tire prematurely. Start out with a 20-minute warm-up, which is just riding along at a moderate pace, or at about 65 percent of your max heart rate (HR), or what would be called your endurance pace. Again, be sure to do the same warm-up, and to use the same intensity in your warm-up, each time you do the test. Then do three fast pedaling efforts at 100 rpm for 1 minute each, with 1 minute of easy recovery pedaling between each, in order to further prepare the muscles for the effort. After these, ride easy for 5 minutes at 65 percent of max HR. Then the true warm-up begins:

5 minutes all out. Punch it and hold it! Make sure that you start at a high pace, but not so high that you die at the end. You should have a little in reserve to kick it to the finish line in the last minute. The goal of this first part is twofold: first, to "open" up the legs for the rest of the effort, and second, to capture your ability to produce watts in what is called VO_2max power, or Level 5 (discussed later in this chapter). Doing this initial 5-minute effort also helps to dispense with the initial "freshness" that always exists at the beginning of a ride. Then, when you do your next effort, you will be able to produce power that is more likely to be truly representative of your FTP.

10 minutes easy at endurance pace. Ride at 65 percent of max HR.

20-minute time trial. Try to do this on a road that is fairly flat and allows you to put out a strong, steady effort for the entire 20 minutes. Do not start out too hard! That's a common mistake, so make sure that you get up to speed and then try to hold that speed as best you can. If you have never done one of these efforts before, we would suggest trying this on a steady climb or into a slight headwind, where you are forced to do it at a maximum effort for the entire 20 minutes.

10—15 minutes at endurance pace. Again, pedal easy at 65 percent of max HR.

10—15 minute cool-down. Finish the ride at an easy pace.

Your goal in the main portion of the test, the 20-minute segment, is to produce the highest average watts over the entire period. It's not a good test if you go out too hard and suddenly run out of energy, because you will not be able to produce your true maximal steady-state power. It is always better to start out in the first 2 minutes a little under what you believe to be your FTP, build up along the way, and then ride at your maximum level in the last 3 minutes.

Once this test is over and you have downloaded the data, you will need to figure out what your average power was for the entire 20-minute effort. Then you will take this number and subtract 5 percent from it. The number that results will be your functional threshold wattage value. (Hold onto this number, as we will come back to it later in this chapter.) So, for example, if you average 300 watts for the 20-minute time trial, you would calculate that $300 \times 0.05 = 15$, and $300 - 15 = 285$. Thus, your functional threshold power is 285 watts.

The reason for subtracting 5 percent of the watts from your 20-minute test is that FTP is defined as the highest average wattage or power that you can maintain for 60 minutes. Because some athletes have a hard time focusing for 60 minutes on a maximal effort, and those who can learn very quickly that a 60-minute time trial is not that much fun, we have found that 20 minutes is more realistic in terms of getting athletes to do more regular and higher quality tests. Since 20 minutes is a shorter time period, it incorporates more of the athlete's anaerobic capacity, however, and this skews the wattage data by about 5 percent over a 60-minute effort. By subtracting that 5 percent, you will come up with a wattage number that would be very close to your 60-minute power measure.

Since one goal of any training program is to increase power at threshold (FTP), how often threshold power will change significantly will depend in part on an individual's training history and habits. For example, someone who is just beginning to cycle or returning to cycling after a long break may see large and rapid changes in their threshold power at first, whereas an experienced rider who has been training for many years, or an athlete who maintains a high level of conditioning year round, will probably experience much less variation. In general, assessing FTP four to six times a year (e.g., in the dead of winter training, near the start of serious outdoor training as a baseline, partway through the precompetition period to track improvement, a couple of times during the season to determine peak fitness, and finally, after your peak fitness is over for the season to determine how far you have "fallen") is probably sufficient.

Step 2: Power-Based Training Levels

With more and more cyclists using power meters, the need has clearly arisen for power-based training programs akin to those used with heart rate monitors. To help meet this demand, Andrew Coggan, coauthor of this book, developed a series of power-based training levels, or zones. In doing so he drew upon fundamental principles of exercise physiology as well as approximately two decades of experience with power-based training in both laboratory and field settings.

The seven levels are categorized in Table 3.1, and other aspects of the levels are noted in Table 3.2. Factors that were taken into consideration in developing the levels are noted below. At the end of the chapter you will see an example of how a hypothetical cyclist—we'll call him Joe Athlete—could determine his own training levels and use that knowledge in developing a training program.

The Basis for the System

Power at lactate threshold is the most important physiological determinant of endurance cycling performance because it integrates VO_2max, the percentage of VO_2max that can be sustained for a given duration, and cycling efficiency. As such, it is more logical to define training levels relative to an athlete's threshold power than it is to, for example, define them vis-à-vis power at VO_2max (just as it is more logical to define HR-based training levels relative to threshold HR than to use maximal HR). Determining the appropriate number of levels, however, is somewhat tricky; the number is bound to be arbitrary because the physiological responses to exercise really fall on a continuum, with one intensity domain simply blending into the next.

A compromise must therefore be made between defining more levels, thus better reflecting the continuum that exists in reality, and defining

TABLE 3.1	POWER–BASED TRAINING LEVELS			
Level	**Name**	**Average Power**	**Average HR**	**Perceived Exertion**
1	Active Recovery	<55%	<68%	<2

Description: "Easy spinning" or "light pedal pressure" (i.e., very low level exercise, too low in and of itself to induce significant physiological adaptations). Minimal sensation of leg effort/fatigue. Requires no concentration to maintain pace, and continuous conversation is possible. Typically used for active recovery after strenuous training days (or races), between interval efforts, or for socializing.

Level	Name	Average Power	Average HR	Perceived Exertion
2	Endurance	56–75%	69–83%	2–3

Description: "All day" pace, or classic long slow distance (LSD) training. Sensation of leg effort/fatigue generally low, but may rise periodically to higher levels (e.g., when climbing). Concentration generally required to maintain effort only at highest end of range and/or during longer training sessions. Breathing is more regular than at Level 1, but continuous conversation is still possible. Frequent (daily) training sessions of moderate duration (e.g., 2 hours) at Level 2 is possible (provided dietary carbohydrate intake is adequate), but complete recovery from very long workouts may take more than 24 hours.

Level	Name	Average Power	Average HR	Perceived Exertion
3	Tempo	76–90%	84–94%	3–4

Description: Typical intensity of fartlek workout, "spirited" group ride, or briskly moving paceline. More frequent/greater sensation of leg effort/fatigue than at Level 2. Requires concentration to maintain alone, especially at upper end of range, to prevent effort from falling back to Level 2. Breathing deeper and more rhythmic than at Level 2, such that any conversation must be somewhat halting, but not as difficult as at Level 4. Recovery from Level 3 training sessions are more difficult than after Level 2 workouts, but consecutive days of Level 3 training are still possible if duration is not excessive and dietary carbohydrate intake is adequate.

Level	Name	Average Power	Average HR	Perceived Exertion
4	Lactate Threshold	91–105%	95–105% *May not be achieved during initial phases of effort(s)*	4–5

Description: Just below to just above TT effort, taking into account duration, current fitness, environmental conditions, etc. Essentially continuous sensation of moderate or even greater leg effort/fatigue. Continuous conversation difficult at best, owing to depth/frequency of breathing. Effort sufficiently high that sustained exercise at this level is mentally very taxing—therefore typically performed in training as multiple "repeats," "modules," or "blocks" of 10–30 minutes in duration. Consecutive days of training at Level 4 are possible, but such workouts are generally only performed when cyclist is sufficiently rested/recovered from prior training so as to be able to maintain intensity.

(continues)

Level	Name	Average Power	Average HR	Perceived Exertion
TABLE 3.1	*POWER-BASED TRAINING LEVELS (continued)*			
5	VO$_2$max	106–120%	>106%	6–7

Description: Typical intensity of longer (3–8 minute) intervals intended to increase VO$_2$max. Strong to severe sensations of leg effort/fatigue, such that completion of more than 30–40 minute total training time is difficult at best. Conversation not possible due to often "ragged" breathing. Should generally be attempted only when adequately recovered from prior training. Consecutive days of Level 5 work not necessarily desirable even if possible.

| 6 | Anaerobic Capacity | 121–150% | N/A | >7 |

Description: Short (30-second to 3-minute), high-intensity intervals designed to increase anaerobic capacity. Heart rate generally not useful as guide to intensity due to non-steady-state nature of effort. Severe sensation of leg effort/fatigue; conversation is impossible. Consecutive days of extended Level 6 training usually not attempted.

| 7 | Neuromuscular Power | N/A | N/A | |

Description: (Maximal) Very short, very high-intensity efforts (e.g., jumps, standing starts, short sprints) that generally place greater stress on musculoskeletal rather than metabolic systems. Power is useful as a guide, but only in reference to prior similar efforts, not TT pace.

*Percentages of average power and average HR are at functional threshold power.

fewer levels, for the sake of simplicity. In the present system, seven levels were felt to be the minimum needed to represent the full range of physiological responses and to adequately describe the different types of training required and used to meet the demands of competitive cycling. Table 3.2 lists the primary physiological adaptations expected to result from training at each level, although these will obviously be influenced by factors such as the initial fitness of the individual, the duration of each workout, the time taken between each interval effort, and other factors.

Heart Rate Guidelines

Relating the specified power levels to corresponding heart-rate ranges or zones is somewhat difficult to do owing to the inherent variability of heart rate as well as individual differences in the power-HR relationship (even when referenced to threshold power). Nonetheless, approximate

TABLE 3.2 *EXPECTED PHYSIOLOGICAL/PERFORMANCE ADAPTATIONS RESULTING FROM TRAINING AT LEVELS 1—7*

	1 Active Recovery	2 Endurance	3 Tempo	4 Lactate Threshold	5 VO$_2$max	6 Anaerobic Capacity	7 Neuro-muscular Power
Average power as percent of functional threshold power	<55%	56–75%	76–90%	91–105%	106–120%	121–150%	N/A
Intensity factor	<0.75	0.75–0.85	0.85–0.95	0.95–1.05	1.05–1.15	>1.15	N/A
Typical length of continuous ride	30–90 min	60–300 min	60–180 min	N/A	N/A	N/A	N/A
Typical length of interval effort	N/A	N/A	N/A	8–30 min	3–8 min	30 sec–3 min	<30 sec
Increased plasma volume		+	++	+++	++++	+	
Increased muscle mitochondrial enzymes		++	+++	++++	++	+	
Increased lactate threshold		++	+++	++++	++	+	
Increased muscle glycogen storage		++	++++	+++	++	+	
Hypertrophy of slow-twitch muscle fibers		+	++	++	+++	+	
Increased muscle capillarization		+	++	++	+++	+	
Interconversion of fast-twitch muscle fibers (type IIb -> type IIa)		++	+++	+++	++	+	
Increased stroke volume/maximal cardiac output		+	++	+++	++++	+	
Increased VO$_2$max		+	++	+++	++++	+	
Increased muscle high energy phosphate (ATP/PCr) stores						+	++
Increased anaerobic capacity ("lactate tolerance")					+	+++	+
Hypertrophy of fast-twitch fibers						+	++
Increased neuro-muscular power						+	+++

Note: The plus signs represent the magnitude of adaptation. The more the "+" signs, the greater the adaptation.

HR guidelines have been provided in Table 3.1 so that they can be used along with power to help guide training, if desired.

Perceived Exertion Guidelines

The values used in Table 3.1 for perceived exertion are from Gunnar Borg's ten-point category-ratio scale, not the original twenty-point scale that is more commonly used (see Table 3.3). We use this scale because it explicitly recognizes the nonlinear response of many physiological variables (e.g., blood and muscle lactate) and thus provides a better indicator of overall effort. Since perceived exertion increases over time even at a constant exercise intensity (power), the suggested values or ranges refer to perceived effort

TABLE 3.3

GUNNAR BORG'S TEN-POINT CATAGORY-RATIO SCALE OF PERCEIVED EXERTION

Percieved Exertion	Description
0	Nothing at all
0.5	Extremely weak
1	Very weak
2	Weak (light)
3	Moderate
4	Somewhat strong
5	Strong (heavy)
6	
7	Very strong
8	
9	
10	Extremely strong
*	Maximal

as determined relatively early in a training session or series of intervals.

Other Issues

Although this method of determining an individual's power level is based on the average power that an individual produces during a workout or interval effort, consideration must also be given to the distribution of power. For example, average power during mass-start races typically falls within Level 3, but racing at Level 3 is often more stressful than training at Level 3 because in racing there is greater variability (and therefore higher peaks) in power. Similarly, because of soft-pedaling and coasting, the average power achieved during a hilly ride or group training session is not equivalent to the same average power achieved during a completely flat ride or solo workout.

In part, this variability in power is already taken into account in the definitions of the various levels, especially Levels 2 and 3 (training at the higher levels will tend to be much more structured than training at the

TABLE 3.4	JOE ATHLETE'S WATTAGE LEVELS: HYPOTHETICAL WATTAGE RANGES BASED ON FTP OF 290		

| | | Wattage Range | |
	% of Theshold Power	Low	High
Active Recovery Level 1	<55%	1	160
Endurance Level 2	56–75%	161	218
Tempo Level 3	76–90%	219	261
Lactate Threshold Level 4	91–105%	262	305
VO₂max Level 5	106–120%	306	348
Anaerobic Capacity Level 6	121–150%	349	435
Neuromuscular Power Level 7	N/A		

lower levels, thus limiting variations in power). Furthermore, there is obviously an inverse relationship between power output and the duration that this power can be sustained. Thus, it is axiomatic that power during shorter training sessions or efforts will fall toward the higher end of a given range, whereas power during longer sessions or efforts will fall toward the lower end of a given range. Nonetheless, a workout consisting of 30 minutes of cycling at Level 1 (a warm-up, for example), 60 minutes of cycling at Level 3, and then another 30 minutes of cycling at Level 1 (a cool-down) would best be described as a Tempo training session, even though the overall average power might fall within Level 2.

How to Determine Your Training Levels

If you performed the test described in Step 1, you have defined your power at 20 minutes and derived your 60-minute power from that. Now, you can take this value and plug it into the percentages for each level to obtain your wattage range at each level.

Let's look at a hypothetical example to see exactly how this works. Say there is a cyclist, Joe Athlete, who has a threshold of 290 watts. His training levels are defined in Table 3.4.

Because 55 percent of 290 is 159.5 (290 x 0.55 = 159.5), we can say that at Level 1 Joe's wattage range will be from 1 to 160. At Level 2, his wattage range will be between 161 and 218 (because 161 is about 56 percent of 290, and 218 is about 75 percent of 290). Calculating the other percentages, it turns out that Joe's range will be from 218 to 261 watts at Level 3, from 262 to 305 at Level 4, and so on. To come up with your own ranges, you can do the same calculations using your own threshold figure instead of Joe's 290.

Once you've constructed your own table, what do you do with it? Again, let's look at what our hypothetical Joe Athlete could do. Now that he knows his training levels, he can begin to train with a specific wattage range in mind as a goal. This will allow him to improve in the specific areas that need work. If Joe needs help on his VO_2max power, then he can begin to specifically address that "hole" in his fitness by working in the 306–348 watt range. Joe also knows that if he is to go on a recovery ride, then he must stay below 160 watts in order to really help his body to recover. Otherwise, he would risk riding too hard and not getting sufficient recovery.

Since Joe has used a heart rate monitor before, he can also begin to understand the relationship between his heart-rate zones and his new wattage levels. For Level 3 (Tempo) riding using wattage, Joe will see watts between 218 and 261. He may find that his heart rate fluctuates all the way from his Level 2 (Endurance) heart-rate zone to his Level 4 (Lactate Threshold) heart-rate zone, while his power is still in the Tempo level. Joe can now see how fatigue, dehydration, and low blood sugar might impact his wattage dramatically even when it does not impact his heart rate, or vice versa. Each individual is different, and knowing the different training levels will allow Joe to train effectively. He may find that he was not training as hard as he could have in the past, and he can make sure his wattage does not drop below the training level he is targeting. Joe can now begin to make the shift from his previous heart rate–based training into a power-based training scheme.

Step 3: Collect More Data

We'll address specific workouts in Chapter 5, but at least for now, you have taken the first two steps in training with a power meter. Step 3 is the fun part of training with a power meter: All you have to do is go out, ride and stomp on the pedals, and see what you can do. It will bring new meaning to training rides and training loops that you have done hundreds of times. Meanwhile, you'll be collecting data on yourself and learning how many watts it takes to get up your local hill or how hard you have to go during the Tuesday Night World Championships in order to win the sprint coming back into town.

You can also begin to learn which roads in your area are the best stretches to do specific intervals that require you to hold a small wattage range. If you are doing a threshold workout (Level 4), you may find that you can easily hold your watts steady on a long, gradual climb, for example, and that might be your best place to do this type of a workout. By collecting all this data, you will be on your way to learning your strengths and weaknesses as a cyclist, giving you a head start on the next step in your training.

P EOPLE—ESPECIALLY ATHLETES—are always sizing themselves up, and cyclists are no exception. On rides you may have heard other cyclists saying, "Oh, I am a bad climber," or "I have no snap or sprint." You may have said these types of things yourself. And maybe there have been times when you correctly assessed your relative weaknesses, or when those other cyclists were able to pinpoint exactly what was holding them back. But oftentimes, such guesses are just not on target. By using the power meter data that you collect in races, in training rides, and in tests, it is possible to create a "Power Profile" of your strengths and weaknesses. We have developed a method of doing just that, and in this chapter you will learn how to use this method—which incorporates power meter technology, of course—to create a profile of your own strengths and weaknesses as a cyclist—based on the facts, rather than your subjective opinion.

The Power Profile

When we first began collecting data on various riders, it was because we simply wanted to get a clearer picture of the power that different types of cyclists could produce. What levels could be attained by elite pro riders?

What could masters riders do? What about beginners? From these datasets, we were able to create the Power Profile chart (see Table 4.1). Our original intention was to compile enough information that we would be able to see whether the athletes we were coaching were on track with their training. However, when we started to plot riders' profiles, it quickly became evident that this way of looking at things gave us powerful clues to the relative strengths and weaknesses of individual riders and their physiological systems.

If a rider had a strong anaerobic capacity as compared to his or her lactate threshold, for example, then we would see this easily in his or her profile. If a rider was talented neuromuscularly, but challenged cardiovascularly, this, too, was easy to quantify in the Power Profile. What started out as a way to compare an individual's performance against others turned out to be one of the most effective ways to quantify the relative strengths and weaknesses of each rider.

There have been other attempts to generate guidelines or benchmarks for power output. These have usually been based on racer category (i.e., Cat. I, Cat. II, etc.). Aside from satisfying people's natural curiosity, though, such category-based values have seemed to be of limited practical use—after all, the best measure of a racer's competitive ability relative to others is found in actual race performance, not power output. If, however, valid standards were available for power across different durations that represented different physiological characteristics or abilities, rather than simply racing categories, then it would be possible, we reasoned, to identify a particular individual's relative strengths and weaknesses. In other words, we would be able to see how a cyclist was doing in one area compared with how he or she was doing in other areas, rather than how he or she was doing in comparison with others. This is where the true value of Power Profiling comes in. When you know your relative strengths and weaknesses, you can develop a program to improve in the weak areas, and that is when you will see real progress. And it may even be possible to identify events where you could be expected to achieve the greatest success, and thereby build on your strengths. Our goal was to develop rational guidelines that could be used for these purposes.

The Approach

In theory, tables of standards for power output for different durations could be generated by simply collecting data on a large number of cyclists of widely varying ability. However, it is highly unlikely that any coach or researcher would have access to a sufficiently large database for this approach to be very accurate. As an alternative, estimates of power output for riders of differing abilities could be derived from actual performance—for example, in time trials. This approach, however, would require one to make somewhat tenuous assumptions regarding body mass, aerodynamic drag, and so on, and such a method would become particularly complex when applied to shorter duration, non-steady-state events (e.g., kilometer track event).

We therefore used a third approach, which was to "anchor" the upper and lower ends of each range based on the known performance abilities of world champion athletes and untrained persons, respectively. For example, a world-class cyclist would produce between 22.66 and 24.04 watts per kilogram in a 5-second sprint, whereas an untrained beginner might produce only 10.57 to 11.95 watts per kilogram. We assigned ranges in between these extremes to six other divisions (exceptional, excellent, very good, good, moderate, and fair). (See Table 4.1.) In addition, we used our own data on the wide variety of athletes with whom we worked to provide confirmation of these figures. The advantage of this approach is that it enhances the validity of comparisons across event durations—for example, a "world-class" power output should be equivalent regardless of whether the duration over which it is measured is 5 seconds or 1 hour.

Choice of Target Durations

We chose index efforts of 5 seconds, 1 minute, and 5 minutes and a fourth measure at functional threshold power because we believed they would best reflect neuromuscular power, anaerobic capacity, maximal oxygen uptake (VO_2max), and lactate threshold (LT), respectively. However, this does not imply that a 1-minute all-out effort is completely anaerobic (in fact, roughly 40–45 percent of the energy expended during such exercise is derived aerobically), or that it fully utilizes anaerobic capacity (which generally requires 1.5–2.5 minutes to deplete). Nor does it mean that a 5-minute all-out effort entails exercising at precisely 100 percent of VO_2max (most athletes can sustain a power that would

TABLE 4.1 *POWER PROFILE OUTPUT (IN WKG)*

	Men				Women			
	5 sec.	1 min.	5 min.	FT	5 sec.	1 min.	5 min.	FT
World class (e.g., international pro)	24.04	11.50	7.60	6.40	19.42	9.29	6.61	5.69
	23.77	11.39	7.50	6.31	19.20	9.20	6.52	5.61
	23.50	11.27	7.39	6.22	18.99	9.11	6.42	5.53
	23.22	11.16	7.29	6.13	18.77	9.02	6.33	5.44
	22.95	11.04	7.19	6.04	18.56	8.93	6.24	5.36
	22.68	10.93	7.08	5.96	18.34	8.84	6.15	5.28
Exceptional (e.g., domestic pro)	22.41	10.81	6.98	5.87	18.13	8.75	6.05	5.20
	22.14	10.70	6.88	5.78	17.91	8.66	5.96	5.12
	21.86	10.58	6.77	5.69	17.70	8.56	5.87	5.03
	21.59	10.47	6.67	5.60	17.48	8.47	5.78	4.95
	21.32	10.35	6.57	5.51	17.26	8.38	5.68	4.87
	21.05	10.24	6.46	5.42	17.05	8.29	5.59	4.79
Excellent (e.g., cat. 1)	20.78	10.12	6.36	5.33	16.83	8.20	5.50	4.70
	20.51	10.01	6.26	5.24	16.62	8.11	5.41	4.62
	20.23	9.89	6.15	5.15	16.40	8.02	5.31	4.54
	19.96	9.78	6.05	5.07	16.19	7.93	5.22	4.46
	19.69	9.66	5.95	4.98	15.97	7.84	5.13	4.38
	19.42	9.55	5.84	4.89	15.76	7.75	5.04	4.29
Very good (e.g., cat. 2)	19.15	9.43	5.74	4.80	15.54	7.66	4.94	4.21
	18.87	9.32	5.64	4.71	15.32	7.57	4.85	4.13
	18.60	9.20	5.53	4.62	15.11	7.48	4.76	4.05
	18.33	9.09	5.43	4.53	14.89	7.39	4.67	3.97
	18.06	8.97	5.33	4.44	14.68	7.30	4.57	3.88
	17.79	8.86	5.22	4.35	14.46	7.21	4.48	3.80
	17.51	8.74	5.12	4.27	14.25	7.11	4.39	3.72
Good (e.g., cat. 3)	17.24	8.63	5.01	4.18	14.03	7.02	4.30	3.64
	16.97	8.51	4.91	4.09	13.82	6.93	4.20	3.55
	16.70	8.40	4.81	4.00	13.60	6.84	4.11	3.47
	16.43	8.28	4.70	3.91	13.39	6.75	4.02	3.39
	16.15	8.17	4.60	3.82	13.17	6.66	3.93	3.31
	15.88	8.05	4.50	3.73	12.95	6.57	3.83	3.23
Moderate (e.g., cat. 4)	15.61	7.94	4.39	3.64	12.74	6.48	3.74	3.14
	15.34	7.82	4.29	3.55	12.52	6.39	3.65	3.06
	15.07	7.71	4.19	3.47	12.31	6.30	3.56	2.98
	14.79	7.59	4.08	3.38	12.09	6.21	3.46	2.90
	14.52	7.48	3.98	3.29	11.88	6.12	3.37	2.82
	14.25	7.36	3.88	3.20	11.66	6.03	3.28	2.73
Fair (e.g., cat. 5)	13.98	7.25	3.77	3.11	11.45	5.94	3.19	2.65
	13.71	7.13	3.67	3.02	11.23	5.85	3.09	2.57
	13.44	7.02	3.57	2.93	11.01	5.76	3.00	2.49
	13.16	6.90	3.46	2.84	10.80	5.66	2.91	2.40
	12.89	6.79	3.36	2.75	10.58	5.57	2.82	2.32
	12.62	6.67	3.26	2.66	10.37	5.48	2.72	2.24
Untrained (e.g., non-racer)	12.35	6.56	3.15	2.58	10.15	5.39	2.63	2.16
	12.08	6.44	3.05	2.49	9.94	5.30	2.54	2.08
	11.80	6.33	2.95	2.40	9.72	5.21	2.45	1.99
	11.53	6.21	2.84	2.31	9.51	5.12	2.35	1.91
	11.26	6.10	2.74	2.22	9.29	5.03	2.26	1.83
	10.99	5.99	2.64	2.13	9.07	4.94	2.17	1.75
	10.72	5.87	2.53	2.04	8.86	4.85	2.07	1.67
	10.44	5.76	2.43	1.95	8.64	4.76	1.98	1.58
	10.17	5.64	2.33	1.86	8.43	4.67	1.89	1.50

elicit 105–110 percent of their VO_2max for this duration). Rather, power output over these target durations would be expected to correlate well with more direct measurements of these different physiological abilities. Second, the index efforts were chosen in an attempt to increase the reproducibility of the data, as well as for convenience in gathering the data.

THE POWER PROFILE TEST

Conducting the Test

To create a Power Profile of your own strengths and weaknesses in cycling, you will need to complete the Power Profile Test described below. You have already gathered one figure for your Power Profile: You'll use the result from the FTP test described in Chapter 3 for the FT (Functional Threshold) column of the profile. To do the test described below, it is again important to find a section of road where you will not be interrupted by stop signs or intersections, and again, it should be a place that you can return to periodically for retesting. The wind conditions should be similar every time you conduct the test, and you should be at a similar place in your training block. It is also good idea to do the test right after a "rest week" so that you will be fresh and also relatively fit.

Be sure to always perform the same warm-up routine on the way to your "testing grounds." This warm-up should last about 45 minutes and should include three 1-minute drills of fast pedaling with your cadence at about 110 rpm. Rest for 1 minute between each drill, with easy spinning. These fast pedaling drills will help to warm up your muscular and cardiovascular systems. Also do one 5-minute effort at your FTP, and then one all-out 1-minute effort. Rest for 3–5 minutes between these. These sprints will help you to get warmed up further and prepare you for the real testing. The majority of your warm-up should be in Levels 2–3 (Endurance to Tempo from the categories listed in Table 3.1). Make sure you have at least 10 minutes of easy pedaling before the first effort.

When you begin your test efforts, do not worry about cadence, heart rate, or anything besides the stop clock, and make sure you drive it to the end of each timed effort. In other words, just do the work, and what happens, happens. Record your efforts as intervals on your power meter, if possible. For the actual test, take these steps:

5 minutes all out. Start from about 20 mph, and really hammer it in the last 45 seconds!

10-minute rest. Ride at Level 2 (Endurance) pace.

1 minute all-out. Start from about 20 mph. You should be out of the saddle and hammering at the beginning, and then seated and driving it all the way to the finish.

5-minute rest. Ride at Level 2 (Endurance) pace.

1 minute all-out.

5-minute rest. Ride at Level 2 (Endurance) pace.

15-second sprint. Start from a slow speed, about 15 mph, and sprint as hard as you can, out of the saddle.

2-minute rest. Ride at Level 2 (Endurance) pace.

15-second sprint. Sprint as hard as you can, out of the saddle.

That's it. Go for a short cool down ride and then get in at least 300–500 kilojoules more at Level 2 to call it a good training ride.

Now, download your data and pick out the best watts for each time period.

Application and Interpretation

Since weight influences how many watts you can produce, it is important to find out your power-to-weight ratio. How many watts per kilogram can you produce? A rider who weighs 200 pounds and produces 350 watts up a hill, for example, will be able to ride side-by-side with another rider who weighs 125 pounds but is only producing 218 watts. Why? Because for each of these riders, the power-to-weight ratio is the same, at 3.850 watts per kilogram.

The power-to-weight ratio is very important in cycling. The higher your power-to-weight ratio is, the stronger you are as a cyclist. That is why in cycling, it can be said that one of the main goals is to be as light as possible in weight, but to produce the highest possible watts. The trick is figuring out at what weight you produce the most watts.

In order to find out your ratio, you will first need to know how much you weigh in kilograms. To do this, divide your weight in pounds by 2.2. For example, if you weigh 165 pounds, you would divide 165 by 2.2 to discover that you weigh 75 kilograms. Now, take your wattage numbers at each time period and divide them by your weight in kilograms. If you held 423 watts for 5 minutes, for example (and you weigh 75 kilograms), divide 423 by 75. In this case, you would get 6.64, which would mean that you produced 6.64 watts per kilogram. The Power Profile chart is stated in watts per kilogram because it is the standard scientific power-to-weight ratio measurement used around the world.

Since weight influences how many watts you can produce, it is important to find out your power-to-weight ratio.

To use the Power Profile table (Table 4.1), simply locate the peak or maximum power that you can generate for 5 seconds, 1 minute, and 5 minutes and at functional threshold power, and then find corresponding values in the rows of the table. You can make a copy of the table from this book and circle or highlight where your performance falls in the list of ranges. If your performance falls between tabled values, which will often be the case, assign the nearest ranking. It is critical that the values used in this analysis be truly reflective of your very best effort over that duration; otherwise, the resultant profile may be distorted, leading to inappropriate conclusions and decisions about training.

What emerges as you highlight your results will be a unique pattern that shows your relative strengths and weaknesses in cycling. You may find that you are at a higher level in sprinting, for example, than in efforts requiring endurance, or vice versa. The pattern may change slightly over time as you train and work on the weak areas. Although every Power Profile is unique, there are some typical patterns. These patterns are illustrated in Table 4.2. However, in considering these examples, keep in mind that performance at each duration is being evaluated in light of the world's best cycling performances. Thus, road cyclists will tend to appear relatively weak in 5-second sprints in comparison with match sprinters, and nonendurance track racers will likely have relatively low 5-minute and FTP levels relative to their abilities at the shorter durations. (Though we considered the possibility of developing road- and track-specific tables, we decided not to, in part because many riders compete in both disciplines.)

Also keep in mind that, based on physiological considerations, an inverse relationship might be expected to occur between anaerobic and aerobic efforts—that is, someone who is great in aerobic forms of exercise, such as the Tour de France, may not be as strong in anaerobic forms, such as the match-sprint event on the track. At the same time, however, a positive association might be expected between each pair. (Although the scientific literature is in fact split on whether there actually is an inverse relationship between short-term and long-term power, there is clearly a positive association within each category.)

Examples of Power Profiles

All-Rounder

The cyclist who is an all-rounder will have a generally horizontal plot across all the categories. That is, all four values will fall at about the same point in that individual's range. The all-rounder does not necessarily excel at any one thing but is likely competitive in his or her category across a broad range of events.

Given the fact that only specialists will likely truly excel at the extreme durations, very few individuals will show this pattern and still fall at the upper end of each range. Instead, the vast majority of nonelite athletes will likely show a generally horizontal Power Profile because they have not yet developed specific strengths. This is a very common profile for beginning racers; as a racer or other rider trains more and more, those areas of strength will begin to reveal themselves.

Sprinter

A good sprinter will typically have a distinctly down-sloping plot (especially between the 1-minute and 5-minute categories). This pattern is characteristic of an athlete whose natural abilities are skewed toward success in short-duration, high-power events. Since aerobic ability is quite trainable, such an individual may be able to become more of an "all-rounder" through focused training; however, if the individual is a sprinter who has already been training hard for many years, he or she may always still be better at anaerobic efforts than at aerobic ones. If so, focusing on events that favor these abilities, such as track racing and criteriums, may result in the most success.

Time Trialist

A distinctly up-sloping plot (again, especially between the columns for 1 minute and 5 minutes, but also between 5 minutes and FTP) is typical for the classical time trialist. This is because most time trialists are weak

TABLE 4.2 *POWER PROFILE: ALL-ROUNDER*

	Men				Women			
	5 sec.	1 min.	5 min.	FT	5 sec.	1 min.	5 min.	FT
World class (e.g., international pro)	24.04	11.50	7.60	6.40	19.42	9.29	6.61	5.69
	23.77	11.39	7.50	6.31	19.20	9.20	6.52	5.61
	23.50	11.27	7.39	6.22	18.99	9.11	6.42	5.53
	23.22	11.16	7.29	6.13	18.77	9.02	6.33	5.44
	22.95	11.04	7.19	6.04	18.56	8.93	6.24	5.36
	22.68	10.93	7.08	5.96	18.34	8.84	6.15	5.28
Exceptional (e.g., domestic pro)	22.41	10.81	6.98	5.87	18.13	8.75	6.05	5.20
	22.14	10.70	6.88	5.78	17.91	8.66	5.96	5.12
	21.86	10.58	6.77	5.69	17.70	8.56	5.87	5.03
	21.59	10.47	6.67	5.60	17.48	8.47	5.78	4.95
	21.32	10.35	6.57	5.51	17.26	8.38	5.68	4.87
	21.05	10.24	6.46	5.42	17.05	8.29	5.59	4.79
Excellent (e.g., cat. 1)	20.78	10.12	6.36	5.33	16.83	8.20	5.50	4.70
	20.51	10.01	6.26	5.24	16.62	8.11	5.41	4.62
	20.23	9.89	6.15	5.15	16.40	8.02	5.31	4.54
	19.96	9.78	6.05	5.07	16.19	7.93	5.22	4.46
	19.69	9.66	5.95	4.98	15.97	7.84	5.13	4.38
	19.42	9.55	5.84	4.89	15.76	7.75	5.04	4.29
Very good (e.g., cat. 2)	19.15	9.43	5.74	4.80	15.54	7.66	4.94	4.21
	18.87	9.32	5.64	4.71	15.32	7.57	4.85	4.13
	18.60	9.20	5.53	4.62	15.11	7.48	4.76	4.05
	18.33	9.09	5.43	**4.53**	14.89	7.39	4.67	3.97
	18.06	**8.97**	5.33	4.44	14.68	7.30	4.57	3.88
	17.79	8.86	**5.22**	4.35	14.46	7.21	4.48	3.80
	17.51	8.74	5.12	4.27	14.25	7.11	4.39	3.72
Good (e.g., cat. 3)	17.24	8.63	5.01	4.18	14.03	7.02	4.30	**3.64**
	16.97	8.51	4.91	4.09	13.82	**6.93**	**4.20**	3.55
	16.70	8.40	4.81	4.00	**13.60**	6.84	4.11	3.47
	16.43	8.28	4.70	3.91	13.39	6.75	4.02	3.39
	16.15	8.17	4.60	3.82	13.17	6.66	3.93	3.31
	15.88	8.05	4.50	3.73	12.95	6.57	3.83	3.23
Moderate (e.g., cat. 4)	15.61	7.94	4.39	3.64	12.74	6.48	3.74	3.14
	15.34	7.82	4.29	3.55	12.52	6.39	3.65	3.06
	15.07	7.71	4.19	3.47	12.31	6.30	3.56	2.98
	14.79	7.59	4.08	3.38	12.09	6.21	3.46	2.90
	14.52	7.48	3.98	3.29	11.88	6.12	3.37	2.82
	14.25	7.36	3.88	3.20	11.66	6.03	3.28	2.73
Fair (e.g., cat. 5)	13.98	7.25	3.77	3.11	11.45	5.94	3.19	2.65
	13.71	7.13	3.67	3.02	11.23	5.85	3.09	2.57
	13.44	7.02	3.57	2.93	11.01	5.76	3.00	2.49
	13.16	6.90	3.46	2.84	10.80	5.66	2.91	2.40
	12.89	6.79	3.36	2.75	10.58	5.57	2.82	2.32
	12.62	6.67	3.26	2.66	10.37	5.48	2.72	2.24
Untrained (e.g., non-racer)	12.35	6.56	3.15	2.58	10.15	5.39	2.63	2.16
	12.08	6.44	3.05	2.49	9.94	5.30	2.54	2.08
	11.80	6.33	2.95	2.40	9.72	5.21	2.45	1.99
	11.53	6.21	2.84	2.31	9.51	5.12	2.35	1.91
	11.26	6.10	2.74	2.22	9.29	5.03	2.26	1.83
	10.99	5.99	2.64	2.13	9.07	4.94	2.17	1.75
	10.72	5.87	2.53	2.04	8.86	4.85	2.07	1.67
	10.44	5.76	2.43	1.95	8.64	4.76	1.98	1.58
	10.17	5.64	2.33	1.86	8.43	4.67	1.89	1.50

in neuromuscular power and anaerobic capacity, but have relatively high aerobic power and an especially high lactate threshold. Though such athletes may be able to improve their performance by spending lots of time practicing sprints, this may not be the case if the training results in a decline in strength, which is sustainable power. A time trialist could indeed improve his sprint, but the small improvements in his sprint may not result in more race wins; meanwhile, the time spent working on sprints would mean less time spent on improving FTP—therefore, by practicing sprints, the time trialist could lose fitness and perform worse in their time trial races.

> *A sharply inverted "V" pattern represents an athlete who has both relatively high anaerobic capacity and high aerobic ability.*

Pursuiter

A sharply inverted "V" pattern represents an athlete who has both relatively high anaerobic capacity and high aerobic ability, and who is thus well suited for events such as the pursuit. Alternatively, a potential "all-rounder" who simply hasn't focused on raising his or her lactate threshold to its highest possible level may exhibit this same pattern.

On the other hand, a sharp "V" pattern is a relatively unlikely combination, given the expected inverse relationship between neuromuscular power and lactate threshold and the positive relationship expected between VO_2max and lactate threshold. Should such a pattern be observed, care should be taken to assure that the values being used are truly representative of the athlete's abilities.

Limitations and Caveats

The Power Profile standards are based on the performance capacities of young adults and thus do not account for the effects of aging (or development). We considered developing age-specific standards, but rejected this idea because it would be difficult to collect sufficient data. Attempting corrections based on known physiological changes would also be difficult. For example, starting around age 30, VO_2max declines a little each year. In men it declines annually by about 0.5 ml/kg/min (that is, milliliters per kilogram per minute, the standard measure used for VO_2max); in women, it declines at a slightly slower rate, about 0.35 ml/kg/min a year. Muscle strength and power, in contrast, can generally be well maintained, with training, until around age 50, but they begin to decline somewhat more rapidly thereafter. Therefore, for maximum accuracy, different age-based correction factors might need to be applied to the different columns. It is unlikely, however, that these differential changes with age are sufficient to significantly alter a rider's own profile, and we suggest that the table simply be applied "as is" regardless of a rider's age.

What Next?

Now that you have created your own Power Profile, you can easily see the areas in your own cycling that need to be addressed. Use these tables to motivate yourself to make improvements and also to race or ride to your strengths. If you are a world-class sprinter, it might be futile to try and break the Mt. Evans hill-climb record. You may even have limitations in certain areas because there is a genetic basis to your strengths and weaknesses. But in most cases, it is possible to focus your training and make strides toward specific goals. It's also important that you revise your chart on a regular basis (such as once every four to six weeks) in order to note any improvements from your previous training block. This is an excellent way to make sure all your hard work is going in the right places.

USING POWER TO CHANGE YOUR WORKOUTS

5

OW THAT YOU KNOW your functional threshold power and power levels, and you have determined your strengths and weaknesses as a cyclist by constructing a Power Profile, you can begin to change your training to better address your unique situation. You can improve in the weak areas, and you can track your fitness increases. By developing specific workouts based on wattage, you will be able to monitor your efforts in training more accurately. You will be able to make better decisions about when to stop an interval, when to take a rest day, or when to tackle greater challenges. The tips presented in this chapter are not meant to last for only a season; nor do we present a "one size fits all" workout plan that every cyclist can follow. Rather, our goal is to help you to discover how to develop your own training program to meet your unique set of objectives, and how to reevaluate and revise that program as you make progress.

Training Opportunities

Simply said, you can use your power meter on every ride, but some rides are more useful than others for optimizing the technology as a tool in achieving your peak performance. Specifically, you should use your power meter:

On an indoor trainer. On a trainer, it is easy to regulate your wattage, as there are no external influences, such as wind or traffic, to interfere, and you can easily hold to a specific wattage range.

On flat roads. This is also an excellent place in which to utilize a specific wattage protocol, as the terrain allows for a steady power output.

In time trials. Using your power meter to help maintain your pace right at lactate threshold is one of the greatest ways to incorporate it into racing. You can stick to your power goal like glue and also select the best cadence. Use your power meter to follow the cardinal rule of time trialing: "Don't start too hard, don't start too hard, don't start too hard!"

In hill climbs. When climbing a gradual grade, you can stay within a small range of power and use watts to maintain an optimal pace. You can determine your optimal climbing cadence by doing multiple repeats on a climb, selecting different cadences each time, and seeing which cadence produces the most watts for the lowest heart rate.

While doing specific intervals and training protocols. Using your power meter to do, for example, a 5-minute interval at 295–305 watts is a perfect example of being able to really dial in your training. Using heart rate as a guide for doing the same 5-minute interval could cause you to go too hard in the beginning, thus reaching a higher power level than you wanted and overshooting your goal for the effort.

While doing "race-winning intervals" and other wattage-based workouts. You will begin to put together your own favorite workouts using wattage, and that will help motivate you to achieve even more success. By using the "interval" or "set" function to mark an interval, you can watch your average wattage while executing the interval, and this can become a great "carrot" for you to push harder than before.

The "Stochastic" Nature of Cycling

One of the first things you may notice when you begin riding with a power meter is the highly variable nature of your wattage. One second, it's 500 watts, the next second it's 0 watts, and the next it's 220 watts. Although your power seems "stochastic," or random, it is actually just highly variable because of the nature of the terrain, the wind, the riders around and in front of you, and so on. This seeming randomness makes it very hard to maintain your watts in a narrow range. Only on the flattest of roads, with little to no wind, or on an indoor trainer is it possible to adhere strictly to a small range of wattage.

Because of this inherently stochastic nature of cycling, it is important not to become discouraged if you are unable to hold a perfect 300 watts while doing, for example, a lactate threshold interval. Rather than trying to hit a specific wattage target, you should attempt to stay within a particular range. Avoid overdoing the maximum watts for a particular effort. For example, you might focus on producing at least 300 watts, but not exceeding 320 watts, while holding a 90 rpm cadence, if your goal is to work the lactate system but not go too hard. The importance of correctly pacing your efforts during a specific interval will become very evident, because it is pacing that will allow you to successfully complete the interval correctly.

As you read through the workout suggestions that follow and begin to incorporate them into your training, make sure that you also choose the correct terrain for each type of effort. In this way, you will activate the appropriate physiological systems. If you are trying to improve your anaerobic system with 1-minute efforts at 475–500 watts, for example, then make sure you are attacking a slight uphill for that minute or a flat road without any downhills. If you are focusing on a 60-minute effort in your Tempo level, then make sure that you keep your watts in this range 90 percent of the time. There may be times when you have to go up a hill and your watts will be over your Tempo range, and this is fine; just make sure that you apply steady power and come back to the Tempo range when you crest the hill. The same applies on the downhills, where it's nearly impossible to push hard enough on the pedals to create a high wattage number, and that's okay; just make sure you are on the gas as much as possible and back to your Tempo range soon.

If you live in an area that offers only one type of terrain, then you will have to make adjustments in your training to overcome this. For example, if all the roads available to you are flat, you could use the wind to your advantage in generating more resistance for you to push against. Rolling hills present the greatest challenge to holding a smooth and steady power output. If you live in an area with only rolling hills, focus on staying within your target wattage range on the uphills. It would be difficult, in any case, to make rolling terrain into a Tempo ride: If you wanted to end your ride with your average watts in the Tempo level, then you would have to hammer up every hill, because your watts would go down on every downhill run. Unfortunately, this would not be a Tempo workout! It would be a hill-repeat workout, and most likely you would be primarily working on your VO_2max or your anaerobic capacity system. The nature of hilly terrain also makes it very tough to do easy recovery rides and endurance rides without having to put your power in the upper training levels. If you live in such an area and you need a rest, then ride on an indoor trainer so you can more easily adhere to the recovery wattage guidelines.

How Many Efforts to Complete?

When should you stop doing repeats? Is there a point at which doing just one more interval is actually not helping you anymore? Can you do too many intervals? And at what point do you experience diminishing marginal returns? These questions have probably been asked by every cyclist and coach a thousand times over, and they have been the source of many an argument between sports scientists. But there is an easy answer to all of them: It depends!

It depends on your goal for that particular workout, your current level of fitness, the big picture of how that session fits into the goals you have for your training, and your own ability to dig deep and put out a 110 percent effort. Since there are so many factors involved in making a decision about when to "end" an interval session, it is difficult to provide precise guidelines, and any guidelines put forth will likely not address all the issues. Nevertheless, we have presented a way to determine the optimum number of repeats in Table 5.1. These numbers are based on our review of more than a thousand power meter files and our experience of working with more than 250 athletes in training with power. It is with some hesitation, however, that we provide these guidelines. Being able to quantify a rider's percentage wattage reduction after each interval by using a power meter has opened up the possibility of truly narrowing down the factors that de-

TABLE 5.1

WHEN TO STOP INTERVAL REPEATS, BASED ON WATTS ACHIEVED IN THIRD EFFORT

Intervals	Avg. Drop in Power
20 min.	3–5%
10 min.	4–6%
5 min.	5–7%
3 min.	8–9%
2 min.	10–12%
1 min.	10–12%
30 sec.	12–15%
15 sec.	When peak power drops by 15–20%, or when average power for the interval drops by 10–15%

Note: The percentage drop in average watts is based on the number of watts achieved in the third effort. For example, when doing 5-minute intervals, a rider is ready for a rest when his or her average watts for an interval are 5–7 percent lower than they were for the third effort.

cide when interval sessions should be stopped; however, more research needs to be done in this area. Therefore, keep in mind that the guidelines presented in Table 5.1 should be adjusted according to your own situation, fitness level, and goals.

In the table, we have based the percentage drop-off on the third interval that you complete because typically, the effort that a rider can put forth in his or her first two intervals will be much higher than what that rider could actually repeat multiple times. Since we assume you are "fresh" when you begin your interval session, we throw out those first two efforts for the purpose of determining when to stop a workout. Obviously, if you are doing longer intervals in which you might only complete two intervals total, then this rule does not apply.

Sample Workouts

The following sample workouts correspond to different cycling goals. Here, we use the fictitious "Joe Athlete" once again to give you some ideas about how to train at the specific training levels that you learned about in Chapter 3 (see Table 3.1). By reading the following workouts and charting out the best routes for them where you live, you'll be better prepared to adhere to the intended philosophy of each workout. Be sure to always be safe and careful in your workouts and think about the big picture: Don't just focus on the numbers.

Joe Athlete is a Category III racer, and his functional threshold power is 290. His heart rate at this level is 175 bpm, and his max heart rate is 200. Joe weighs in at 160 pounds, and his ratio of watts per kilogram at threshold is about 4 w/kg. He is a very good sprinter and has very good anaerobic capacity as well. His Power Profile is downward sloping to the right (the typical "sprinter" described in Chapter 4).

In these workouts, we are assuming the best of conditions, from weather to road surface to a strong and healthy Joe. Joe also pedals at his normal "self-selected" cadence, unless the workout description says otherwise. To find the correct number of watts for your workouts, you will have to calculate the percentages from your own functional threshold power (FTP) using the instructions presented in Chapter 3.

Level 1: Active Recovery

Joe Athlete does his Active Recovery (Level 1) workout when he needs to recover from a hard workout the day before or cool down at the end of a hard workout.

There are two options that Joe might choose for a Level 1 ride. The first one lasts for about 1.5 hours. Joe warms up for 15 minutes, holding his average watts under 148 (that is, staying within 48–51 percent of his threshold power of 290 watts). Then he rides for the next hour with his average watts under 160 (55 percent), keeping his cadence nice and smooth at 90–95 rpm. He cools down for 15 minutes, again maintaining his average wattage below 140 (48 percent).

For the second option, Joe rides for a total of 1 hour, warming up for 10 minutes, with his watts under 140 (a range of 45–48 percent), then keeps his cadence about 5–8 rpm higher than his normal, self-selected cadence for

LEVEL 1	RIDE A, 1.5 HOURS	
Warm-up	15 min.	48–51%
Ride, 90–95 rpm	1 hr.	55%
Cool-down	15 min.	< 48%

the next 40 minutes, maintaining his watts at 145–160 (50–55 percent). He cools down at his normal cadence, with watts under 140 (48 percent).

This may seem like an embarrassingly slow pace, and that is why too many elite racers do not do enough riding at this level. When you are going out for a recovery ride, it should really be slow and all about recovery. If you go above the upper limit of the wattage range for this level, then you are riding too hard to recover properly, but not hard enough to train. It is very important physically to do Active Recovery rides because they help to "flush" your system of built-up waste products, keep your body in a rhythm of riding, and maintain suppleness in your muscles.

Reminder: It is okay if your watts go above the 55 percent level a few times during the ride. When you get back from your ride and download the data, however, the average power should be under the 55 percent level.

Level 2: Endurance

When Joe wants to build a base of endurance and enhance his aerobic fitness, he emphasizes Endurance rides (Level 2). Over time, training in this range will lead to the development of a stronger heart muscle, increase mitochrondrial levels in the cells, develop more capillarization in his muscles, and result in an overall increase in his stamina.

LEVEL 2	RIDE A, 2.5 HOURS	
Warm-up	15 min.	56%
Ride	2 hr.	69–75%
Cool-down	15 min.	<56%

For this workout, Joe may take a 2.5-hour ride, starting with a warm-up of 15 minutes with his output in watts at less than 162 (less than 56 percent of FTP, or Active Recovery pace). He then rides at a level of 200–220 watts (69–75 percent) for 2 hours. His cadence is self-selected. He cools down for 15 minutes, with his watts under 162 (56 percent).

Alternately, he may ride for 3.5 hours total, warming up for 15 minutes while keeping his watts under 190 (65 percent). He then rides with his watts at 200–220 (69–75 percent) for 3 hours, but includes some bursts of faster riding once every 10 minutes (8 seconds, seated, taking rpm to 130 and watts to 300, or 103 percent). The rest of the ride is at a normal, self-selected cadence, and he cools down for 15 minutes, keeping his watts under 150.

LEVEL 2	RIDE B, 3.5 HOURS	
Warm-up	15 min.	< 65%
Ride w/ bursts every 10 min.	3 hr.	69–75%
Bursts: remain seated, 130 rpm	8 sec.	103%
Cool-down	15 min.	< 55%

It is very important that you do enough of these longer rides to prepare your body for harder levels of riding. The longer you can ride, the better. The workouts described for Levels 3–7 are on the short side; therefore, to receive the benefits of riding at an Endurance level, long Level 2 rides are the best.

Level 3: Tempo

The Tempo level is the "meat and potatoes" of every cyclist and is probably the level ridden by most cyclists. A Tempo ride should be done at a pace that feels fast and also takes some work.

Do not underestimate the amount of work that training in this level requires. However, this level of training is also one of the most beneficial for most cyclists. Riding in Level 3 causes some of the greatest adaptations to your training stress. It's the "best bang for the buck," so to speak. There are a variety of ways to effectively train in Level 3, two of which are described below. But remember to keep the importance of seeing the big picture in mind. Do not worry, for example, if your watts go above 90 percent of your threshold (the upper limit of Level 3) on a few hills or in a short headwind section. That's okay: It's the average watts (or normalized watts—discussed in more detail in Chapter 7) that are important.

The Tempo level is the "meat and potatoes" of every cyclist.

Many a coach has referred to this level as a cyclist's "no-man's-land," and it's true that training in this level will not make you either a better sprinter or a better hill climber. If you spend too much time here, you just get very good at riding at Level 3 and not much else. It is wise not to get caught in the trap of constantly spending valuable training time in this level. If you want to improve your power at VO_2max, then you are going to have to train at VO_2max power: Tempo power just won't be sufficient.

If you have limited time, however, or if you are trying to increase your muscular endurance, then this level is for you. If all you have is 3 hours a week to ride, then drill it in the upper range of Level 3 and get in a great workout; or if you are getting prepped for a long 100-mile race, then being able to ride in this zone for up to 2.5–3 hours will pay off with a possible podium finish.

That said, when our fictitious Joe Athlete takes a Tempo training ride, he chooses from two 2.5-hour rides. For the first ride, he warms up for 15 minutes, keeping his watts under 200, or 68 percent, which is a good intensity to begin warming up the muscles. It's not as easy as recovery pace, but it's not so hard that it will undermine the entire workout. Joe then nails it at between 76 and 90 percent of his threshold, at about 220–260 watts. He tries his best to hold this range over hills, on flats, and even on downhill runs. The emphasis is on spending as much time as possible in the 240–260 (82–90 percent) range. He keeps his cadence at his self-selected level, metering his efforts on hills. He may go over 260, and that's fine, but he does not sprint up hills.

For the other option, Joe warms up for 15 minutes with his watts under 200 (68 percent), then rides at between 76 and 90 percent of his threshold, 220–260 watts. However, this time he does two 20-minute segments of specific cadence work. The first one is at a cadence 15 rpm lower than his self-selected cadence to emphasize strength endurance; the second is at a cadence 15 rpm higher than his self-selected cadence, emphasizing leg speed and muscle endurance. Again, he goes steady and smooth, metering his effort on hills.

LEVEL 3	RIDE A, 2.5 HOURS	
Warm-up	15 min.	< 68%
Ride	2 hr.	76–90%
Cool-down	15 min.	< 55%

An alternative approach to Tempo workouts is to treat the Level 3 ride as a fartlek workout. That is, deliberately vary the power to try to replicate the "stochasticity" of mass-start racing. In other words, as you ride in Tempo pace, randomly accelerate and vary your power within that Tempo wattage to better simulate the demands of racing. Although this may or may not

LEVEL 3	RIDE B, 2.5 HOURS	
Warm-up	15 min.	< 68%
Ride	40 min.	76–90%
Cadence work, −15 rpm	20 min.	76–90%
Ride	40 min.	76–90%
Cadence work, +15 rpm	20 min.	76–90%
Cool-down	15 min.	< 55%

be necessarily better than following the option described above, training in this manner will tend to be highly specific to the demands of racing. Since mass-start racing is not limited to a specific level of training, applying a fartlek-type philosophy will definitely help foster improvement. If you take this approach, your rides should be shorter, however, since you will be creating more training stress than in just a nice, solid, steady Tempo ride.

Lower Level 4: Sub-Threshold, or the "Sweet Spot"

Training in the lower part of Level 4 is what we call the Sub-Threshold level, or the "sweet spot." This sweet spot occurs at about 88–94 percent of your functional threshold power. That means that it is on the "cusp" of both the Tempo level and the Lactate Threshold level. Although this is not exactly an official level of its own, it is an excellent place to begin building your FTP and pushing it higher.

In our coaching, we encourage the athletes we work with to train heavily in this area at the beginning of the racing season, before moving into training right at their FTP (95–105 percent). This intensity level is also great to revisit right around the middle of June in order to achieve a second peak in the fall. Even if an athlete is not trying to achieve a second peak, we incorporate this sweet spot training into his or her schedule at least once or twice every fourteen days. Figure 5.1 shows this important training zone.

FIGURE 5.1: THE "SWEET SPOT"

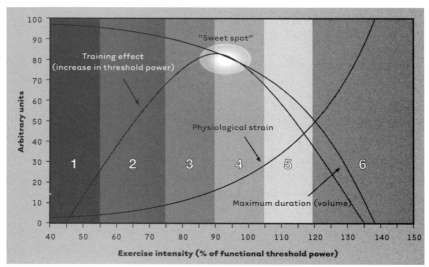

Riding in this range certainly does not help significantly with your sprint, your power at VO_2max, or your anaerobic capacity. Nor is it going to make you the best criterium racer. But at the same time, if all your training were in this area, at least you probably wouldn't get dropped. All in all, it's one of the most beneficial places to spend your training time. Just make sure that you are training the other systems as well.

To train at this level, Joe Athlete would ride for 2–2.5 hours, warming up well for 15 minutes at below 200 watts (68 percent), then do one 5-minute effort at 290 watts, or 100 percent of threshold power. This is to get his body ready for some solid work. He would then do two efforts of 20 minutes each with his watts at a range of 255–272 (88–94 percent of threshold power). It is critical for him to stay in this range as best he can. He would rest for 15 minutes between each effort. He uses a gear that allows him to keep his cadence in his self-selected range, or challenges himself to pedal just a touch faster than he normally would. He finishes the workout with several (eight or ten) 1-minute intervals of fast pedaling with a high cadence (over 105 rpm), holding his watts under 280 (85–95 percent range) and resting for 2 minutes between each. The goal is not to go super-hard, but to spin a high cadence at Sub-Threshold power. Then, he goes into his cooldown.

LEVEL 4	*RIDE A, 2–2.5 HOURS*		
Warm-up		15 min.	< 68%
Ride		5 min.	100%
Ride, 15 min. rest int.		2 x 20 min.	88–94%
Ride +105 rpm, 2 min. rest int.		8–10 x 1 min.	85–95%
Cool-down		15 min.	< 55%

There are other options to Joe's workout at this level. Depending on his fitness level, the time of the year, and his experience in cycling, it might be better for him to start at out at a shorter time period and build up as he gains more fitness. For example, for the main part of the workout, he could start with three 12-minute efforts and build up to four 12-minute efforts, then start over at three 15-minute efforts, build to four 15-minute efforts, and then move to two 20-minute efforts. A Category III racer like Joe Athlete should not need to do more than two 20-minute efforts, but cyclists rated in higher categories should strive to build to four 20-minute segments.

In any case, he should do at least six to eight of these workouts before moving to specific threshold work. This type of workout is a good base upon which to build threshold work, so he should be sure to make it a base that is wide and strong. If he moves to upper Level 4 work and above too soon, he could compromise the solidity of this foundation.

Remember: When you are working at this level, don't hammer over hills; instead, keep your pedaling pressure steady up to the crest of the hill.

Typical Level 4: Threshold

Threshold-level workouts are meant to focus directly on improving your FTP, and they are done right at FTP. They are strenuous and require a solid recovery between each effort and also between workouts. Otherwise, they are very similar to the previous level, Sub-Threshold. The only difference is that the intensity is increased a notch to hold you right on your "edge." These are important workouts to perform, not only so you can increase your ability to handle the level of intensity needed to maintain this type of effort, but also so that you can continually improve your threshold power.

Joe Athlete will ride for 2–2.5 hours to train at this level, with a 15-minute warm-up in which he holds his watts under 200 (68 percent). He then gets in one "blowout" effort with watts at 290 (100 percent), followed by 5 minutes at an easy pace—that is, less than 200 watts (68 percent). After that, he does two 20-minute efforts at 288–315 watts (96–105 percent), with 10–15 minutes of resting in between. After the second effort, he cruises for 15 minutes with his watts below 220 (76 percent).

Joe could have used other options that parallel the options presented under the previous level for building up to the 20-minute efforts. If he chose to do so, he would have simply followed those plans, but at FTP wattage instead of just below that level.

LEVEL 4	RIDE B, 2–2.5 HOURS		
Warm-up		15 min.	< 68%
Blowout effort		5 min.	100%
Easy pace		5 min.	< 68%
Ride, 10–15 min. rest int.		2 x 20 min.	96–105%
Cool-down		15 min.	< 78%

If your goal is to become a strong Category III racer, we suggest building up to riding at least one hour at this power level.

Nontypical Level 4 Workouts

There are some other ways to train at Level 4 that are not so typical. These workouts might give you a different way to think about training at this important level.

For a 2-hour ride, warm up for 15 minutes at 68 percent of your FTP (for Joe Athlete, that would be less than 200 watts). Then do one strong "blowout" 5-minute effort at 100 percent of threshold watts. For the main part of the ride, do a 10-minute effort at 100–107 percent, and then bring up the intensity by 10 watts in

LEVEL 4	RIDE C, 2 HOURS		
Warm-up		15 min.	68%
Blowout effort		5 min.	100%
Ride		10 min.	100–107%
Increase intensity every min. until you reach limit		1.25 hr.	+10 watts
Cool-down		15 min.	

each successive minute until you reach your limit. See if you can increase the number of minutes you can last, as well as your ability to hold a constant load and pace. Follow up with a cool-down.

Another 2-hour ride would also start with the 15-minute warm-up with watts under 68 percent of FTP and the 5-minute effort at 100 percent. Next, however, you would cruise for an easy 5 minutes, then begin a 15-minute effort with specific wattage goals: Begin strong, at 110 percent of your FTP, and hold this for 2 minutes; drop the wattage down by about 10 watts each minute for 4 minutes; bring the watts back up by 10 watts each minute for 2 minutes; and hold it here for the remaining 7 minutes (try to pick it up to 110 percent in the last 45–60 seconds if you can). Repeat this drill two or three times and allow for good recovery between each effort.

LEVEL 4	RIDE D, 2 HOURS		
Warm-up		15 min.	< 68%
Blowout effort		5 min.	100%
Recover		5 min.	< 70%
Drill:			
Ride		2 min.	110%
Back off 10 watts each min.		4 min.	−10 watts
Build 10 watts each min.		2 min.	+10 watts
Hold wattage		10 min.	95–105%
Repeat drill 2–3 times.			
Cool-down		15 min.	

The goal of this exercise is to start out hard in order to load up the system with lactate, demand a steady output for a short period of time, scale back to prevent exhaustion, and then force yourself to hold just at your threshold power or a touch above. In the end, you ramp back up in order to make a final push.

Another nontypical ride at this level could be called the "Hour of Power." It could equally be called the "Hour of Pain." This is a particularly hard workout that has been popularized by Bill Black, an elite masters athlete. He created it to combat the boredom of indoor training during a long Maine winter. Give it your best shot!

Begin this 1.5-hour work out by ramping up to your threshold power level (100 percent of FTP), reaching it by the 20-minute

LEVEL 4	RIDE E, 1.5 HOURS		
Warm-up		15 min.	< 68%
Ramp up to threshold power		20 min.	80–100%
Hold wattage with bursts			
every 2 min.		1 hr.	100%
Out of the saddle, shift down,			
drop or raise cadence by 20 rpm	10 sec.		
Cool-down		15 min.	

mark. If you want to work on muscle tension, then do 80 rpm; otherwise, pedal at a self-selected cadence. Now hold this wattage for the rest of the hour, as you are now training correctly to enhance you FTP. Every 2 minutes, get out of the saddle for 10 seconds, shift down a gear, and drop or raise the cadence by 20 rpm. Then cool down at the end of the hour.

FIGURE 5.2: BILL BLACK'S "HOUR OF POWER"

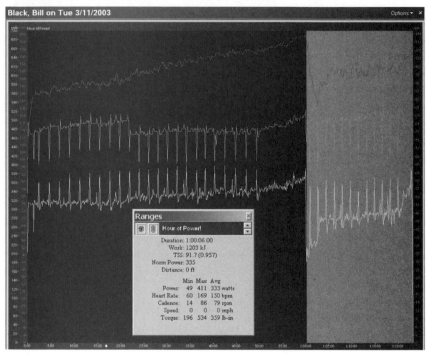

Figure 5.2 shows a graph of Bill Black's "Hour of Power." In this screenshot, you can see how he gradually builds up to his FTP, incorporating small bursts during this time. Note how his heart rate gradually increases throughout the workout, showing the effects of possible overheating and/or dehydration.

Level 5: VO$_2$max

Designed to elicit improvements in your VO$_2$max, or the maximal volume of oxygen uptake, workouts for Level 5 range from 3 to 8 minutes, with the majority of work typically done in the lower end of this range of time.

LEVEL 5	*BOOST VO$_2$MAX, RIDE A, 2 HOURS*	
Warm-up	15 min.	< 68%
Blowout effort	5 min.	100%
Recover	5 min.	70%
Intervals, 3 min. rest int.	6 x 3 min.	117%
Recover	10 min.	70%
Intervals, 4 min. rest int.	4 x 2 min.	113–120%
Cool-down	15 min.	

Joe Athlete, for example, out on a 2-hour ride, may want to work at this level to boost his VO$_2$max. If so, he would begin with a 15-minute warm-up, keeping his wattage at less than 200 (that is, less than 68 percent of FTP). Then he would do one 5-minute interval at 300 watts (100 percent), followed by 5 minutes at an easy pace. The main part of the workout would then begin. He would do six 3-minute efforts, trying for an average of 340 watts (117 percent of FTP or greater) in each effort. He would rest for 3 minutes between each one. Following the sixth one, he would cruise easy for 10 minutes, and then do four 2-minute efforts with 4 minutes of rest between each. In these four efforts, he would try to average between 330 and 350 watts (113–120 percent). Finally, he would cool down.

LEVEL 5	*RIDE B, 2 HOURS*	
Warm-up	15 min.	< 68%
Blowout effort	5 min.	100%
Recover	5 min.	70%
Drill:		
Interval 1	5 min.	113%
Interval 2	5.5 min.	113%
Interval 3	6.0 min.	113%
Interval 4	6.5 min.	113%
Interval 5	7.0 min.	113%
5-min. rest between intervals		
Hard efforts, 5-min. rest int.	2 x 3 min.	> 100%
Cool-down	15 min.	

Another 2-hour ride at this level would start out the same way—the same 15-minute warm-up, the same 5-minute interval at 100 percent of FTP, and the same easy 5 minutes. The main part of the workout, however, would be different. Joe would start out with five efforts in which he pushed his level of watts to 330 (113 percent), and in each successive effort, he would try to extend the time by 30 seconds. The first effort would last 5 minutes, the second would last 5.5 minutes, the third would be for 6 minutes, and so on.

If you try this workout and cannot extend these efforts by an additional 30 seconds each, then try reducing the intensity by 10–15 watts (3–5 percent) so that you can do these for the full recommended times.

Do not reduce the intensity below 106 percent, however. Instead, go ahead and start with shorter periods of time, but work toward extending these. Do 5–8 minutes of Recovery-level riding between each effort. Finish the workout with two hard all-out 3-minute efforts reaching 100 percent or greater of FTP (340 watts for Joe Athlete), and rest for 5 minutes between each effort.

VO_2max is an important factor in racing, and therefore, training at this level is essential for cyclists who race. This fact became obvious to Hunter when examining the downloaded power meter files of the athletes with whom he worked who had won races. He began to see a pattern, and once he noticed it, he realized that it was appearing again and again. In these files, the race-winning move always contained an initial attack to create separation from the field—that is, a breakaway—then a continued high effort to establish the separation, followed by a relative settling in at threshold power and a finish with a short burst of speed. This type of race-winning effort is considered a VO_2max effort because of the short amount of time available to complete the effort and the average power that the breakaway move elicits. Practicing this exact pattern is the perfect race-winning simulation. It is a series of moves that plays out just as easily in a criterium as it does in a road race or even a track points race. Because the power meter data reveals how they work, it is possible to put these efforts inside a solid, endurance-paced workout

FIGURE 5.3: RACE-WINNING INTERVAL

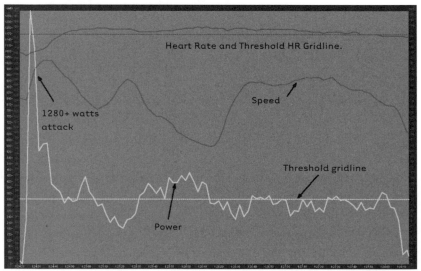

LEVEL 5	*RIDE C, 2 HOURS*		
Warm-up		15 min.	
Drill, repeat 5–8 times:			
Sprint, 15 sec. out of saddle	30 sec.	avg. 200%	
Ride	3 min.	100–104%	
Burst	10 sec.	100–205%	
Rest interval	5–6 min.		
Cool-down	15 min.	56–75%	

to increase your chance of winning and create a super workout.

In Figure 5.3, it is easy to see the initial explosive effort that was needed to create a separation from other racers. At the same time, the upper line, which represents heart rate, climbs up to respond to this quick burst of power. As the effort continues, the watts come down to hug the threshold power line (bottom dashed line), and then the effort ends with a short increase in wattage. The speed line (middle) provides a perspective about the terrain. Notice that as the speed goes down right in the middle of the graph, the power goes up dramatically, indicating that the rider is going up a hill.

A workout that duplicates these race-winning efforts includes five to eight efforts, following a sensible warm-up. Each effort begins with a 30-second sprint (15 seconds out of the saddle), and you must average approximately 200 percent of your threshold power in these, peaking at around 300 percent (for Joe Athlete, this would be a 600-watt average and a peak of 900–1,000). Then you would ride for 3 minutes at 100–104 percent of your FTP (290–300 watts for Joe) and finish with a 10-second burst, trying to reach 200–250 percent of FTP. Rest for 5–6 minutes, then cool down for 15 minutes at Level 2.

Level 6: Anaerobic Capacity

Anaerobic Capacity (AC) efforts are usually completed in time intervals of 2 minutes or less. These are very intense, short, hard efforts, and they are difficult to do correctly without the use of a power meter. The intensity of these efforts is far beyond what can be maintained aerobically. It is a supra-maximal intensity—that is, it requires more than 100 percent of your VO_2max.

Level 6 efforts are much higher in intensity than Level 5 efforts, and they are carried out long enough to stress the anaerobic capacity system, which means they hurt! Training at this level includes the greatest variety of efforts, however. There is huge difference between a 30-second effort and a 2-minute effort, although both train the AC system. This variety makes it exciting to create many different intervals and workouts. The key is to reach the required intensity; the duration of the effort can change somewhat. These Level 6 exercises should be performed when you are relatively fresh in the week.

LEVEL 6	RIDE A, 2 HOURS	
Warm-up	15 min.	
Ride, with 2–3 min. rest int.	8 x 2 min.	avg. 135%
Stop intervals when you can no longer reach 120–122%		
Recover	2–3 min.	
Ride, with 3-min. rest int.	8 x 1 min.	avg. 145%
Stop intervals when you can no longer reach 128–131%		
Cool-down	15 min.	

To add some Anaerobic Capacity work to your training diet in a 2-hour ride, start with a standard warm-up, then set your power meter to show average watts in "interval" mode. Then do about eight 2-minute efforts pedaling as hard as you can, using average watts as a "carrot" to push all the way to the end. The goal? Average 135 percent of FTP (390 watts for Joe Athlete). Reach for that, and stop when you can no longer reach 120–122 percent of FTP, which would be a 10–12 percent drop in power, in your average. Joe Athlete, for example, would stop when he could no longer reach an average of 348–355 watts. Recover for at least 2–3 minutes, more if needed, then finish with eight 1-minute efforts, trying to average at least 145 per-

LEVEL 6	RIDE B, 2 HOURS	
Warm-up	20 min.	< 68%
Hard hills:	45 sec.–	
Sprint final 25m, explode at top	1.5 min.	avg.140%
Repeat hills 8–10 times, 4–5 min. rest interval.		
Stop when you experience a 10% drop in power.		
Cool-down	20–30 min.	

cent of FTP (420 watts, for Joe), with 3-minute rest periods in between each effort. Do all of these efforts unless you are unable to reach 128–131 percent, which would represent a 10–12 percent drop in power (370–380 watts in our hypothetical example).

Another 2-hour ride includes hill repeats. Get in a 20-minute warm-up, and then do eight to ten hard hills. Each should be between 45 seconds and 1 minute 30 seconds long. Try to average around 140 percent of FTP for each effort, and sprint in the last 25 meters or so to explode at the top of each hill. Rest for 4–5 minutes between each attempt. Stop the efforts

LEVEL 6	RIDE C, 2 HOURS	
Warm-up	20 min.	
Ride, with 1-min. rest int.	3 x 2 min.	avg. 135%
Recover	5 min.	
Ride, with 1-min. rest int.	3 x :30 sec.	> 200%
Cool-down	15 min.	

when you experience a 10 percent drop in power from your performance in the second or third interval. Finish with a 20–30 minute cool-down at endurance pace.

Finally, a third way to approach the 2-hour Level 6 ride, following the 20-minute warm-up, is to do three 2-minute efforts, striving for 135 percent of FTP, with 1 minute of resting between each, then 5 minutes of easy pedaling. Then do three efforts of 1 minute each, striving for 150 percent of FTP, with a 1-minute rest between each. Finally, pedal easy for 5 minutes and finish with three 30-second all-out efforts to reach over 200 percent of FTP for each, with 1-minute rests, and cool down with 15 minutes of easy spinning.

Level 7: Neuromuscular Power

Level 7 exercises are super-short, high-intensity efforts usually lasting less than 10 seconds each. They place a larger load on the musculoskeletal system than on the metabolic systems. In these short efforts, it would be difficult to use power as guide for training, since the efforts themselves are so explosive and short that you would have to focus more on handling the bike than on reading your power meter.

Quite literally, there are hundreds of ways to do these workouts. Anytime you do a sprint workout, you are working in your Neuromuscular Power (NP) zone, and you will want to perform these workouts when you are the most "fresh" during the week, as the intensity of the workout is very high, and you will need to be highly energized for them.

When you do these efforts, do not concern yourself with looking at your power meter. You can review the data

LEVEL 7	PEAK SPRINT, RIDE A, 1.5 HOURS
Warm-up	15 min.
Small-ring sprints, 3–5 min. rest int. Begin out of saddle, then wind out gears and shift *Start at 10mph and finish at 120 rpm.*	6 x sprint int.
Recover	3–5 min.
Big-chain sprints, 3–5 min. rest int. Jump out of saddle at start in the 53:17 from 20 mph. *Wind out gear and shift, finishing at 110–120 rpm.*	3 x sprint int.
Recover	3–5 min.
Big-ring sprint, 3–5 min. rest int. Start at 53:16 at 23mph, include two gear changes, winding out each.	3 x sprint int.
Cool-down	20–30 min.

later, while you are cooling down between sprints. The most important thing is to get all the sprints done and continue to add more repetitions as you get stronger.

A good "peak sprint" workout might take 1.5 hours. Warm up for 15 minutes, and get ready for some hard efforts. Start out with six small-ring sprints from 10 mph, and pedal for only 50 meters, with no gear changes. In these sprints you should wind the gears out: Jump out of the saddle to begin and make sure you are spinning at 120 rpm by the finish. Rest for about 2 minutes between each effort. Then do three big-ring sprints with one gear change. Start by jumping out of the saddle in the 53:17 from 20 mph, then wind out the gear and shift. Finish at 110–120 rpm. Rest for 3–5 minutes between each big-ring sprint.

Then do three more big-ring sprints. For these, start with 53:16 at 23 mph and include two gear changes, again winding out each gear. Finish with one big-ring sprint in the 53:15, from 26–28 mph, jump hard, and continue the sprint until you wind out that 53:13 gear. This last series can be performed on a slightly downhill grade to help you get up to speed.

One of the goals of this workout is to show that you do not need to "dump" the chain into the hardest gear for a sprint. Sprinting starts out with a hard jump in a gear that you can turn over. Then, as you wind out each gear, you shift down one. It's just like driving a car with a stick-shift: You work down the gears when the rpms reach the correct range.

Another Level 7 workout that has become very popular is called the "micro-burst workout." It is an excellent exercise to do on the indoor trainer, and it really focuses on improving your neuromuscular power.

FIGURE 5.4: MICRO-BURSTS FROM A WORKOUT
AND FROM A CRITERIUM

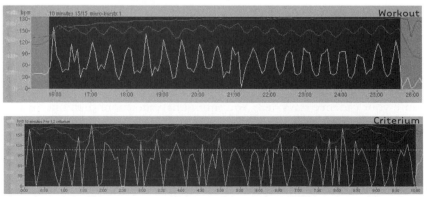

LEVEL 7	*MICRO-BURST, RIDE B 2 HOURS*
Warm-up	20 min.
Micro-bursts, 15 sec. on, 15 sec. off, with 20 min. rest int. sets	2 x 10 min.
Ride at 150% of FTP for the "on " burst, then drop to 50% of FTP for "off" burst. Try to reach 300–350% of threshold power.	
Cool-down	15 min.

Since the efforts are 15 seconds each, using an indoor trainer makes them highly controllable. You can easily use your power meter for pacing. The micro-burst workout is designed to improve your ability to produce the explosive power that is needed for the initial "snap" in a sprint, for the jump out of the saddle in a criterium, or for the standing start in a track event. When you view data from this workout and compare it to data from a criterium, you can easily see that the downloaded files are very similar in nature. This shows the importance of specificity in training (see Figure 5.4).

For a standard 2-hours micro-burst workout, do a standard warm-up and then do two sets of micro-bursts lasting 10 minutes each. A micro-burst effort is 15 seconds "on" and 15 seconds "off," repeated continually for the 10 minutes. For the "on" segment, go to 150 percent of FTP (for our fictitious Joe Athlete, that would be 450 watts), and draw back to 50 percent of FTP (150 watts) for the 15-second "off" segment. Follow this up with 20 minutes of easy spinning, and then begin your next block. This block includes ten 10-second sprints out of the saddle, with at least 2 minutes of easy pedaling between each effort. Try to reach 300–350 percent of threshold power as your max wattage. Then cool down for 15 minutes.

A slight variation of this workout that still attacks the NP system is also a good exercise. Again, it is a 2-hour ride that begins with a standard warm-up. Then, set a pace at the lower end of Level 3—approximately 76–80 percent of FTP, and hold this pace for the next hour. Within this hour, do a 10-second, out-of-the-saddle burst every 3 minutes, trying to reach 150 percent of FTP, and hold it there for the 10 seconds. Make sure your cadence stays high. You should have no more than one or two gear changes, if any. Cruise for the rest of the ride at below 80 percent of FTP, and then cool down.

In summary, all the training levels are continuous: There is no definitive starting or stopping point for any of them. You just do not go from training your aerobic capacity while you are riding in Level 3 (76–90 percent of FTP) to magically training your threshold at 91 percent of FTP in Level 4. The physiological systems in the human body that you are training meld into one another; if you are training in Level 3, that just means that you are using a larger percentage of that particular system than you are using for other systems at that intensity. It does not mean that the other systems are unaffected, however. It's important to remain aware of the big picture, or the philosophy of the workout, and not to get too caught up in becoming a slave to the numbers.

These workouts should help you to begin using your power meter in training. They are by no means the only workouts you can do, however. There are hundreds of ways to design a workout using wattage, and we encourage you to create others that will help you to achieve your goals. When you begin to design your own formats, make sure that you are aware of the different training levels that you will be addressing and the impact these factors will have on your goals for the given workout.

UP TO THIS POINT, you have been getting familiar with your new power meter, and if you have followed some of the steps presented in previous chapters, you have learned a lot about how to train with it. You know your training levels and your functional threshold power, you have evaluated your cycling skills using the Power Profile, and you know how to create workouts with wattage. The next step in conquering this learning curve is to understand what the downloaded data mean. How should you interpret all of this information, and what actions, if any, should you take based on these conclusions?

Interpretation of the data is the key to understanding your current level of fitness, how it has changed over time, and how you might need to adapt your training to make progress in your cycling. Every chart and graph has meaning, just as every ride has meaning in your overall training program. Your rest days are just as important as your hard training days, and it is the same with your power meter data: All your data are significant and important. Record every ride, every race, every time you get on the bike, and make sure to download that file. It's remarkable how many cyclists there are who profess to be "training with power," but then confess that they've never even downloaded their power meter data! Download your data. It's important. Race with your power meter. That is important, too. Your best data will come from your races, and you'll learn the most from those files.

We will mainly use CyclingPeaks software in this analysis, partly because it provides the greatest ability to "drill down" into the data. If you are using other software, it is important that you work with it and take the time to analyze the information fully. Only by downloading and correctly interpreting your own data will you be able to utilize your power meter to the utmost extent. By taking these steps, you will discover a whole new world of possibilities in training and racing.

What to Look at in Your Downloads

First, let's do some housekeeping in order to make your data the best it can be. Make sure to set your power meter on the smallest sampling interval you can do in order to get the greatest accuracy in recording your ride. For some power meters, this limits the total time that it can record your ride, so set the recording rate higher if you are doing a longer ride. When you have your wheel circumference measured (and make sure to measure it precisely, with your weight on the bike and correct tire pressure in the tire), you are ready to go for a training ride. Make sure that you zero the power meter before you begin. There is nothing more frustrating than coming home from a ride only to see that your zero-offset point was not at zero when you started and your data are essentially worthless. Finally, make sure that your power meter is calibrated. With an SRM, you can do a calibration process that is on the SRM Web site; with PowerTap, you can use the "stomp" test, which is on the Wattage FAQ Web site, referenced in Appendix A of this book; and with ergomo you can test by mounting a correctly calibrated PowerTap on your bike and comparing the downloaded files. Unfortunately, this means that for the ergomo calibration you must have access to another power meter, which makes it doubly important that your "control" is accurate.

Later, when you are viewing the graph of your data, either look at the data without any "smoothing" or with just 5-second smoothing. There are some inherent issues in how power meters measure power, as discussed in Chapter 2, so smoothing the data in your software application might be the best way to get rid of any "noise" that may be misleading. The problem is that, though smoothing gets rid of some of the jaggedness in the data, many times it obfuscates the true peaks and valleys in the data. In "5-second smoothing," the data is smoothed over 5-second time periods. This is short enough that you lose little of the meaning contained in the data, and it is easier on the eye to comprehend than if you do not smooth the data at all; thus, 5-second smoothing might be best in all but a few cases.

We'll start by looking at each individual file; later, we'll come back to the larger perspective of how to manage your training over time using the "Athlete Home Page."

Thinking About the Big Picture

Once you begin to download your power meter data and view the graphs, you will no doubt have many questions, such as:

- What should I do now that I have all this great data?
- What should I be looking for?
- How can I make sense of the data?
- How can I use this information to organize my next day of training? My next week of training?
- How do I pick out what is important?

The rest of this chapter is devoted to answering these questions. The list below suggests a few areas that you might be interested in, for starters:
- Periods of significant efforts. For example, you might look at a 15-minute interval that you did at sub-threshold.
- Max wattage and average wattage for a selected duration of interest.
- Significant fluctuations in power during the workout (see "What Is a Match?" later in this chapter).
- Cadence, especially when you have times of high power output.
- Kilojoules of energy burned.
- Training Stress Score (TSS) and Intensity Factor (IF) (more on these in Chapter 7).
- Heart rate during significant time periods.
- The relationship between total work done and time spent at varying levels of intensity.

Try to pinpoint areas of a race that may be significant and determine the exact power demands of those areas, and compare them to your training data. For example, what level of power would have been needed to stay with the front group when the winning split occurred? Look at your power output during the portion of a race where you got dropped, and see what happened at that point. Maybe your cadence was too low for the previous 10 minutes; or maybe your pedaling stroke became sloppy as you became more fatigued, and your torque got too high compared to the power output. How does the ride fit in with previous rides or races? All of this analysis will help you to gain insight into the ride itself.

Your analysis can begin with a look at power distribution.

Power Distribution

Let's open a workout file and begin to look at the "Journal" page of your workout. The first thing to do is to view your power distribution chart. If it is from a race, then check out how much time you spent not pedaling. That is an interesting fact to know because you may have even spent too much time pedaling in a race. The name of the game is saving energy. Most winning road racers do not pedal at least 15 percent of the time. If you are pedaling more than 85 percent of the time in a race, then you need to think about where you are sitting in the peloton. The downloaded power distribution charts of road-race winners usually look like the one shown in Figure 6.1.

In this chart, you can see that the cyclist spent lots of time at under 60 percent of his or her FTP (that is, saving energy and resting) and then lots of time at FTP. For this rider, this translates into lots of time under

FIGURE 6.1: POWER DISTRIBUTION CHART

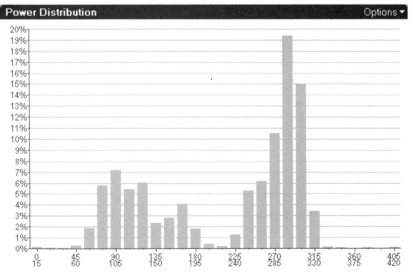

180 watts and lots of time over 285 watts. That means the winners usually pedal the least, but when they pedal, they pedal the hardest. Read that again: This is imperative to remember.

On a normal training ride, the time spent not pedaling is not that important. Instead, what is important is how much time you spend in your power zones. Therefore, you should also begin to look for the time drop-off around your functional threshold power level. Notice that in Figure 6.1, there is a huge drop-off in the amount of time that this rider spent at 315–330 watts compared to the amount of time that he or she spent at 300–315 watts. Based on this information, one could make a ballpark guess that this rider's FTP is probably somewhere on the upper end of the 300–315 bar; it is unlikely to be over 315 watts. How do we know this? Well, most athletes can spend plenty of time at or just below FTP, but limited time above it, so it's easy to make a case for a winning racer to spend lots of time just at FTP, but not much above it, because they know how to pace themselves well. Similar trends may show up in your power meter download.

Most winning road racers do not pedal at least 15 percent of the time.

Percentage of Time in Power Levels

The next thing to consider in looking at the power distribution chart is whether you spent enough time in the level that you were interested in. If you were trying to make strides in an area in which you are weak, did you ride at that level long enough to achieve your overall goal? Examine your power distribution chart by levels. This will enable you to make sure you trained in the correct level to maximize your training time. It is important to set up your training levels correctly first, as regards your FTP, in order to make sure that the calculations will be correct.

Since your fitness changes over time, and your power levels are calculated on the threshold value, these absolute numbers will change throughout the year. For example, say that in January your FTP was 200 watts. This would mean that your Tempo level (Level 3) (76–90 percent of FTP) would be between 152 and 180 watts. Anytime you are riding within this range, you will be accumulating time in Level 3, and you will see this in the corresponding bar in the power distribution chart. By June, however, you may have raised your FTP to 260 watts. Your corresponding Level 3 watts will now be 197–234. Because your fitness has

Determining Functional Threshold Power (FTP) from the Power Distribution Chart

One of the interesting things that we have observed after poring over thousands of power meter files is that it's possible to closely estimate a rider's FTP from just looking at the power distribution chart. Since we know that, by definition, you can ride "right up" to your FTP, but not much over it, then we should expect to see a larger percentage of time in the "bin" that most closely represents that FTP edge. If your ride has been variable enough, contained hard efforts at what you think your FTP is, and also efforts above that level (a mass-start road race or hard group ride is perfect for this), then your power data might be good enough to simply estimate your FTP from the power distribution chart.

In Figure 6.2, for example, notice that there is a sharp "step-down" in the wattage levels after the 330–345 watt bin. This means that this athlete has been able to spend a much larger percentage of time in this bin than in the next bin (345–360). So much more time, in fact, that the difference has created the longest step-down in the power distribution chart. It is easier to recognize the step-down if you do not include zero power in the data and if you mark the width of the bins at 15 watts.

FIGURE 6.2: DETERMINING FTP FROM
POWER DISTRIBUTION CHART

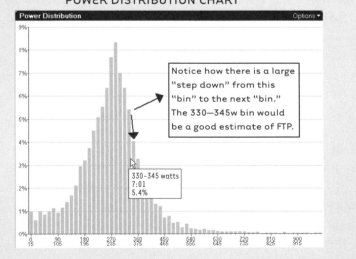

increased so dramatically, 152–180 watts is now in your Level 2, or Endurance level. This is great news. But you will have to adjust your settings, and your training, to make further progress. Remember to update these associations as your fitness changes.

One Caveat

There is one issue that you should be aware of when looking at your power levels. Consider, for example, that if you alternated between pedaling for 15 seconds at 400 watts and pedaling for 15 seconds at 100 watts, and kept this up for an entire hour, you would end up spending 30 minutes pedaling at 400 watts, which is a power that you might be able to maintain for only about 4 minutes if you were pedaling at this level continuously. Obviously, there's something going on that is not evident when you look at just "time in level," and that is the impact of how long each "foray" into a particular power level actually lasts. This is not an issue when using heart rate because: (1) heart rate lags behind changes in power—that is, it is automatically smoothed by your physiology so that very short forays get averaged into the mix; and (2) you can only use heart rate for levels requiring less intensity than $HRmax/VO_2max$. In other words, "time in level" is much more meaningful when applied to heart rate than when applied to power.

Heart-Rate Distribution

Once you have determined your power output in relation to your ride, the next thing to look at is your heart-rate distribution chart. This graph reveals how much time you spent in your heart-rate zones and also includes different "bins." It is possible to estimate your threshold heart rate by looking at the largest "step-down" between bins. Make sure that you have the range of the bins set at three to five heartbeats to more easily see where this step-down occurs. In the heart-rate distribution chart, just as in the power distribution chart, if you look at a large enough data set that includes time spent at and above FTP, you can see where the heart-rate threshold would be. In Figure 6.3, it is easy to see the step down from the 160–165 heart-rate bar to the 165–170 heart-rate bar.

Cadence Distribution

By examining the cadence chart, you can start to see how much time you typically spend in different cadence ranges (see Figure 6.4). This can be informative if you are actively trying to increase or decrease

FIGURE 6.3: DETERMINING THRESHOLD HEART RATE
FROM DISTRIBUTION CHART

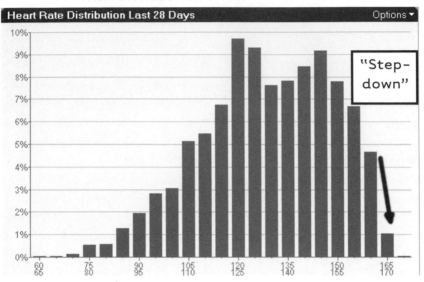

FIGURE 6.4: DISTRIBUTION OF CADENCE IN A TRAINING RIDE

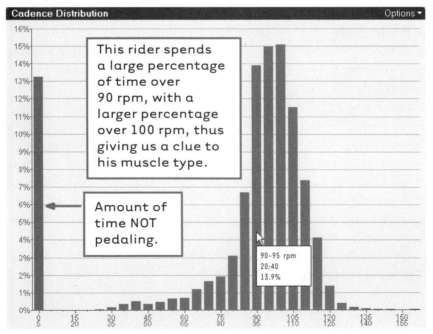

What Are CP Values?

Critical power as defined by exercise scientists refers to the power in watts that you could maintain indefinitely. This is in theory, of course, as ultimately there isn't any level of power you would be able to maintain indefinitely because eventually you would fall off your bike in extreme fatigue! However, world-renowned author and coach Joe Friel has popularized a different meaning to the term "critical power" (CP) among cyclists and coaches using power meters. Friel defines critical power as the best average power that you can maintain for a given amount of time. Another term with the same meaning is "mean maximal power." Friel described the critical power principle in his booklet *Training with Power* (2001). For the description below, we have borrowed heavily from this booklet with his permission.

To further understand this concept, let's look at an example. Say that you did an Olympic distance triathlon with a 40 km bike leg. In that leg, you averaged 300 watts over exactly 60 minutes. We might conclude that your FTP is 300 watts. But would you be able to average a higher wattage if you were riding for only half that time period? Most likely, the answer would be yes, because you would have energy in reserve at 30 minutes. Therefore, the best average power output (300 watts) in the 40 km race was "critical" to the time duration of 60 minutes. In the same way, you would have best average power outputs that would be critical to 30 minutes, 12 minutes, 1 minute, and so on. Your critical power would be different for each time period.

Training at each critical power level produces physiological adaptations and fitness results specific to that workload. When you know your critical power at 6 minutes (CP6), for example, you can train very precisely by using your power meter to optimally stress the physiological systems that limit the VO$_2$max system. Friel suggests critical power zones for 12 seconds (CP0.2), 1 minute (CP1), 6 minutes (CP6), 12 minutes (CP12), 30 minutes (CP30), 60 minutes (CP60), 90 minutes (CP90), and 180 minutes (CP180). To determine your critical power for these times, you *(continues)*

(continued)
simply do time trials at those durations and then create a zone
around them by adding and subtracting 2.5 percent of the average
power. For example, if your CP6 is 390 watts, then your CP6 zone
would be 380–400 watts.

You can also simply view the "Mean Maximal Power Curve" in
CyclingPeaks Software. As long as you have a large enough sample
of files to pull from, you will be able to easily pick out these durations
and their corresponding critical power. CP values may be applied to
heart-rate zones during training, a principle that is described in
Friel's books, which include *The Cyclist's Training Bible, The Mountain
Biker's Training Bible*, and *The Triathlete's Training Bible*.

your cadence for a specific workout or for overall physiological
change. It also tells you something about yourself and may provide a
clue as to the percentages of fast-twitch and slow-twitch muscle fiber
in your body.

This chart also provides further information about how much time
you spend not pedaling. The power distribution chart will show you this
as well, but the cadence chart is more accurate, and here's why. Since the
bins are smaller in the cadence chart than in the power distribution chart
(you should view this chart in increments of 5 rpm), you will see, for example, the time you spent pedaling at between 1 and 5 rpm, between 6
and 10 rpm, and so on, which is more precise than looking at the 0–20
watt bin in the power distribution chart.

Mean Maximal Power, or Critical Power

Now that you have examined the overall ride, you should narrow the
perspective to look at your peak power for the ride. By plotting your
peak power over small slices of time, you can view a telling graph of your
mean maximal power, or "critical power," as Joe Friel calls it (see sidebar,
"What Are CP Values?"). This is quite literally a plot of your best average
power for each second of the ride.

The Mean Maximal Power Curve (MMPC) Chart is important and
revealing for a variety of reasons. One is that it gives you the ability to
confirm that you are working in the correct training level when working

FIGURE 6.5: MEAN MAXIMAL POWER CURVE FOR SPRINTER

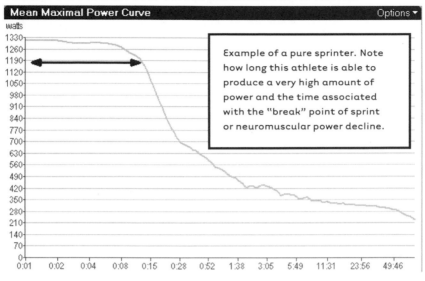

out. In an intense race file, the chart helps you to pinpoint weaknesses and strengths. When you examine maximal power for a relatively large set of data (six months or greater), the shape of the curve will be based on your personal set of abilities. Distinctive changes in the slope of the curve may reveal how much you rely on different physiological systems.

For example, the slope of your maximal power curve might be very consistent from 20 seconds out to 2.5 minutes but run at a lower angle from 2.5 minutes out to 25 minutes. This might tell you that at 2.5 minutes your body shifts emphasis from the anaerobic capacity system to the VO_2max and lactate systems. Each rider is different, and this is one reason why it is important to read and interpret this graph regularly. If you see a distinct "hump" in the curve at around 3–6 minutes, that is, a very high output of power in that section in relation to the rest of the curve, this indicates your strength at VO_2max power. Or, if you see a "plateau" in the curve, you may have a weakness in your ability to produce power at the time period where the plateau occurs.

It is important to remember, though, that if you did a workout with 5-minute efforts, and then looked at the watts you produced at 6 minutes, the data may not be indicative of your overall ability. To obtain valid data, you would need to do specific 6-minute efforts. That is, you must compare similar time periods together from workout to workout. Also, if you did not do sprints or lactate threshold intervals, then your max power on the chart would not be representative of your true max when you do sprints, and your lactate threshold would not be representative of your true FTP. If you are looking to see the "big picture" from this curve, then it is important to create the MMP Curve over a larger period of time—maybe even looking at an entire year's worth of data in order to get that true picture. Figure 6.5 shows a classic example of an MMP Curve for a sprinter. Note the relatively long period of time at a very high power output. In this example, the rider weighed only 135 pounds, so based on his Power Profile, he is considered a world-class sprinter. We'll examine these charts in more detail in Chapter 9.

Line Graphs

There are many ways to view your ride in the power meter software, and each can reveal more information about you as a rider and about the workouts you complete. The graph of your ride tells the story of your ride second by second. Examining these graphs, which at first may look like a bunch of squiggly lines, and discerning this story to glean helpful information is what this section is all about.

FIGURE 6.6: STACKED VIEW OF WATTAGE, HEART RATE, AND SPEED

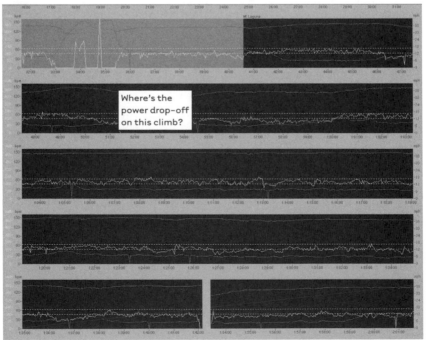

Stacked or Horizontal?

Each type of software represents the data a little differently in graph mode, and each type has its pluses and minuses. When we were creating CyclingPeaks software, we faced a dilemma about how to show the graph. A stacked view would present raw data that had not been interpolated, smoothed, or "smashed together." However, there are times when it is also useful to view the data all on one screen, or "horizontally." When viewing the stacked graphs, it may be difficult, for example, to see a small decrease in power over a period of 60-minutes or longer. A horizontal view is better for this type of analysis. Therefore, we decided to include both options in CyclingPeaks software. In Figures 6.6 and 6.7, you can see that the "stacked" view makes it difficult to find the decrease in power right at the end of the climb, whereas the horizontal view makes this easy to locate and analyze.

We recommend that you begin with the horizontal view with no smoothing or with 5-second smoothing, as this will enable you to see your ride from a broad perspective. From this view you can easily determine the segments of the effort that you want to examine in more detail. Many times we begin to "mark up" the file in this view and then switch over to the stacked view in order to better define the exact start and finish of each period of work. If it is a road ride, then we view the watts, heart rate, and speed lines. Viewing speed allows you to determine whether the work was being done on an uphill or on the flats. If the workout was aimed at specific cadence

FIGURE 6.7: HORIZONTAL VIEW OF WATTAGE, HEART RATE, SPEED

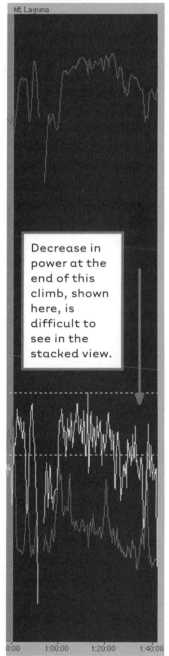

Decrease in power at the end of this climb, shown here, is difficult to see in the stacked view.

FIGURE 6.8: HIGHLIGHTED OR "MARKED," RANGE OF
A 20-MINUTE MOUNTAIN BIKE CLIMB

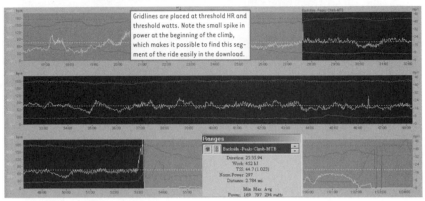

goals, we take out speed and add in cadence in order to better understand the power-to-cadence relationship. If it is a trainer ride, then we view watts, heart rate, and cadence, as speed is largely irrelevant on a trainer.

Areas of Interest

Begin analyzing your data by scanning through your ride and finding areas of interest. You can create a "range" around a specific area of interest (that is, mark an interval) to gain further insight into the numbers. You can also mark intervals while you are on your bike so they will be easy to find and view later. However, if you did not mark a particular effort—maybe it was an intense mountain bike race, for example, and you couldn't afford to take your hands off the handlebars to mark it—then you can find that area later. For example, let's say you went over a 20-minute climb in your mountain bike race. This should be easy to view, as your heart rate will be high, your speed will be low, and your power fairly constant. The graph of this portion of your ride might look something like the graph presented in Figure 6.8.

Notice that when the climb begins, the power line becomes smoother, the speed line is lower, and the heart-rate line goes right to the roof! Even though this is a mountain bike file, the power is relatively smooth despite undulations in the trail.

Interval Shape and Meaning

The line for each interval that you do will have a slightly different shape, and this shape means something about how you paced yourself in the

FIGURE 6.9: VO$_2$MAX WORKOUT SESSION WITH SEVEN 3-MINUTE INTERVALS

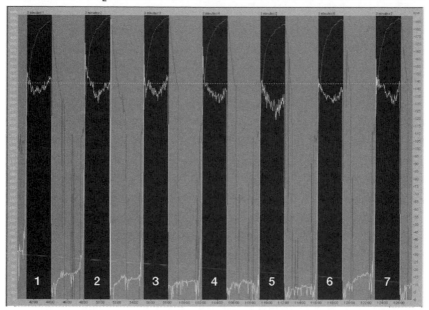

interval, how relatively fresh or tired you were, and whether you gave it your all or didn't quite get the job done. By comparing the different shapes of the interval lines with each other, you can learn much about your efforts, and this will help you to determine a better pacing strategy, set a bigger wattage goal, or plan the number of intervals to do.

Let's look at the various shapes of the intervals and what they mean. Figure 6.9 shows 3-minute intervals done by an elite track racer in her preparation for the Canadian Track Nationals. In this example, the graph is in the horizontal view so that we can see all the intervals at one time. We have created a range around each interval in order to pull out the data for just that interval. One of the first things you may notice is the shape of the power lines. Notice that there is a general trend that each one follows. Each interval starts with a hard effort; the power drops down about 1 minute into the effort, however, and then the wattage rises again at the end of the interval. We might call this pattern a "twin peak interval."

Humans adapt easily to stress, and good athletes quickly learn pacing after they have done only a few intervals. But this pacing may be arbitrary instead of deliberate, and analyzing the files may enable you to make better pacing decisions. That is the case here: A closer look at the files provides interesting clues into how this track racer could improve.

FIGURE 6.10: CLOSE-UP VIEW OF INTERVAL 1, PERFECT PACING

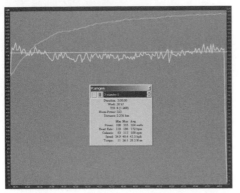

FIGURE 6.11: CLOSE-UP VIEW OF INTERVAL 2, STARTING OUT TOO HARD

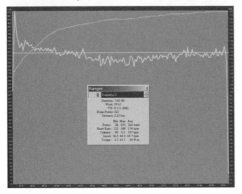

FIGURE 6.12: CLOSE-UP VIEW OF INTERVAL 6, GOOD PACING WITH DROP IN POWER

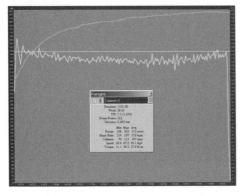

To be fair to this athlete, even though she is an elite-level Canadian track racer, this is the very first time she had ever tried this specific workout, and so she was learning just how hard she could go for each interval. The goal in this workout was to do seven 3-minute repeats as hard as she could, with 3 minutes of easy pedaling between each one. We estimated that she would be able to hold VO_2max power (for her 315–325 watts), as this 3-minute time period is perfectly within the VO_2max power level. We told her to just go as hard as she could and didn't give her a specific wattage goal. Since this was her first workout at this time period, we did not want to color her results with some wattage number that might or might not be right for her. We also wanted to see how well and quickly she adapted to the effort so that we could uncover any weaknesses that she might have at this level. The workout was performed on an indoor trainer.

In Interval 1, notice how there is a peak at the beginning and end, with a little valley in the middle (see Figure

6.10). This is perfect pacing, and it's her first interval. She's very fresh, and as a result she does very well. This shape also indicates that she was a little conservative, so as not to blow, and then she realized that she had more to give and throttled it at the end. So, in terms of going all out, she didn't, but in terms of giving it her best time and watts, she was dead on. This is a textbook example of how to create your best average watts in an interval.

FIGURE 6.13: CLOSE-UP VIEW OF INTERVAL 7, STRONGER THAN EXPECTED

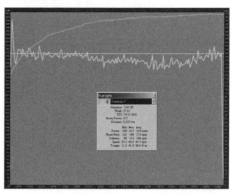

In Interval 2, our Canadian cyclist went too hard (see Figure 6.11). The power drops off very quickly, and she has no power in the end. In the first interval she was a little worried about going too hard, so she held back, and at the end of the interval she realized she could have gone harder. In the second interval, she drills it from the start, but "blows up." At this point, she must have realized that she started the interval pedaling too hard.

By the time she does intervals 3, 4, 5, and 6, she's got this figured out (see Figure 6.12). Perfect! This is as hard as she could go; she's got these intervals nailed. However, we are starting to see an intriguing pattern: Note how each effort has this little power "hole" in it at around 1:05 to 1:25, mainly around that 1:20 mark. This tells us that our track racer is having a hard time transitioning from her purely anaerobic capacity, which requires fast-twitch muscle to using a larger percentage of her slow-twitch muscles, every time she hits a certain point in the interval. It's as if her "depth" of anaerobic capacity is not "deep" enough. We should be seeing that drop-off occur closer to the 2:30 mark instead of at 1:05 to 1:20.

But this is exactly why we did not give her a wattage goal in the beginning of the workout, and the strategy worked. Now we can see that she might possibly have a weakness in this transition period, and we can determine how to address this issue. To do that, it helps to look at Interval 7 (see Figure 6.13). In this last interval, she held back and did not push it hard enough. At this point, if she was at her limit and feeling fatigued, we would have seen a quicker drop-off in power from the start to the finish. In addition, she would not have been able to bring up the power at the end of the final effort. Instead, Interval 7 presents a profile that is very similar to the profile for Interval 1; however, since it is not the first effort but the last one, we need a different interpretation. That interpretation is this: Ultimately, she could have done a few more of these efforts before reaching a point of diminishing marginal returns.

We can conclude that this rider has good average pursuit power and good cruising power in pursuit. Her repeatability is good, as evidenced by the relatively low drop-off in power from Interval 2 and Interval 3 to Interval 7. (When looking for "repeatability," always compare the second and third intervals to the last one to really see the drop-off in power, because the first interval always takes place when the athlete is fresh, and the wattage is therefore not one that can be repeated multiple times.)

Training specifically for your discipline is very important.

From this analysis, we can suggest areas for improvement. Because this athlete seems to fade too fast if the initial effort is too high, practicing her pacing from the start would be important. By holding back a hair more on the start, and then consciously focusing on that time period from minute 1 to minute 2, she could begin to eliminate the quick drop in power during that time period. If she can boost her ability to keep the pressure on throughout that time and then dig deep for the last minute, she will really reduce her time.

Training for Specific Demands of the Course

Once you have created areas of interest, you can compare these to previous efforts or to the efforts of others (such as teammates). Or you can look deeper into that specific effort—to examine your cadence, for example. Training specifically for your discipline is very important. If you always train on the flats, but most of your races are in the mountains, then you are not training for the specific demands of the races that you are competing in.

An interval workout done by a mountain biker in preparation for a race would show significant portion of the ride at threshold power, but there would also be short periods of time requiring bursts in order to power up and over drainage ditches.

"Fast Find"

Another way to create areas of interest is by using the "Fast Find" feature, which currently is exclusive to CyclingPeaks software. Let's say you did several 3-minute efforts, then some 30-second efforts, a 10-minute effort, and a few 1-minute fast-pedaling efforts. You can easily find these efforts by defining them based on the length of the interval and the watts that were held during that time. The "Fast Find" feature can help you to find these efforts quickly.

What Is a "Match"?

A "match" is an elusive term used by riders and coaches within the bike-racing world. When you "burn a match," you have done a hard effort. It's an effort in which you had to dig deep or really push yourself. Any bike racer knows what it feels like to have burned a match, but until now, no one has really tried to quantify exactly what a match is.

Why do you need to know what a match is? Think of it this way: As a rider, you start out the day with a full set of matches in your matchbook, but every time you go hard, do an attack, or hammer over a hill, you burn one of your matches. The size of the matchbook is different from one cyclist to the next, but nobody has an infinite number, so it is important to burn your matches at the right time, whether you are competing in a race or just training. Otherwise, you may be left with an empty matchbook when you still might need to use some matches to finish well, and your chances of performing at your best may have been drastically reduced. If you burn all your matches before the end of the race, it's doubtful you will win. Indeed, if your matches are burned prematurely, it's certain that you won't win.

So, with regard to matches, your goals are fourfold: (1) figure out exactly what a match is for you; (2) figure out the size of your matchbook; (3) try to increase the number of matches you have; and (4) burn your matches at the right time in the race in order to optimize your chances for success.

For most riders and racers, a match can be defined as an effort in which one goes over threshold power by at least 20 percent and holds it there for at least 1 minute. Of course, burning the proverbial match

TABLE 6.1	"BURNING A MATCH": EXAMPLE OF MATCHES BURNED AT VARIOUS DURATIONS FOR FTP	
Time	**Percent over Threshold Power**	**Power Needed to "Burn a Match" if FTP is 300 Watts**
1 minute	20+%	360 watts
5 minutes	15–20%	345–360 watts
10 minutes	8–12%	324–336 watts
20 minutes	0–8%	300–324 watts

could involve an effort longer than 1 minute, but as the time period gets longer, the percentage above threshold power would be lower. Table 6.1 estimates the power required to burn a match for different time periods for all riders. Remember, however, that there is no exact definition of "match," and these numbers would be different for every individual. You may be able to use the power meter software to determine exactly when and how you burn your own set of matches. It may be illuminating, for example, to make a chart for yourself like the one presented in Table 6.1. With this chart, you would be able to attempt to quantify your own matches.

Now that you have a general idea of what a match is, you need to figure out how many matches you have at your disposal. There are only two ways to do this: You could do a super-hard training ride in which you have planned out the matches that you are going to burn, or you could do a tough race that requires a lot of match burning. The great thing is that you now know, based on your rating of perceived exertion and rate of exhaustion, when you have burned a match and when you are out of matches. Listen to your body as you ride, and then go back through your downloaded data to find your matches.

If you are using the "Fast Find" feature, under the Edit button, in the CyclingPeaks Software, you can enter some parameters that will help you find those matches. For example, let's assume that your threshold power is 300 watts. Take 120 percent of 300 watts, which is 360 watts, and enter that into the "Leading Edge." Then take 300 watts and enter that as your "Trailing Edge," since you are still going hard at that point. Select 1 minute as the minimum duration, and 5 minutes as the maximum duration.

FIGURE 6.14: PLACING GRIDLINES TO "FIND A MATCH"

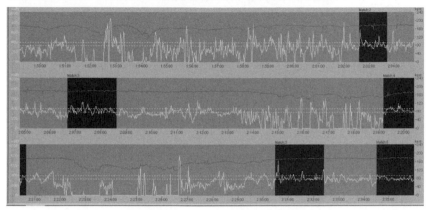

All of your matches will be highlighted. You can then review the graph of your ride and type notes in the text area that provide some description about that match. For example: "Hard attack on hill," or "Preme sprint." Or you could simply label each "Find" as a match and then use the Linking button to link them all together. It might look like the screenshot shown in Figure 6.14.

This screenshot shows another way of viewing a match. We placed a gridline at 330 watts (this rider's threshold power), and then another gridline at 396 watts (120 percent of his FTP) so we could visually scan the graph and look at any area above the 396-watt gridline. These are definite matches. The space under the power line (watts), but above the 330-watt line, is the time spent burning a match. Any significant time spent above 396 watts is like sending up a "flare"!

When you have more insight about when your matches occur, and how many you have before you are "cooked," you can make changes in your training that will increase both the size of your matchbook and the intensity of the flame from each match. At the same time, by using a power meter in a race, you can review the data postmortem and determine whether you spent too many matches in the beginning of the race, or spent them at the correct times to optimize your chances for success. This is one of the great benefits of racing with a power meter. It allows you to see your performance objectively and determine whether you are using the right tactics. At the same time, you can begin to develop a better training plan based around your weaknesses in order to better "toast" your competition.

Other Ways to Analyze the Data

In race files, you can use the power data in the following ways:

- Use "Fast Find" to count the number of laps that you did in a race and define them.
- Look at your Training Stress Score and Intensity Factor (defined in Chapter 7) for the ride and see how they fit into your entire season so far.
- Look for your peaks powers and determine where they are in the file. This will help you to gain insight into the hardest parts of your race.

If you got dropped, find the time just before this occurred and begin to work backward to see what types of efforts you had to do, the number of watts for these efforts, and where the breaking point was. This helps you to see exactly how and why you got dropped in the race, and you can use this information to tailor your training plan.

In training files, you can do the following:

- See how many kilojoules of energy you used during your ride and determine whether you refueled enough to supply the energy you needed.
- View your Normalized Power for the ride (defined in Chapter 7).
- Determine when your wattage began to decrease during the ride. How many kilojoules of energy had you expended up to this point?

Compare your intervals with one another. How many repetitions were you able to do before there was a major drop-off in power? Did you do enough intervals? Or did you do too many? If your power dropped off by more than 5–10 percent, and you continued doing intervals, then it is possible that you were not working intensely enough to produce the physiological adaptations.

These suggestions should help to get you started in looking at your data in a more productive manner. Every time you ride, your data will help to teach you something new about yourself and also further define your abilities as a cyclist. You do not need to do a full markup on every file, but it will still be important to review each ride and make notes about that ride and how it fits into the big picture of your fitness goals. The downloaded data from your races will provide important information about the specific demands of the event, and when you understand these demands, you will be able to create a training program that addresses issues specific to your needs and the requirements of the next race. The data that you capture are priceless for helping you to become even more successful in the future and reach your athletic potential.

7 BEYOND AVERAGE POWER

I T'S *NOT* ABOUT AVERAGE POWER. . . . One of the first things that catches the attention of any beginning power meter user is how variable, or jumpy, the power output tends to be. This aspect of the data is largely due to the constantly changing levels of resistance that must be overcome when cycling outdoors. The resistance may come from small changes in elevation, gusts of wind, and other external factors. Because of this variability, training with a power meter is not directly comparable to training with a heart rate monitor. In particular, it is very difficult (as well as often counterproductive) to try to keep power constantly within a certain range or zone during a training session.

Just as important, this variability means that the overall average power for a ride or part of a ride is often a poor indicator of the actual intensity of the effort. For example, you could go out and do two 20-minute intervals at your FTP, and your average power for those 20-minute segments might be 300 watts, but since you rode easily on the way to and from the place where you did the intervals, the average power for the entire ride might be only 180 watts. Does this mean that this workout would have the same effect on your body as an easy recovery ride in which you averaged 180 watts for 2 hours? Obviously not: Both rides may have had the same average power, but they were entirely different in terms of the physiological systems that they called upon and the overall training stress they required.

This limitation to using average power as a measure of intensity is even more apparent in racing because power can vary dramatically from one moment to the next in a race. Most good racers try to conserve energy and then attack, and these extremes skew the averages. For example, after the hardest road race of the year in which you hung on for dear life, you may download your power meter data and find that you only averaged 200 watts for the entire 4 hours of racing. Since you know that this was the hardest race of the year, obviously there must be something more going on that simply is not reflected in your average power.

And It's Not About Total Work...

In early 2002, we began discussing an idea that we had about coaching. We theorized that we should be able to develop an athlete's entire annual training plan based on some measurement that quantified overall training load. There had to be a better way than just arbitrarily deciding how many hours a rider should train each year based on his or her category.

We, then, briefly considered using the total work performed (in kilojoules, or kJ), since this is a function of both volume (i.e., frequency and duration) and intensity (i.e., average power). However, this idea was fundamentally flawed, because: (1) it did not account for the limitations of average power; and (2) it did not account for the non-linear relationship between many physiological responses and exercise intensity. For example, you might go out and ride for 3.5 hours and in the process perform 2,000 kJ of work, which would require pedaling at an average power of 159 watts. For the average serious rider, this would be a "garden variety" Level 2 Endurance workout. It probably would not result in undue fatigue on the following day. But you could go out and perform that same 2,000 kJ of work during a ride that lasted only 2 hours by sustaining an average of 278 watts. For all but the most talented athletes, this would be a much more difficult workout, most likely falling into Level 3 or Level 4, and it would probably leave them rather tired for one or more days afterward. Two very different

Two very different workouts may require the same amount of total work, but the impact they would have on your body would be completely different.

workouts may thus require the same amount of total work, but the impact they would have on your body would be completely different.

Periodization of Training Using Power Meter Data

It seemed obvious that if each ride could be scored to take proper account of both duration and intensity, it would be possible to look at an athlete's past data, correlate that with his or her successes and failures, and draw some conclusions about whether his or her training had been appropriately structured. Ultimately, it was the authors' desire to be able to predict when an athlete would achieve a "peak" of fitness, such that this information could be used to optimally design an individualized training program.

The inspiration for this idea came from a number of scientific studies showing that it was possible to accurately model, or predict, training-induced improvements in performance using Dr. Eric Banister's heart-rate-based training impulse (TRIMP) score to quantify the overall training load. In essence, it was a search for the Holy Grail of periodization—that is, a way to apply the appropriate amount of training stress at the appropriate time, such that an athlete would peak for his or her most important competition(s). For a long time, coaches all around the world have relied on intuition and trial-and-error to determine how to do this. However, technology provided us with the capability to precisely measure what a rider was doing during each and every training ride, and we believed that it would be possible to make these decisions far more accurately and confidently.

With this goal in mind, we developed a number of unique analytical tools designed to provide greater insight into the true demands of training and racing a bicycle. The first three—Normalized Power (NP), Intensity Factor (IF), and Training Stress Score (TSS)—are interrelated, and we developed them in an attempt to quantify the metabolic demands and overall training load more accurately than would be possible using average power and total work. Normalized Power is integral to the calculation of IF and TSS and serves as means of accounting for the variability in power during a ride. Intensity Factor is an athlete's NP expressed as a fraction of his or her functional threshold power, and as such it is designed to aid in comparisons across individuals. Finally, Training Stress Score quantifies the overall training load, similar to the way that TRIMP quantifies training based on heart-rate data. Once these three concepts were developed and integrated into CyclingPeaks software, it became possible to capture considerable information regarding the demands of a workout based on just these three metrics. The fourth tool, Quadrant Analysis, is described later in the chapter. Let's look at Normalized Power first, and then we'll introduce the rest of the "beyond average power" concepts.

Some of the reasoning behind these concepts is quite technical. It draws on advanced research in exercise physiology and requires some math knowledge to really understand. If you'd rather skip the technical details, that's fine: You can still get a general idea of how to use these tools by reading through this chapter. But we did not want to leave out the nitty-gritty. If you are the type of cyclist or coach who wants to be thoroughly informed, you will not be disappointed: You are about to get a crash course in some very useful concepts.

Normalized Power™

As stated before, the act of riding, training, and racing a bicycle is a highly variable, almost stochastic, exercise. There are many factors that affect every ride you take: wind, uphills, downhills, quick accelerations, long steady grinding, and so on. Because of this variability, average power is just not a sufficient indicator of the true metabolic demands of your ride. To account for this variability, we developed a special algorithm to calculate an adjusted (or "normalized") power for each ride or segment of a ride (longer than 30 seconds) that you may want to analyze.

The algorithm is somewhat complicated but it incorporates two key pieces of information: (1) the fact that physiological responses to rapid changes in exercise intensity are not instantaneous but follow a predictable time course; and (2) the fact that many critical physiological responses (e.g., glycogen utilization, lactate production, stress hormone levels, and the like) are curvilinearly, rather than linearly, related to exercise intensity. We calculate Normalized Power by (1) starting at 30 seconds into the wattage data and calculating a 30-second rolling average for power; (2) raising the values obtained in step 1 to the fourth power; (3) taking the average of all the values obtained in step 2; and (4) taking the fourth root of the number obtained in step 3. This is Normalized Power, which Cycling Peaks software calculates automatically. Basically, it's an estimate of the wattage you would have averaged if you had pedaled smoothly for the entire effort—the power that your body "thinks" it is doing, though in reality the effort could have been a very sporadic "on/off" race. In other words, it is an estimate of the power that you could have maintained for the same physiological "cost" if your power output had been perfectly constant (such as on a stationary cycle ergometer), rather than variable. Because of the factors it takes into account, Normalized Power provides a better measure than average power of the true physiological demands of a given training session.

Keeping track of NP is therefore a more accurate way of quantifying the actual intensity of training sessions and races. For example, it is common for average power to be lower during criteriums than during equally difficult road races, simply because of the time spent soft-pedaling or coasting through sharp turns during a criterium. The NP for a criterium and a road race of about the same duration, however, will generally be very similar, reflecting their equivalent intensity. In fact, NP during a hard criterium or road race of about a 1-hour duration will often be similar to what a rider can average when pedaling continuously for a flat 40 km time trial. The NP from mass-start races can therefore often be used to provide an initial estimate of a rider's threshold power.

Figure 7.1 shows the difference between average power and NP in a road race. In this figure, the power line is very jagged and constantly fluctuating, indicating that this section of the race contained times of high wattage and times of low wattage. This is typical of road races, where the range of power that cyclists produce is very wide and constantly changing. Since these changes from high power to low power occur so quickly, various physiological systems do not have enough time between them to recover. Thus, although the muscles get very short breaks, the overall body does not, and therefore, the body experiences the same amount of stress that it would if you did one hard constant effort. Note that in Figure 7.1 the NP is 357 watts, whereas average power is 319 watts. In this case, the stress, or physiological "cost," to the body was approximately equivalent to what it would experience at 357 watts. The greater the difference, the more variable and less continuously aerobic the effort was. Charles Howe, editor and author of the Wattage FAQ (http://midweekclub.ca/power-FAQ.htm), coined the term "Variability Index" (VI). To obtain the VI, he

FIGURE 7.1: NORMALIZED POWER VERSUS AVERAGE POWER IN A
MASS-START ROAD RACE

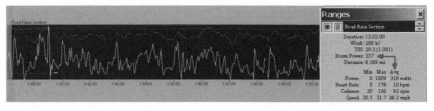

simply takes the NP number and divides it by the average power number.
The more variable your ride is, the higher the "Variability Index."

The reason all of this is important is that, used correctly, NP can help
you to better define the demands of your event. Table 7.1 shows typical VI
values for some common types of cycling events. However, the table is just
a rough guideline for helping you to think more critically about variability in cycling. Knowing the demands of your event is one of the key factors to training specifically for that event. If you are a mountain biker and
you are only training on the
road, then most likely you will
not be ready to handle the
constant change in power, cadence, and speed that you will
encounter in your next mountain bike race. You'll learn more
about this variability in the section on "Quadrant Analysis"
later in this chapter.

Figure 7.2 shows NP and
average power on a steady, relatively constant gradient climb.
It is clear that this type of climb
has a much smaller effect on
the variability of a rider's
power output than the mass-
start road race shown in Figure

TABLE 7.1	VARIABILITY INDEXES FOR COMMON RIDES
Type of Ride	*Variability Index*
Steady isopower workout	1.00 to 1.02
Flat road race	1.00 to 1.06
Flat time trial	1.00 to 1.04
Hill-climb time trial	1.00 to 1.06
Flat criterium	1.06 to 1.35
Hilly criterium	1.13 to 1.50
Hilly road race	1.20 to 1.35
Mountain bike race	1.13 to 1.50

7.1 did. The wattage line shows how much smoother and more stable the
power output was in this effort. The NP for this section of the ride was
304 watts; the average power, at 300 watts, was only 4 watts lower. Therefore, the VI for the ride depicted in Figure 7.2 is very different from the VI

FIGURE 7.2: NORMALIZED POWER VERSUS AVERAGE POWER ON A
STEADY CLIMB

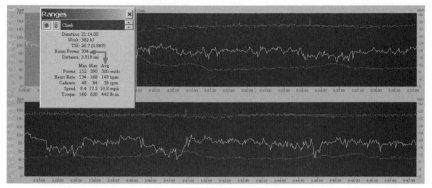

for the ride shown in Figure 7.1 (1.01 for Figure 7.2, versus 1.12 for Figure 7.1). Although these two very different efforts might have a similar physiological cost, their NP and AP values are very different.

Intensity Factor™

Although Normalized Power is a better measure of training intensity than average power, it does not take into account changes in fitness in an individual over time or differences between individuals. It is also important to be able to quantify the intensity of your effort relative to your own abilities, as this plays a key role in the adaptations to training that occur as a result. That is where Intensity Factor comes in.

IF is simply the ratio of your NP to your functional threshold power—that is, the fraction of your functional threshold power that you maintained for that workout or part of a workout (IF = NP/FTP). (Ratios can always be expressed as fractions or decimals: For example, the ratio 1 to 5, or 1:5, could be written 1/5, that is, 1 divided by 5, or 0.2. NP to FTP (NP:FTP) means the same thing as NP/FTP, or NP divided by FTP.) So, for example, if the NP for a long training ride that you performed early in the year is 210 watts, and your threshold power at the time was 280 watts, then the IF for that workout would be 210 divided by 280, or 0.75. However, if you did that same exact ride later in the year, when you were fitter, and by then your threshold power had risen to 300 watts, then the IF would be lower—0.70. IF therefore provides a valid and convenient way of comparing the relative intensity

| TABLE 7.2 | *TYPICAL INTENSITY FACTOR VALUES IN TRAINING AND RACING* | |

Exertion	IF Value	Notes
Level 1, Active Recovery	< 0.75	
Level 2, Endurance	0.75–0.85	
Level 3, Tempo	0.85–0.95	Also includes road races lasting less than roughly 2.5 hours.
Level 4, Lactate Threshold	0.95–1.05	Also includes road races lasting less than roughly 2.5 hours, criteriums, circuit races, and longer time trials.
Level 5 and higher	1.05–1.15 > 1.15	Shorter time trials Prologue time trial, track pursuit, track miss-and-out.

of a training session or race either over time for one rider or from one rider to the next, taking into account changes or differences in threshold power. Table 7.2 shows typical IF values for various training sessions or races.

Training Stress Score™

Although exercise intensity is clearly an important factor in determining the type and magnitude of physiological adaptations to training, exercise frequency and duration—which together determine the overall training volume—are important factors as well. However, there is obviously an interaction between training intensity and volume—that is, at some point, as your intensity goes up, your volume must come down, and vice versa, or you will become overtrained. To quantify the overall training load and help to prevent such a situation, the authors developed Training Stress Score.

TSS can be calculated for every workout, and you can view a graphic summary of your recent TSS in a spreadsheet program or in Cycling-Peaks. The new ergomo Pro computer also has the ability to calculate and display TSS as you ride, which could prove to be a big help to serious cyclists in modeling performance. TSS takes into account both the intensity (i.e., IF) and the duration of each training session, and might be viewed best as a predictor of the amount of glycogen utilized in each workout. If you know the TSS from a certain workout, you can make decisions about how to proceed in your training. A very high TSS resulting from a single race or training session, for example, would indicate that one or more days of rest should be scheduled. The formula for TSS is:

$$\text{TSS} = (s \times W \times IF)/(FTP \times 3{,}600)$$

Using Intensity Factor to Recognize Changes in Fitness

Note that one particularly useful application of IF is to check for changes in functional threshold power. Specifically, an IF of more than 1.05 for a race that is approximately 1 hour in duration is often a sign that the rider's threshold power is actually greater than that presently entered into the CyclingPeaks software program or a spreadsheet program. Thus, by simply examining a rider's IF for various events during the course of a season, one can often discern increases or decreases in threshold power without the need for frequent formal testing.

For example, let's say that Joe Athlete has set his threshold power at 290 watts and has been training smart for the past eight weeks. However, he hasn't done any formal testing or races lately. Joe heads out to his local district criterium race and gets in a breakaway for about an hour. He comes home and downloads his power meter. Looking at his graph, he creates a range around his time "spent off the front," and he sees that his TSS score is 114 and his IF was 1.07, with his normalized watts at 310.

Joe knows that this can't be right because, by definition, an hour at threshold should equal 100 TSS points and an IF of 1.0. Joe adjusts his threshold value up to 310, lets the software recalculate his TSS and IF, and sees that the TSS is now 100 and the IF is now 1.0. That tells Joe that his functional threshold power has probably increased to 310 watts. Since Joe knows that a 20-watt increase in FTP is relatively large, he decides to raise his FTP setting in the software to 300 watts, and then confirm this number through formal testing as soon as possible.

where "s" is for duration in seconds, W is Normalized Power in watts, IF is Intensity Factor, FTP is functional threshold power, and 3,600 is for the number of seconds in 1 hour.

Training Stress Score is based on a 1-hour time trial at your threshold. An athlete riding for an hour at FTP would score 100 TSS points, and the IF from this ride would be 1.0. Most serious cyclists know what it feels like to do a time trial for an hour, and they also know how important it is to recover from such an effort. Each year, there are many 40 km time trials held in the United States, and riding a 40k in under 1 hour is and has been the goal of many an aspiring cyclist. This effort was therefore chosen to be the "gold standard" for TSS and IF because it is such a well-known event. Almost all riders are familiar with it, and it's a perfect place to establish the "anchor" of TSS. From this knowledge, just about any rider can understand that a 200 TSS ride would represent the same overall "dose" of training as two 40 km time trials. In contrast, a 100 TSS ride could be a long 2-hour ride at a lower Intensity Factor (0.71), which would still produce the same training stress as a 40 km time trial at an Intensity Factor of 1.0.

A very high TSS would indicate that one or more days of rest should be scheduled.

One of the exciting things about TSS, since it is calculated based on functional threshold power, is that beginning riders can work at a level that is right for them to optimize their own training. Although a 300-TSS ride for a beginning rider will be very different, in terms of distance and duration, from a 300-TSS ride for Lance Armstrong, it will put the same degree of stress on the beginner's physiological system and produce an equivalent positive impact. What this means is that as long as you know the FTP of the athlete, you can easily understand the amount of stress created by his or her efforts, no matter what the category of the rider. The amount of training load that individuals can tolerate, however, will differ. Lance Armstrong can do 300–400 TSS at 0.85 IF for twenty-one days in a row and continue to get stronger, whereas a beginning cyclist may find that just two days of training at that level might severely "over-reach" his or her abilities. Because of this difference, we created a scale that can be used as an approximate guide to training:

TABLE 7.3	TRAINING TEST SCORES (TSS) AND INTENSITY FACTORS (IF) FOR DIFFERENT RIDES		
Event Description	**Duration**	**TSS**	**IF**
Easy Level 1 recovery ride, flat terrain - Male Category 3 rider	1 h 0 min	12	0.37
Easy Level 2 endurance ride, rolling terrain - male category 2 rider	2 h 30 min	60	0.49
C-X race, Female masters age 40–45 age group	0 h 45 min	61	0.92
Division 1 Pro in an American Pro 1, 2 criterium	1 h 0 min	73	0.86
Women's Pro Criterium	0 h 45 min	80	1.06
40k TT- Category 2 Male	0 h 53 min	89	1.02
Typical SuperWeek Cat 3 crit (same race as above)	1 h 57 min	109	0.75
Typical SuperWeek Pro 1/2 Crit	2 h 35 min	118	0.67
2005 Mount Evans Hill Climb, Cat 1	2 h 2 min	126	0.79
Masters National RR- 2005, 55–59 age	2 h 29 min	136	0.76
SuperWeek 2005, Schlitz Park Criterium, Cat 1	2 h 28 min	166	0.82
Category 4 Road Race, rolling terrain, in one small break, rest of time in field	2 h 50 min	185	0.81
Level 2/3, with 1 hour of threshold climbing	2 h 50 min	241	0.92
Category 2 Dead Flat Road Race	3 h 35 min	246	0.829
SuperWeek 2005, Holy Hill Road Race, Cat 1, small chase group	4 h 55 min	266	0.74
2005 US Elite National Championships Cat 1	5 h 22 min	272	0.71
2003 Redlands: Oak Glen Stage, Cat 1	4 h 55 min	292	0.78
Category 2 Hilly Road Race	4 h 16 min	305	0.85
2005 Philadelphia USPro Championships	5 h 41 min	307	0.74
Tour De Georgia Stage 1, 2005, easy day, Divison 3, US Pro	6 h 0 min	317	0.72
2004 San Francisco Grand Prix	4 h 20 min	327	0.87
2005 Lake Placid Ironman, Fast Woman Age Grouper, fell apart on run	5 h 30 min	330	0.73
TDF stage 14- 2004	6 h 24 min	464	0.85
24 Hour MTB race, Elite Masters Male	24 h 0 min	1058	0.74
1000k Brevet- done over 3 days, only 5 hours sleep total, woman- age 40	42 h 0 min	1610	0.62

- Less than 150: low (recovery generally complete by following day)
- 150–300: medium (some residual fatigue may be present the next day, but recovery is generally complete by the second day)
- 300–450: high (some residual fatigue may be present even after two days)
- Greater than 450: very high (residual fatigue lasting for several days is likely)

Once you are able to associate your different rides with TSS and IF scores, you will be able to understand the type of ride that someone else did just by hearing what the TSS and IF scores were for that ride. Table 7.2 lists some different types of rides and their corresponding scores.

By tracking NP, IF, and TSS for each workout and over time, individual athletes and coaches will gain a powerful tool for analyzing the enormous amount of data gathered by training with a power meter. The results of such analyses can then serve as the springboard for improvements in training and, ultimately, race performance.

Quadrant Analysis™

In order to be successful at racing, you must train in ways that are highly specific to the events in which you compete. That is why it is important to consider the moment-by-moment power fluctuations that occur in cycling. But power fluctuation is also related to an athlete's neuromuscular power—and that is the issue that we wanted to address when we developed the concept of Quadrant Analysis.

By now you know that when you ride with a power meter, the power fluctuates dramatically. One moment you may be producing 500 watts, the next moment 50 watts, then 250 watts, and so on. These fluctuations are all due to changes in speed, wind, road or trail gradient, and the like. And this can happen in just a few seconds of your ride! Think about these power fluctuations compounded over the entire ride, and then over multiple days of riding. Then consider the power differences between different events within the sport, which arise not because of wind or road conditions but because of the nature and duration of the event. The highly variable nature of cycling power has significant physiological implications, not only in terms of the acute responses to a single ride, but also in terms of the chronic adaptations to repeated training sessions.

Tools such as Normalized Power, Intensity Factor, and Training Stress Score explicitly recognize the seemingly stochastic nature of cycling power output and help coaches and athletes better understand the actual physiological demands of a given race or workout. Even so, to completely understand the physiological consequences of large variations in power, one must also understand how they impact neuromuscular function—that is, the actual forces and velocities that the leg muscles must generate to produce a given power output. Such effects are recognized by the algorithm used to calculate Normalized Power, but only to the extent that they influence metabolism (e.g., via altering fiber-type recruitment patterns). Although strength (or maximal force) per se is rarely a limiting factor in cycling, neuromuscular factors nonetheless can still sometimes play an important role in determining performance. Thus, we realized that it would be useful to be able to analyze power meter data that captures this important information in a form that could readily be grasped even by nonexperts.

Neuromuscular What?

"Neuromuscular function" may sound complicated, but it simply means how fast you can contract a muscle, how strongly you can contract it, and how long you can contract it before relaxing it again. When someone learns a new movement pattern—it could be anything from learning how to type on the keyboard to pedaling a bicycle—those movement patterns are governed by that individual's ability to transfer the information from his or her brain to the muscles that are involved. We all take this for granted, and when it comes to cycling we just pedal, but in reality each of us is different in our ability to make these contractions occur. With your power meter, you can begin to understand your neuromuscular ability, and you can determine whether you are training correctly for cycling success and then begin to improve your neuromuscular power.

Measuring Neuromuscular Power

Some information about the neuromuscular demands of a given workout or race can be obtained by examining a frequency distribution histogram of the rider's cadence. Such plots are automatically prepared by most, if not all, power meter software programs, and thus provide a con-

FIGURE 7.3: CADENCE DISTRIBUTION CHART OF A WORKOUT

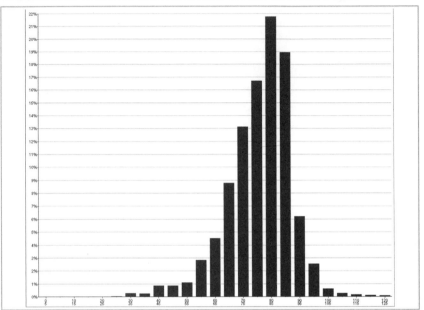

venient means of data analysis. Figure 7.3 shows how the cadence from a workout is distributed in the different "bins," or bars. In this particular workout, the rider spent a large percentage of his time in the 80–90 rpm range.

However, the velocity of muscle contraction (as indicated by cadence) is only one of two determinants of power, with the other, of course, being force. Unfortunately, at present no power meter directly measures the force applied to the pedal. However, it is possible to derive the average (i.e., over 360 degrees) effective (i.e., tangential to the crank) pedal force (both legs combined) from power and cadence data. The equation looks like this:

$$\text{AEPF} = (P \times 60) \div (C \times 2 \times \pi \times CL)$$

In this formula, AEPF stands for average effective pedal force (in newtons, or N); P is power, in watts; C is for cadence (in revolutions per minute); CL is for crank length (in meters); and the constants 60, 2, and π, serve to convert cadence to angular velocity (in radians/second).

Additional insight into the neuromuscular demands of a race or training session can then be obtained by preparing a frequency distribution
histogram for AEPF that is similar the one for cadence, as shown in
Figure 7.3. (Note that, as with all such plots, graphs like this one do not
take into consideration how long AEPF was continuously within a
given "bin," or range. This is not an issue, however, because unlike, for
example, heart rate, neuromuscular responses and demands are essentially instantaneous. Indeed, it is the generation of specific velocities
and forces via muscle contraction that essentially drives all other physiological responses.)

FIGURE 7.4: SCATTERPLOT OF FORCE AND VELOCITY FOR SAME
WORKOUT AS DEPICTED IN FIGURE 7.3

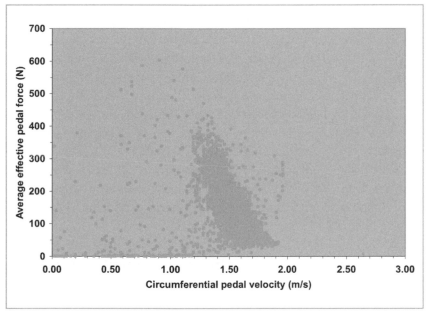

Although simply examining the frequency distributions of AEPF
and cadence provides insight, it does not reveal the relationship between
these two variables. This relationship can only be quantified by plotting
force versus velocity. Muscle physiologists have used such force-velocity
diagrams to describe the contractile properties or characteristics of muscle ever since the early 1920s. Figure 7.4 therefore provides an example
of a force-velocity (that is, AEPF–circumferential pedal velocity) scatterplot for the same training session as used to generate Figure 7.3.

Circumferential pedal velocity—that is, how fast the pedal moves around the circle it makes while pedaling—is derived from cadence as follows:

$$\textbf{CPV} = \textbf{C} \times \textbf{CL} \times \textbf{2} \times \boldsymbol{\pi} \div \textbf{60}$$

Here, CPV stands for circumferential pedal velocity (in meters/second); C is for cadence (in revolutions per minute); CL represents crank length (in meters); and the constants 2, π, and 60 serve to convert the data to the proper units. Although technically, muscle-shortening velocity, or at least joint angular velocity, should be used instead of CPV, CPV has proven to be an excellent predictor of both of these. Indeed, since crank length is generally constant, especially for a given individual, one could just as well use cadence instead of CPV. However, we have used the latter here to be consistent with scientific convention and to emphasize the relationship of cycling-specific plots to the more general force-velocity curve of muscle. A scatterplot of force and velocity, such as that shown in Figure 7.4, therefore presents information that cannot be obtained from just frequency distribution plots of AEPF and CPV.

However, it can be difficult to detect subtle and sometimes even not-so-subtle differences between roughly similar rides based on such "shotgun blast" patterns, especially if the scaling of the X and Y axes is allowed to vary. Furthermore, without additional information, such force-velocity scatterplots are entirely relative in nature because there are no fixed anchor points or values that can be used as a frame of reference. It is the latter issue that Quadrant Analysis was specifically developed to address.

Once again, threshold power (and the associated cadence) provides a useful basis for comparison, and in particular for separating relatively low-force from relatively high-force pedaling efforts. (It cannot be overemphasized that the absolute forces generated while cycling are usually quite low, such that strength is rarely a limiting factor to performance. An example of how Quadrant Analysis can be used to demonstrate this point is provided later in this chapter.) Specifically, one factor contributing to the curvilinear relationship between exercise intensity and various metabolic responses (e.g., glycogen utilization, blood-lactate concentration) is the recruitment of Type II, or fast-twitch, muscle fibers. Specifically, when pedaling at a typical cadence and power output well below lactate threshold, there is little engagement or utilization of fast-twitch fibers, but with progressive increases in power output, a progressively greater fraction of the total motor

FIGURE 7.5: FIBER TYPE RECRUITMENT AS A FUNCTION OF INTENSITY

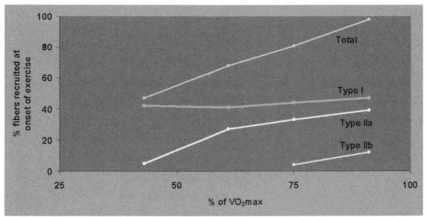

N.K. Vollestad et al., "Effect of Varying Exercise Inensity on Glycogen Depletion in Human Muscle Fibers," *Acta Physiologica Scandinanvia* 125 (1985): 395.

unit pool will be recruited to generate the required force. For example, while riding at Level 2 (Endurance), you could possibly be using 90 percent slow-twitch, or Type I, muscle fibers, and only 10 percent Type II, or fast-twitch, muscle fibers. When you pick up the intensity to Level 4, you will continue to use those slow-twitch fibers, but you will also begin to recruit significant numbers of fast-twitch fibers as well. In other words, the more intense the effort, the greater your reliance on fast-twitch muscle fibers.

Figure 7.5 shows how the different fiber types are recruited in relation to the intensity of the effort, based on the rate at which they use glycogen as determined using muscle biopsies. The Type I fibers are maximally recruited even at a relatively low exercise intensity (i.e., 40 percent of VO_2max), whereas the Type IIa and especially Type IIb fibers are only recruited at much higher exercise intensities.

Scientific studies using a variety of other techniques (e.g., electromyography spectral analysis) also suggest that threshold power represents not only a threshold in terms of the power that an athlete can sustain, but also somewhat of a threshold in terms of fast-twitch fiber recruitment. To state it another way: When pedaling at a typical self-selected cadence, functional threshold power appears to occur at the power (and thus force) at which significant fast-twitch fiber recruitment first begins. Thus, AEPF and CPV at an individual's threshold power can be used to divide the force-velocity scatterplot from any ride into four quadrants, as shown in Figure 7.6. This division is somewhat arbitrary, in part because of the gradation in force, and thus motor unit recruitment, that occurs when cycling. Also, exercise duration

FIGURE 7.6: QUADRANT ANALYSIS OF A ROAD RIDE

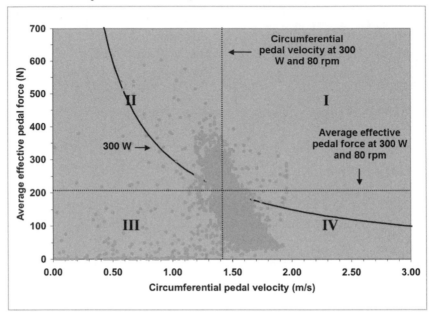

plays an important role in fiber type recruitment, but this is not considered in the figure (to do so would require a three-dimensional plot of AEPF, CPV, and time, which is too complex for routine use). Furthermore, the threshold relationship for fast-twitch fiber recruitment is not really a line as shown, but more of a curve that falls from left to right. Nevertheless, data points that fall into these four quadrants can be interpreted as follows:

Quadrant I (upper right): high force and high velocity. At the extreme, this would be represented by sprinting, but it also includes almost any extended supra-threshold effort on level ground (e.g., an attack or bridge attempt during a race). Perhaps not surprisingly, mass-start racing on the track (e.g., a points race) invariably entails a significant amount of such high-force, high-velocity pedaling due to the typical aggressive nature of such racing and the use of a fixed gear.

Quadrant II (upper left): high force but low velocity. Typically, Quadrant II pedaling occurs when climbing or accelerating, especially from a low speed. Indeed, a standing start, in which the initial CPV is zero, is the one situation in cycling where strength is truly limiting—that is, only when CPV is zero will AEFP be maximal. Racing off-road (e.g., cyclocross or mountain bike racing) also often involves a significant amount of high-force, low-velocity pedaling. However, even a race held on pavement may require a large percentage of such pedaling if the climbs are steep and/or the rider is overgeared. Because AEPF is sufficiently high, pedaling in both Quadrant I and Quadrant II would be expected to entail significant recruitment of fast-twitch fibers.

FIGURE 7.7: QUADRANT ANALYSIS OF A FLAT 40 KM TIME TRIAL

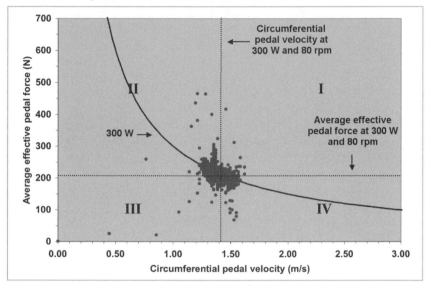

FIGURE 7.8: QUADRANT ANALYSIS OF A CONSTANT-POWER ERGOMETER WORKOUT

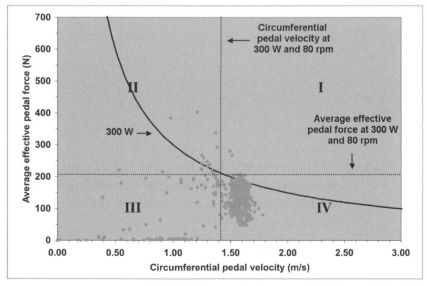

Quadrant III (lower left): low force and low velocity. Rides that entail a very large percentage of pedaling that falls into Quadrant III would typically be those used for recovery or for social purposes (e.g.,

FIGURE 7.9: QUADRANT ANALYSIS OF A "MICRO-BURST" INTERVAL (15 SECONDS "ON"/15 SECONDS "OFF"), ERGOMETER WORKOUT

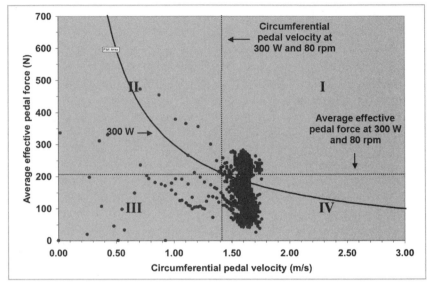

FIGURE 7.10: QUADRANT ANALYSIS OF A ROAD RACE OVER FLAT ROLLING TERRAIN

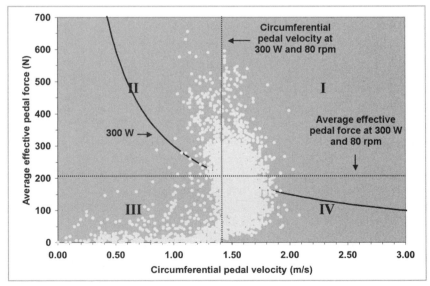

coffee shop rides), not for actual training. However, a mass–start race in which power is highly variable may also involve a good deal of low-force, low-velocity pedaling—for example, when recovering from harder efforts when there is little possibility of an attack, or when soft-pedaling in a large bunch.

Quadrant IV (lower right): low force but high velocity. Perhaps the most obvious example of Quadrant IV pedaling would be the use of a low fixed gear or rollers in an attempt to improve pedaling smoothness. Racing, however, may also involve a significant amount of low-force, high-velocity pedaling, especially during events in which there is a frequent need to accelerate rapidly (e.g., criteriums).

To further illustrate the applications of this method and the insights it may provide, examples from different types of workouts and races are provided below (Figures 7.7–7.12). These examples were specifically chosen because, except for the 40 km time trial provided earlier as a reference, the average (not normalized) power in each case is close to 250 watts. As can be seen, however, the combination and distribution of pedaling forces and velocities accounting for this power output differ significantly. In particular, note the different patterns evident in the plots of the constant power and micro-interval ergometer training sessions. The

FIGURE 7.11: QUADRANT ANALYSIS OF A FLAT CRITERIUM

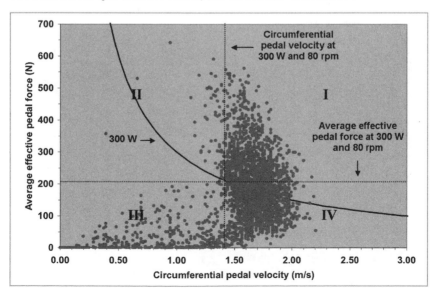

utility of preparing a force-velocity scatterplot is especially evident in this case as it reveals an important difference between the two workouts that cannot really be discerned based on average power, Normalized Power, average cadence, and other analyses.

Although the concepts we have presented in this chapter are rather advanced, they are important, and it is very useful to understand them when training with power. Beginning to associate your rides with how many TSS points you accumulated, and figuring out how that will impact your recovery, can be a profound learning process. Knowing that an hour of work at your FTP equals 100 TSS points with an IF of 1.0 will help you to better associate levels of training load with your rides. You will begin to understand the levels of training load that would be provided in a ride with your local Tuesday night group, the ride you do on your mountain-climbing day, the workout you do to reach Level 3 (Tempo), and so on, and from this knowledge you can use TSS and IF on a daily basis to design a more complete training plan. This is one of the greatest uses you will discover with your power meter. Never before have we been able to so closely and accurately quantify training load for each individual cyclist and for his or her unique individual and cumulative workouts over entire years of time. With these tools, the power

FIGURE 7.12: QUADRANT ANALYSIS OF ALL EXAMPLES PLOTTED TOGETHER

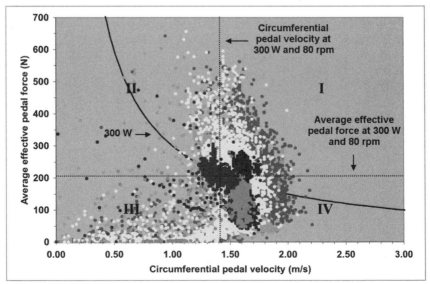

meter allows you to see how your training load will impact you after your ride, two days later, one week later, and even a month later.

Quadrant Analysis provides another level of understanding about the specificity of your workout. If you are a triathlete, and all you are doing are mass-start road races, it is very likely that you would not be ready for your upcoming triathlon, neuromuscularly speaking. By learning how your events fall into the four quadrants, you can determine whether your training is specific to that quadrant. Don't expect to be a successful criterium racer if you spend a majority of your time in Quadrant III riding back and forth to the coffee shop. But make sure that you are in Quadrant III when you are doing your recovery rides. Using Quadrant Analysis on selected rides and races will help to confirm that you are training properly and help you to achieve peak performance at cycling events.

HOW TO DEVELOP A TRAINING PLAN BASED ON POWER

8

SOMETIMES IN CYCLING it's hard to know whether you are indeed improving, or if everyone else is just going slower. Now that you have some tools, tips, and tricks for training with power, you can begin to track your improvement; seeing your wattage improve can, in turn, be a good motivator for continued hard work. In this chapter you will learn how to develop a training plan based on wattage that will take you to the next level of fitness. Rather than looking at methods and theories about training itself—other complete training books are available to cover those issues—we will focus specifically on how to integrate wattage into your training plan. This chapter is also intended to be used in conjunction with Appendix B, which supplies more of the sample workouts that would go with this plan.

Sample Training Plan

In developing a training plan, you must start with the things you know, such as weekly training time constraints, strengths and weaknesses, and goals. From these known items, you can begin to fill in the blanks of your training plan—for example, how hard to train, which roads to train on, and whether to do sprints, endurance rides, or hill climbs. Once you fill in the blanks, you'll end up with a finished product that is your "blue-print" to success. Hunter's training plans are hosted at the Web link www.trainingpeaks.com/hunter. If you are interested in trying an inter-active plan, please visit the site and choose the plan that fits your FTP. The sample workouts described below for Weeks 1–8 are from the "Cy-cling Intermediate 250 Watts Threshold" plan, and the workouts for Weeks 9–16 are from "Cycling Intermediate 250 Watts Threshold, Weeks 9–16."

To give you an example of this process, we'll invent another ficti-tious cyclist. Here, we'll use Bob Rider, a fast cyclist with good bike-handling skills who is already doing well in the local club rides. He wants to start racing and going on the weekly "racing" group rides. Bob has about twelve hours a week to train, including weekends. He is a decent climber, but his skills are lacking in time trialing and sprinting as com-pared with other local racers.

Bob weighs 155 pounds. His current FTP is 250 watts, or 3.55 watts per kilogram. His best 5 seconds is 845 watts, his best 1 minute is 480 watts, and his best 5 minutes is 320 watts. His Power Profile slopes upward to the right, with a slight peak at his 5-minute or VO_2max power. Since he is a good climber, which means he has good power-to-weight ratio, but is a rel-atively poor sprinter, that tells us that he lacks in neuromuscular power. This is also echoed in his Power Profile by his higher than normal 5-minute power and the fact that he does not do as well as others in shorter, hard ef-forts. Of the three main body types, Bob could be characterized as an "ec-tomorph" (the other types are mesomorph and endomorph), which means that he has a thin build with relatively small muscles, and possibly a larger percentage than average of slow-twitch muscle fibers.

Bob is ambitious and excited about cycling, so he has decided to begin racing this season and compete in ten events. He really wants to do well in a 2-day stage race in late May that has a 10-mile time trial and a 25-mile criterium on Saturday, and then a 50-mile road race on Sun-day that has a 5-mile climb on the course.

The Plan

Now, that we have Bob's background information, we can begin to de-sign a training plan for him. We'll begin his plan on February 1 and go through his peak event, giving him a complete sixteen-week program. The plan, described below, has a general pattern. Bob will have a complete rest day every Monday. His Tuesday, Wednesday, and Thursday workouts will constitute the "meat" of the program, and Friday will generally be for Active Recovery (Level 1), although sometimes Bob will do specific workouts on Friday in order to build three strong workouts on consecutive days. The weekend will include a long group ride (or race) on Saturday, and a medium-length ride (or race) on Sunday. We'll build up his fitness in the classic "three weeks on, one week off" periodization model and monitor it along the way with his downloads in case a change in direction is needed. All of his workouts will be based around wattage.

If you miss a day, then it's generally better to move on to the next workout than to try to make it up.

A couple of guidelines to go by when deciding how to write your own training plan:

It's okay to do your Tuesday and Wednesday workouts in the reverse order if you need to. The Thursday workout should be easier because it follows two hard days, and also because it's two days before your big Saturday ride or race. However, if you are not racing on Saturday, or if it's okay to not quite be as sharp on the Saturday group ride, then you can switch your Thursday workouts around with the Tuesday and Wednesday workouts, too.

If you miss a day, then it's generally better to move on to the next workout than to try to make it up. The only caveat to this is that if the workout was a highly specific one, and you look at your plan and see that you will not be performing that workout again for at least two weeks, then you should try to make up the workout as soon as possible.

You should not have any "stacking" of workouts. "Stacking," a term coined by Gale Bernhardt, author of *Triathlon Training Basics* (2004), occurs when an athlete misses one or more workouts early in the week, then tries to make up for lost time on the weekend. A stacker is a close relative to the weekend warrior. For example, the stacker completes the Tuesday workout but takes off the rest of the week—meanwhile, life and business are full throttle on those days. Stackers believe they can make up for lost time by doing all the work in two days. They try to do their Level 4 work, their long group ride and hills, and their sprints all in the same day. The next day, they again go out and overdo it, with more intervals (because they didn't complete all of them on Saturday, because they were too tired . . .). Packing all or most of the work into two days is a recipe for illness or injury. Cycling is not a sport that allows you to "cram" the way you did back in your schooldays before your midterms.

Bob Rider will have some specific days in the plan for "strength" work. This is because one of his limiters is neuromuscular power, and in order to improve on this weakness, he'll need to do some work in this area. This does not mean, however, that this is right for you. If this is not one of your weaknesses, then we suggest you use this time for additional miles on the bike.

If you begin to feel that you are overly tired, then it's okay to move up a rest week. However, many times athletes do not push themselves hard enough; as soon as they get a little tired, they assume they are "overtraining." Sometimes, you have to push through and "dig deep"; otherwise, you may limit your performance potential. So while rest is incredibly important, you should also challenge yourself to push beyond what you thought was possible. On the flip side of the coin, it's also okay to push back a rest week if you are not tired when a rest week was scheduled. If that happens, keep going strong, and be sure to go ahead and take the rest week in the week after it was scheduled.

While rest is incredibly important, you should also challenge yourself to push beyond what you thought was possible.

Download every ride. By now you should know how important it is to view the power meter data, even from your recovery rides.

If your power meter is in need of service during a critical time, don't panic. Remember, you rode without of these "gizmos" for a long time, and now that you have ridden with it, you probably have a good sense of what 400 watts feels like going up a hill and how your heart rate responds to efforts. Fall back on your rate of perceived exertion (RPE) and heart rate, and you'll be able to weather the temporary horror of not having your power meter.

Weeks 1–4

The first part of Bob's training program is designed to introduce him to speed changes and also to work at threshold. Because Bob has a weakness in his short efforts, we will begin to work on his ability to change speeds. We'll work on his threshold as well throughout the sixteen weeks, and on the weekend, even though his FTP is already decent. (For his other workouts in Weeks 1–4, see Appendix B.)

Bob will also start addressing his limiter of neuromuscular power by incorporating some big-gear work. Let's take a look at that specific workout and see how having a power meter will help him to complete his workout correctly.

From Week 2, on Friday, Bob will begin his workout with 15 minutes of pedaling at 90–100 rpm, keeping his watts below 150, or at the bottom of Level 2 (Endurance). This will give him three consecutive days of training for two weeks in a row in order to create a stronger "overload" of work. After he warms up, he'll get his legs ready for some work by doing a hard effort requiring him to hammer out one 5-minute effort at 240–250 watts, right at his threshold power. He'll up the intensity in the last 30 seconds to 270 watts to push himself over the edge, then recover with 5 minutes of easy pedaling, with his watts under 150.

Then, every 5 minutes for the next 60 minutes, Bob will do an effort in the 53:13 gear for 20 seconds, trying to hold 400–500 watts and pushing this big gear. Staying seated the entire effort, he'll try to jump hard into it and try to get it going as fast as he can in 20 seconds. This effort is aimed at developing leg strength and force. Bob's cadence will be low in the beginning and get faster with each second, so he should focus on pushing hard on the pedals and being as smooth as possible. Between each effort, he'll ride for 5 minutes easy, with his cadence in the 90–100 rpm range, using an easy gear, and his wattage should be around 150–200 watts

WORKOUT 8.1	*TEMPO WITH BIG GEAR*	
Week 2, Friday, 1.5 hours		
Warm-up	15 min.	<68%
Ride	5 min.	100%
Last :	30 + to	108%
Rest	5 min.	<68%
Ride	:20	160–200%
Seated, use 53:13, push the gear		
Ride	5 min.	68–75%
Every 5 min, repeat :20 push, for 60 min total		
Cool-down	10 min.	<55%

(Levels 2/3). Then he'll cool down for 10–20 minutes with small-ring spinning (cadence 95–100 rpm, but watts below 140).

As you can see, having the ability to regulate his effort specifically with watts in mind will allow Bob to get the most out of this workout and also keep him from overdoing the efforts and undermining his up-coming workouts.

The weekends are critical for training because they allow Bob to get in a longer ride and improve his overall aerobic fitness. Although Bob isn't a weekend warrior, he also has to take advantage of the additional time in order to build more stamina in his legs. At the end of the cycle, he will be in need of a rest week to recharge and allow his body to adapt. Then he can come back stronger than ever for the next four-week block.

Weeks 5–8

Bob starts off this block with some intensity to work on his anaerobic capacity and increase the length of his threshold power intervals. By Week 6, Bob is ready for a sprint workout and also a time trial workout to focus on improving his "snap" and also his power at VO$_2$max.

Thursday workouts are unique in the fact that they are dependent on what happens on Tuesday and Wednesday and also what is going to occur on Saturday. In general, there is no set pattern to Thursday. Some days Bob will be resting in order to recover from his Tuesday and Wednesday workouts and also to get ready for Saturday. On other Thursdays, he'll get in a strong workout, either because he had an easier day on Wednesday or because we are creating a nice three-day block of training.

Let's take a look at his time trial workout on Thursday of Week 6, a ride that will take 1.5 hours. He'll begin the workout with 15 minutes at Level 2 (Endurance) pace, with his watts from 150–190 and pedaling smoothly at a self-selected cadence. After the warm-up, he'll complete six mock time trials. Each will be 6 minutes long but will reach only 96–102 percent of his FTP. This should be around 240–255 watts. He'll try to start out strong, but not too fast, as he'll need to pace himself in these efforts, and then hold like glue to his wattage goal. These trials will help him to learn pacing, enable him to get in some solid work at threshold power, and also give him enough time

WORKOUT 8.2	LEVEL 5, VO$_2$MAX EFFORTS	
Week 6, Thursday, 1.5 hours		
Warm-up	15 min.	56–75%
Ride	6 min.	96–102%
Rest	6–8 min.	<55%
Repeat 6-min. efforts 5 more times, same rest period		
Cool-down	15 min.	<68%

while at threshold power to develop a solid, powerful rhythm. These intervals are about going fast, but not hammering at max pace. He'll rest for at least 6–8 minutes between each effort with his watts below 120. Bob will then cool down for 15 minutes, holding his watts below 150.

The weekend rides should get progressively longer each week, bringing Bob's endurance up gently and only when he's ready. Bob will do some focused threshold work in Week 7 on Tuesday and Wednesday by getting in multiple intervals at his FTP, and by the end of the week he should be ready for his Week 8 rest week.

Weeks 9–12

Week 9 starts off with a monthly testing protocol to see how much Bob's threshold has improved. It may be time to increase his threshold power number in the software and adjust his workouts accordingly. He should test his threshold when he's still fresh from his rest week; he also still has eight weeks to go before his big event, so knowing threshold power now is critical. The "monthly" power test does not have to be done monthly; however, it is important to do this test at least once every eight weeks.

The testing protocol does not just look at threshold power. It is important to also test the four Power Profile time periods and update the Power Profile chart accordingly. The testing protocol is a great workout in and of itself, so Bob will not be losing anything by completing it.

WORKOUT 8.3	TEST	
Week 9, Monday, 1.5 hours		
Warm-up	20 min.	<68%
Ride	3 x 1 min.	100%
Fast pedaling, 1 min. rest int.		*100rpm +*
Ride	5 min.	Max effort
Rest	*10 min.*	*<68%*
Ride	2 x 1 min.	Max effort
Rest 5 min. between		*<68%*
Ride	3 x :20 sprints	Max effort
Rest 3 min. between		*<68%*
Ride	10 min.	<68%
Ride	20 min.	Max effort
Cool-down	15 min.	<55%

To begin the testing protocol, Bob starts with a 20-minute warm-up. Then he'll do three fast-pedaling efforts at 100 rpm for 1 minute each, with 1 minute between each effort. These are to help open up the legs and finish warming up the muscles. After the fast pedaling, he'll ride for 3 minutes easy with his watts at less than 150. Then he'll go for it—doing one 5-minute all-out effort.

He'll punch it as hard as he can and hold the highest watts he can for the 5 minutes. He should not start too hard though. Then he'll ride for 10 minutes easy at less than 150 watts. The next efforts are a test of his anaerobic capacity: He'll do two 1-minute efforts, with 5 minutes between each effort. He should be out of the saddle and accelerating hard up to speed, and then really pushing until the end of the minute. After the second effort, he'll do 5 minutes easy at watts less than 150. Bob will then finish off the short tests with a test of his neuromuscular power, or sprinting ability, doing three 20-second "super jumps." For these, he should jump as hard as he can out of the saddle and then sprint, as if he were about to win a race, for 20 seconds. We are just going to take the best 5 seconds to look at, but to get that segment he needs to do the full 20 seconds of effort and make sure he gives it his all. He should rest for 3 minutes between each effort with very easy pedaling, with watts less than 120, then ride easy for 10 minutes or so with his watts at 150–190, and then complete a 20-minute time trial. At this point, he should try to produce the best average watts that he can for the entire 20 minutes. If he starts out too hard, he'll blow up in the first 5 minutes, but it's important for him to give it his all, focus, and push hard. After this, he should cool down for 15–30 minutes of easy pedaling with his watts at less than 150.

Bob should also start to race on the weekends and begin to work on more race-specific efforts. Threshold power work will continue on the weekends, both in long training rides and in races. This block is the most important segment for building muscular endurance and overall aerobic endurance; therefore, the weekend rides, if not races, are much longer and intense than before. Bob should be very ready for a rest week on Week 12, as his chronic training load is really starting to build up now.

Weeks 13–16

This is the final block leading up to Bob's goal—racing weekend. Week 13 starts out with three hard days in a row to take advantage of being fresh and to get in some high-quality work. At the end of Week 13, Bob is going to do a practice 20 km time trial in order to get all his gear and his position dialed in, and also so that he can experience the sheer intensity of a 20 km flat-out time-trial effort. This will be an important test for Bob, as up to this point he hasn't done any threshold work over 20 minutes, and he hasn't done such work in his time trial position, either.

Week 14 is another tough training and racing week. Bob should do a hard anaerobic capacity workout on Wednesday, and either two days of racing that weekend or two hard days of training. The week preceding Bob's key goal is a rest week that allows him to rebuild his muscle glycogen stores, rid his body of any residual muscle soreness, and make sure that he comes into his big weekend with plenty of enthusiasm for the event. It's absolutely essential that Bob does not overdo it in this week. If he does, he may compromise his finishing position in his key event.

WORKOUT 8.4	*TUNE-UP*	
Week 16, Friday		
Warm-up	15 min.	<68%
Ride	1.5 hours	65–75%
Within ride do these efforts:		
Ride	3 x 1 min.	Max effort
Rest 5 min. between		*65–75%*
Ride	3 x :30	Max effort
Rest 5 min. between		*65–75%*
Cool-down	15 min.	<68%

The beginning of this final week is a great time to get any work done on his bicycle if it needs maintenance. It's a sure sign of a beginner to wait until two days before the event to try and change old worn-out parts. Bob should take care of any mechanical issues on the Monday of Week 16. After a few days of rest, Bob should shake out the "cobwebs" and get in a solid race tune-up (that is, for his body, not his bike) on the day before his event. This is a critical workout that helps to prepare the muscular and cardiovascular systems for some intense work the next day.

The tune-up is a simple yet very effective workout. Bob will ride 1.5 hours at upper Level 2 (Endurance) pace, 65–75 percent of FTP, and within this 1.5 hours he will do three hard efforts of 1-minute each, with at least 5 minutes of easy riding between them. These are random efforts and can be done toward the beginning, middle, or end of the ride. They can also be done on hills or on a flat road. The key is to really push hard on these in order to prepare the legs for the next day's event. It is also critical that Bob do three hard 30-second sprints on this ride, starting out of the saddle and sprinting for at least 15 seconds, and then settling back into the saddle and driving the bike to the line for the full 30 seconds. A long rest is required between each of these efforts as well in order to completely recover and to be able to reproduce a maximal effort for the next one. Therefore, he should rest, with easy pedaling, at endurance pace for 5 minutes between the sprints. As with the 1-minute intervals, these can be done at any time during the ride, as long as he groups them together. It is important that he leave at least 15 minutes of easy recovery riding before finishing for the day.

Developing Your Power-Based Training Plan

We hope that by reading through this sample plan, you will begin to see how to develop your own plan that addresses your own training needs. The workouts described in Chapter 5 should also give you ideas about how to do this, and, of course, the rest of Bob's plan, which is presented in Appendix B. You have now learned all the steps that are necessary for training effectively with your power meter. To recap all of the steps involved in developing a power-based plan:

- Test for your functional threshold power.
- Set your training levels.
- Define your strengths and weaknesses and test your Power Profile time periods. Plot your Power Profile.
- Try sample workouts and collect data on your power meter.
- Understand your data and what the charts/graphs are telling you.
- Begin developing your power-based training plan.
- Set a goal.
- Understand your training time constraints.
- Work on your weaknesses.
- Write out a training plan!

9 TRACKING CHANGES IN YOUR FITNESS

U P UNTIL NOW, it has been difficult for coaches and athletes to accurately track changes in cycling fitness. Cycling is not like other sports where improvements can be more easily measured. In football, for example, it is easy to track the number of successful catches in the endzone; in baseball, you can record the number of RBIs, and in golf, the number of birdies. But cyclists have usually judged their performances rather subjectively by comparing how they have placed in races or ridden against regular training partners. Some have gone further and regularly timed themselves on set courses or up specific climbs. These methods obviously have their limitations, however, as performance in races depends on tactics and good fortune as well as fitness, and even performance in the "race of truth," i.e., a time trial, can vary significantly depending on environmental conditions such as wind.

With the introduction of the power meter, cyclists have the ability to easily track quantitative changes. You can see how much you have improved in your peak 5-minute power, for example, or your peak 60-minute power. With a few simple charts you can really see the fruits of your labor, as that little line on your graph continues to climb higher and higher. One of the benefits of this new technology is that seeing these changes can be very exciting and motivating. There is no more guessing that "maybe" you are better. It's a definite. There's the number right there in your power meter software. Unfortunately, the opposite can also apply, and when you are riding poorly, it can be really depressing. Quite simply, sometimes the truth hurts! Even in this case, however, it is worth knowing precisely how your fitness has declined, and by how much, so that you can make appropriate changes in your training program to get back on track.

It is important that you understand what the charts and graphs mean, so that with a few simple clicks of the mouse you can see your improvements. Each type of software has different options and ways to view the data. Some of these are more advanced than others, and going through each one is beyond the scope of this book. However, there are some key charts that you should understand and use on a daily basis. Though it is possible to perform some of these analyses using other programs, we have again used CyclingPeaks software to illustrate the ideas. Let's take a look at these charts and explain why they are important.

Mean Maximal Power Periodic Chart

One of the most important charts for you to understand is the Mean Maximal Power (MMP) Periodic Chart. This chart compiles the data from every ride that you have done for a particular time duration. Each data point represents your mean maximal power (that is, average best power) for a particular ride for the time period you select. Figure 9.1 is a graph showing the peak 5 seconds, peak 1 minute, peak 5 minutes, and peak 20 minutes of a masters rider in his second season of training (his first year of training with a power meter). However, as you can tell by just glancing at this chart, there is too much data, and it is difficult to draw any conclusions about his fitness changes from it. Did he improve? It's hard to tell.

How can we see the trees for the forest? By changing the "days per point," we can smooth the data over seven days and look at it week by week (Figure 9.2). This will help us to better see how his fitness has changed over time. Now, each data point represents the peak wattage for each time period over the entire week. So the peak 5 seconds will be the peak 5 seconds for that entire week, the peak 1 minute will be the peak minute for the entire week, and so on.

Now we have a better picture of how this cyclist's fitness changed throughout the year and when it peaked in each of the different time periods. We see that his peak 5 seconds for the year was in early spring, when he almost cracked 1,080 watts. His peak 1 minute for the season was in early May, when he was able to produce 560 watts for 1 minute. Note how his peak 5-minute power stayed relatively the same throughout the entire racing season, finally peaking in early September at 375

FIGURE 9.1: MEAN MAXIMAL POWER PERIODIC CHART, MASTERS CYCLIST

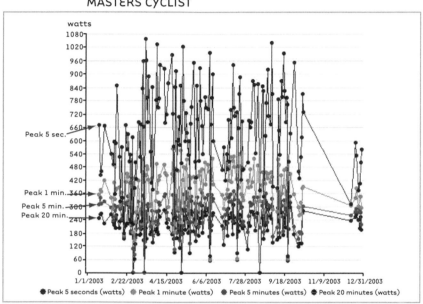

FIGURE 9.2: MEAN MAXIMAL POWER FOR MASTERS CYCLIST, WEEK-BY-WEEK VIEW, 2003

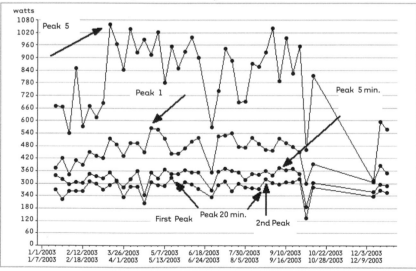

watts. Now look at his peak 20-minute power. In fact, there are two peaks for this duration, one in May and one in August. Both are roughly the same wattage, at 327 and 323 watts, respectively.

A little background information might help to explain this double peak. This athlete wanted to do well in the spring races and also at Masters Nationals. His goal for Masters Nationals was to achieve an FTP of 350 watts in August. He was right on track with his training, he was progressing well in the spring, and he had a great spring campaign, with eight race wins. Unfortunately, he crashed in early June, breaking his collarbone in four places. (Note the sharp drop across all power in June.) This effectively stalled his fitness growth for the season. When he came back to training at 100 percent, he was able to bring his fitness back to his previous level, but there was just not enough time to reach his goal of 350 watts at FTP for the Masters Nationals in August. He still placed in the top twenty of each event. In November, he took one month off completely in order to recover and get ready for a strong winter of work. This all occurred in 2003.

Now, let's look at his 2004 season (Figure 9.3). As the chart shows, in little more than one month he achieved his peak 5 seconds at 1,015 watts, his peak 1 minute at 575 watts, his peak 5 minutes at 387 watts, and his peak 20 minutes at 333 watts. Obviously, his fitness was the greatest in April and May, also evidenced by six race wins in this time period. Now, what this doesn't show is that he also did very well at Masters Nationals in 2004; however, since the event was held at altitude (at an elevation of about 8,000 feet in Park City, Utah), his peak wattages were lower than what might have been expected at sea level. He finished fourth on the time trial and in the top fifteen in the other two events.

Finally, let's look at his 2005 season (Figure 9.4). At the beginning of the season we changed his training so that he could really peak for Masters Nationals, aiming at an FTP of 375 watts. This year the Masters Nationals competition would be held in late June instead of early August, and we shifted his training accordingly. His fitness came up steadily at all levels throughout the season, peaking in mid-June with his peak 1 minute at 631 watts, his peak 5 minutes at 417 watts, and his peak 20 minutes at 375 watts. His peak 5 seconds was the highest in early April, as in previous years.

He did well throughout the season, coming to Masters Nationals with twelve wins under his belt. Again, the Masters Nationals competition was held at altitude, so his true peaks weren't reached in that event. However, his performance there was the best out of the three years. He took the Overall Omnium Win and a criterium championship and had the fastest time in the time trial for his age group

FIGURE 9.3: MEAN MAXIMAL POWER PERIODIC CHART FOR MASTERS CYCLIST, WEEK-BY-WEEK VIEW, 2004

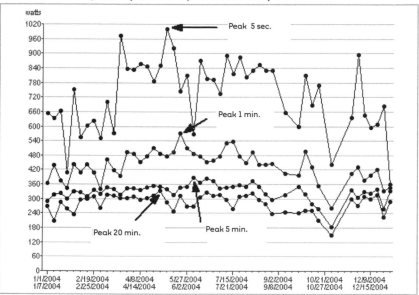

FIGURE 9.4: MEAN MAXIMAL POWER PERIODIC CHART FOR MASTERS CYCLIST, WEEK-BY-WEEK VIEW, 2005

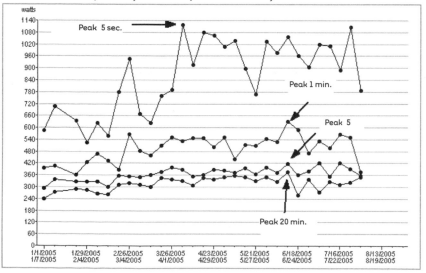

(though, as seen in his downloaded power meter file, he missed his start by 1:30!).

Now let's compare the three years on one chart (Figure 9.5). By charting them together, we can see this athlete's progress from 2003 to 2005. He made some major improvements. His 2004 season was very good, but in 2005 he experienced even more dramatic growth. Some of this growth is obscured, because his peak occurred while at altitude. Nevertheless, having the opportunity to look at all three years of data is very powerful, not only for the athlete, but also for the coach.

Mean Maximal Power Curve

With the Mean Maximal Power Periodic Chart, we can see how an athlete has (or has not) improved in four different significant time periods. A related chart, called the Mean Maximal Power Curve, shows how an athlete has (or has not) improved over every time period. With the MMP Curve, you can gain more insight into the type of rider that you are.

The MMP Curve is a plot of all your "bests."

The MMP Curve is a plot of all your "bests"—your best 39 seconds, your best 56 seconds, your best 1:38, your best 5:42, your best 1:15:32, and so on. By plotting all of your "bests" over the entire selected time span, you can visually grasp the rate of your wattage decay as the duration

FIGURE 9.5: MEAN MAXIMAL POWER FOR MASTERS CYCLIST, JANUARY 2003—AUGUST 2005

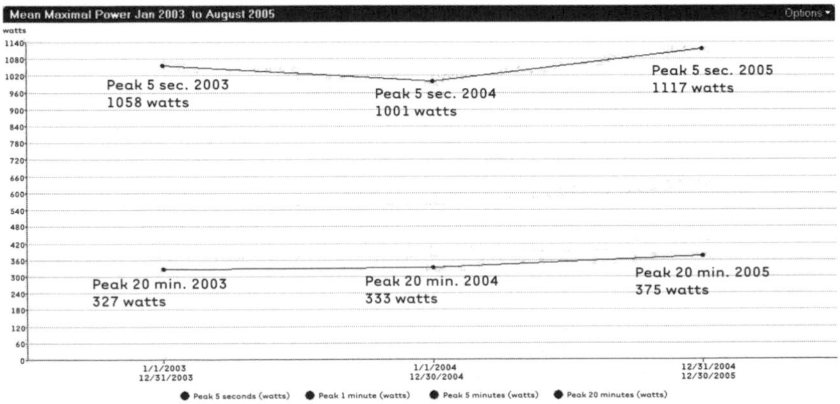

of the intervals increases, and you can determine when it decays the fastest. By looking at the shape of the line and the areas of slope change in a rider's Mean Maximal Power Curve, we can also begin to distinguish the different training levels, their relative strengths and weaknesses, and possible areas for improvement. We can see if a rider is a sprinter, a time trialer, or a climber.

Figure 9.6, for example, shows the Mean Maximal Power Curve of an all-rounder Category II female cyclist with a high VO_2max power. Note how

FIGURE 9.6: MMP CURVE FOR CATEGORY II CYCLIST

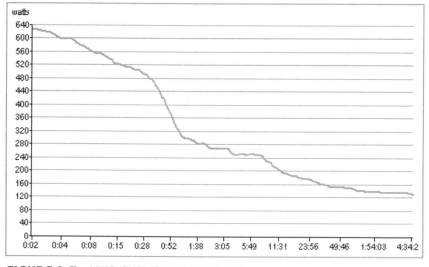

FIGURE 9.7: MMP CURVE FOR SPRINTER

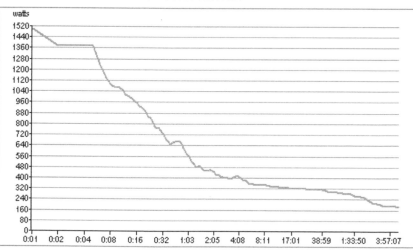

little her power decreases from about 1 minute to 8 minutes, an indication that her strength would be in races emphasizing hard VO₂max type efforts.

Figure 9.7 shows the curve for a sprinter. Notice the high power output from 0–5 seconds, indicating very good neuromuscular power. The power decay is very stable (the slope is constant) all the way to roughly 1 minute. Even at 30 seconds, this athlete is doing 700+ watts.

The MMP Curve is best viewed on a logarithmic scale as this places the most emphasis on the data at the shorter time periods. Most fitness changes typically occur in time periods between 1 second and 30 minutes, so by using a log axis, you can bring out these small but important changes. Notice that in Figure 9.8, which shows a logarithmic view for a road racer, over half of the chart covers only the first 3 minutes of his mean maximal power data.

When you are viewing your own curve, note the exact time at which the slope of the line changes and how that relates to your different physiological systems. For example, in the MMP Curve shown in Figure 9.9, note that at 1 minute 25 seconds, the slope dramatically changes, and the new slope continues until about 7 minutes 25 seconds, at which point it flattens out even more. It could be that this slope shows the athlete mov-

FIGURE 9.8: MMP CURVE, LOGARITHMIC SCALE

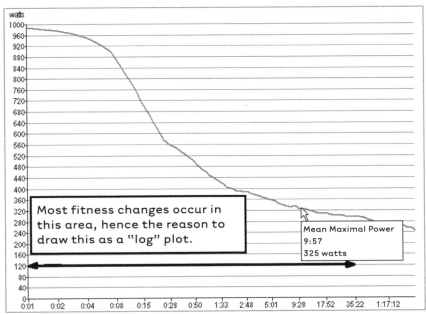

ing from the anaerobic capacity system into the VO_2max system and then transitioning into the lactate threshold system around that 7:25 mark.

When you see the slope change, the steepness of the change could indicate a weakness in your cycling that you could address with some specific training for that time period. In addition, there will be some "dips" in the curve. Does this mean that you cannot do, say, 350 watts for 1:24, but you can do this same wattage for 1:45? No—that would not make sense. How could you produce more power at 1:45 than at 1:24? Remember: This is a curve of the "best" watts you produced for every 2–3 seconds over a long period of time. It's highly possible that you did a hard hill interval for 1:45 at about 350 watts but then did not do any maximal efforts for 1:24. Therefore, it's possible that your chart could show a higher wattage for that longer time period.

It is also important to note that, at longer durations, your average power will tend to be less than the maximum wattage that you can produce, in part because of the time that you spend not pedaling. Thus, beyond about 1 hour (or beyond the longest, generally flat time trial that you have done), Normalized Power will be a more accurate measure of your true ability.

In Figure 9.10, on the left, the upper line shows mean maximal power, while the lower line is the mean maximal Normalized Power. At about

FIGURE 9.9: MMP CURVE, TRANSITIONS BETWEEN TRAINING LEVELS

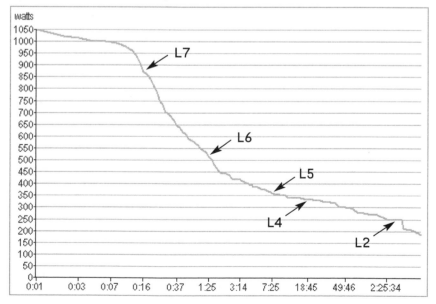

7:25, they switch places and the Normalized Power becomes the upper line. This is an interesting curve because it shows that average power can obfuscate your true abilities. Theoretically, as this MMP line moves farther and farther to the right, it would eventually hit zero, but in real life this most likely will be when you can't throw your leg over your bike and you are heading to the nursing home. For now, there is some level of wattage that you can maintain for even long periods of time, almost indefinitely.

Changes in the MMP Curve Over Time

In 2003, the masters rider who was discussed earlier lost many races in the final sprint when a competitor would just "nip" him, beating him by a hair. So in 2004, he changed his training in order to make his sprint longer, as evidenced by the flatter top portion of the MMP Curve. From 2003 to 2004, the slope of the first 16 seconds of the line drastically changed, and although his overall watts were not as high in 2004, he was able to maintain a much higher wattage for 16+ seconds. Now, compare that first 16 seconds from 2003 and 2004 to 2005 (see Figure 9.11). The slope shifted back to a pattern that was similar to the one from 2003, but now the watts

FIGURE 9.10: MMP CURVE, NORMALIZED VERSUS AVERAGE POWER

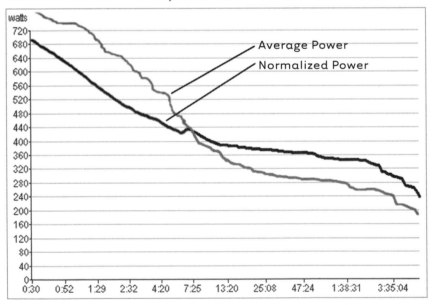

were higher overall. Did this athlete lose any of his sprinting ability in 2005? No, actually it got better! In 2005, he was able to produce more absolute peak watts and also could maintain them longer than in the preceding years. Now, take a closer look at the period from roughly 2 minutes to 30 minutes. The slope of this data did not change significantly from year to year, but it did move upward, indicating overall improvements in fitness.

Changes in the Distribution of Training Levels

You may notice that the areas that you train in shift throughout the season. In the off-season, you might spend more time in Level 2 (Endurance), for example, and as spring approaches, you might spend more time in Levels 3 (Tempo) and 4 (Lactate Threshold). This is natural and indicates that you are indeed taking on more race-specific training as racing season approaches; you are building your fitness one piece at a time. By creating the power distribution charts for more than one duration, you can either confirm this shift in training levels or discover that you need to consciously change your training and begin to address a different training level.

FIGURE 9.11: MMP CURVE FOR MASTERS RIDER, 2003–2005

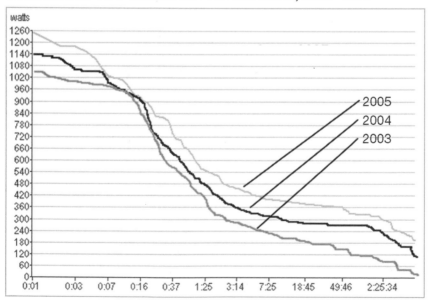

The Power Distribution Chart in Figure 9.12 shows the percentage of time that a particular cyclist spent at each wattage level in January and February 2005, and then the percentage of time that he spent in the different levels. In this example, the rider spent the majority of his time in Levels 1, 2, and 3 (Active Recovery, Endurance, and Tempo), just building a base of fitness.

Figure 9.13 shows what happened in March through May. Notice how the amount of training begins to smooth out in the upper wattage bins. The rider is now spending more time at Level 3 (Tempo) and also in Level 5 (VO$_2$max) and Level 6 (Anaerobic Capacity).

By June, the amount of time he spends in Level 6 (Anaerobic Capacity)

FIGURE 9.12: POWER DISTRIBUTION FOR SAMPLE CYCLIST, JANUARY AND FEBRUARY 2005

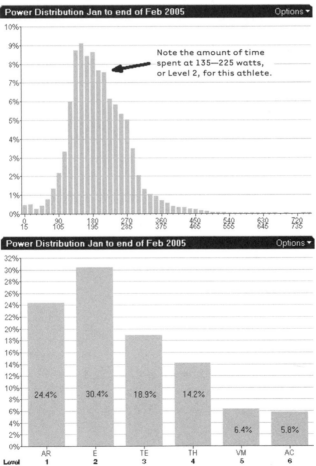

is really increasing (Figure 9.14). Also note the drastic increase in the amount of time that he spends in Level 1 (Active Recovery). As this rider begins to ride in more criteriums, he increases his emphasis on Anaerobic Capacity.

The chart for July shows how much racing influences the amount of time spent at or near FTP (Figure 9.15). The big "step-down" after Level 4 (Lactate Threshold) is clearly evident now. Racing data, primarily road races and time trials, constitute much of the data. Although initially it appears that the increase in Level 4 riding is not that drastic, a 2 percent increase can be very significant in terms of creating chronic training stress. (Remember the "caveat" about the "time in levels" from Chapter 6.)

FIGURE 9.13: POWER DISTRIBUTION FOR SAMPLE CYCLIST, MARCH TO MAY 2005

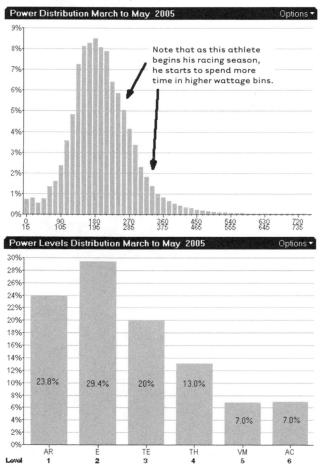

Chronic Training Load Versus Acute Training Load

One of the biggest advantages of training with power is that it gives you the ability to quantify your training based on each and every pedal stroke that you make. By quantifying your training using TSS, you can better understand how the cumulative effects of training load are influencing your body and use that knowledge to better determine when to rest and when to continue to push further with your training. The complex ways in which different types of training stress affect your overall fitness and

FIGURE 9.14: POWER DISTRIBUTION FOR SAMPLE CYCLIST, JUNE 2005

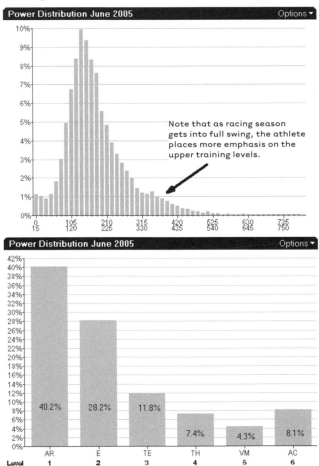

fatigue levels is an area currently under study; in fact, theories about training load are on the cutting edge of exercise physiology theory, and the vote is still out on how it all works.

Chronic Training Load (CTL) is the cumulative training "dose" that builds up over a long period of time. The basic idea behind all the research is that an ideal level of CTL is beneficial because it causes your body to undergo positive fitness adaptations. The period of time involved can be anywhere from three weeks of hard

An ideal level CTL is beneficial because it causes your body to undergo positive fitness adaptations.

FIGURE 9.15: POWER DISTRIBUTION FOR SAMPLE CYCLIST, JULY 2005

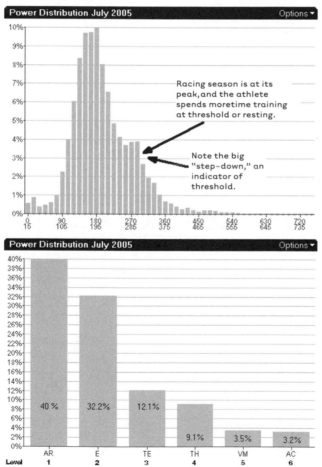

training to six weeks, six months, or two years. Every "old school" cycling coach out there will say that you "just need another 20,000 km in your legs" and you'll be at the top. In many ways, they are correct, as it takes years and years to develop the physiological systems needed for racing at the highest levels. The more kilometers you have in your legs, the more training stress you'll be able to handle and the stronger you'll become.

Acute Training Load (ATL) is the dose of training that you accumulated over a shorter period of time. This might be the training you have done in

FIGURE 9.16: CHRONIC TRAINING LOAD, EXAMPLE 1

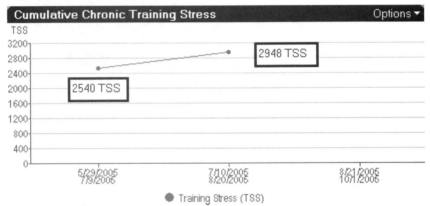

Note: Over the past 42 days, this athlete has increased his CTL level fairly significantly. This indicates that he must be building fitness.

FIGURE 9.17: CHRONIC TRAINING LOAD, EXAMPLE 2

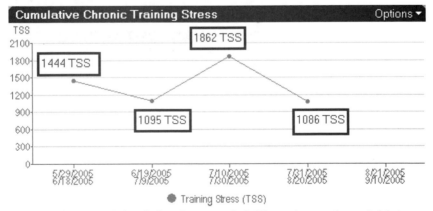

Note: This chart zooms in for a look at the same cyclist's CTL over the same time period, but now divided into four 21-day periods. His TSS score has actually dropped down from a three-month all-time high. This could indicate that his training load has peaked and that he is now beginning a tapering-off phase.

the past three days, over the past seven days, or over the past ten days. Your accumulated ATL is what forces you to rest after a hard week of training, and it is what builds your CTL. Without those hard, intense training blocks, you would never achieve a high enough CTL to create meaningful, long-term fitness adaptations. On the one hand, it is important that you naturally build your CTL; on the other hand, it is the rest periods that enable your body to recover from the ATL. ATL and CTL go hand in hand, and trying to manage these two essential components of your training program can be one of

FIGURE 9.18: ACUTE TRAINING LOAD, EXAMPLE 1

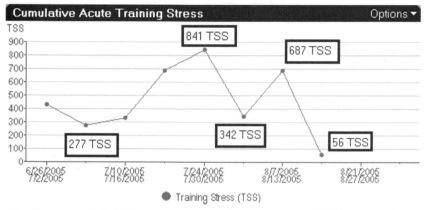

Note: The same cyclist's ATL hit a peak at the end of July with a score of 841 TSS. A rest week immediately followed it, and then another relatively hard week of training in which he accumulated 687 TSS points for the week. In the last week, we see a very low TSS score as his training tapers off for a key event.

FIGURE 9.19: ACUTE TRAINING LOAD, EXAMPLE 2

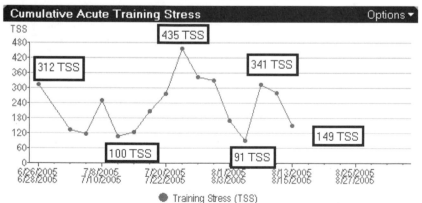

Note: Here it is easy to see the effect of multiple 3-day blocks of training. The cyclist's training load was greatest in the last week of July, and even though early July's training load was relatively low, the hard training at the end of the month is what drove the high CTL in Figure 9.16.

the toughest things to master. And yet it can have a more profound impact on your overall fitness than any other aspect of training.

Using the charts in CyclingPeaks Software, you can begin tracking your ATL and CTL scores. Keep in mind that it is difficult to interpret these charts. There are many factors that affect how ATL and CTL interrelate and how they ought to be managed. You should take other factors about your training, such as specificity, into account when looking at these charts. We have presented some examples of the charts, with possible interpretations, as a way to help you start thinking about the possibilities, and not as an in-depth analysis of CTL and ATL (Figures 9.16 through 9.19). These charts were created for the same masters racer referenced in Figures 9.1 through 9.5.

In summary, by looking at your cumulative (or average) TSS over varying periods of time, you will have a better understanding of how much CTL your body can handle before breaking down. As your ATL builds through focused blocks of training, it will be important for you to be careful to document all the factors influencing your fitness; this will help you to avoid "over-reaching" and going into a downward spiral of "overtraining." Looking at these cumulative TSS scores is definitely a very promising and exciting new frontier for training with a power meter, and as you learn more from these tools, your performance will continue to improve.

Fitness Changes Over Time

Taking all the examples in this chapter as a guide, you can now begin to track your own fitness changes. Looking at your mean maximal power over the past twenty-eight days is a reliable method of seeing how you are improving in different areas. Learning the intricacies of Chronic and Acute Training Load is more complicated; if you are interested in the concept, you can find out more by keeping abreast of new research. In any case, it should be clear that your power meter data can help you to achieve more. The simple collection of data is one of the most "zen" ideas about training with power. Ride, collect data, do nothing extra. Even though this motto may sound simplistic, it also brings out a concept some cyclists may find helpful: a minimalist approach to training with a power meter. The interpretation of the charts and graphs is not complex in most cases, and we hope that this chapter has helped to illuminate the simplicity of tracking fitness changes.

10 RACING WITH A POWER METER

WE ARE GOING TO SHIFT GEARS now and go into some of the ways that you can use your power meter while in races. So far, we have focused on training, not racing per se, although we have alluded to some of the ways that you can use your power meter for racing. But in bicycle racing, awards aren't given to those who can produce the greatest number of watts per kilogram; they are given to those who finish first. More and more athletes are using power meters on their bikes in the races themselves, and it is exciting to think that they may be using them to help coordinate their racing strategy, their nutritional intake, and their pacing. Power meters can also serve as a post-race analysis tool and enable a racer to communicate more effectively with a coach about the race experience. Indeed, the data that you get from racing with your power meter is some of the most valuable data you will collect.

For starters, racing with your power meter is a great way to help pace yourself during very demanding times of the race. When you are riding in the breakaway, how do know whether you should pull or just "sit on" (that is, draft behind the rider in front of you and never help in the workload)? How hard should you pull? If you pull too hard, you risk getting dropped, but if you don't pull hard enough, the peloton will inevitably catch your break. A power meter is more than just a great pacing tool for time trials; it is also perfect for any mass-start bicycle racing event. Second, racing with a power meter is a great way to define the physiological demands of the event. Just by capturing the data with your power meter while competing, you will begin to understand what it takes to ride in the peloton, to escape from the peloton, and even to win the race. Finally, by reviewing the data after the race, you will be able to better prepare yourself for your next race and for next year's racing season.

In this chapter, we will take a look at power meter files from different disciplines, races, and events and tell the stories behind them so that you can begin to understand how power meters can be used to achieve success. In fact, your own power meter data is incomplete without the "story" behind each ride, so it's important for you to take a couple of minutes after each race to write the story of your ride in your ride diary. It does not need to be a dissertation, but it should contain the key points of your ride, any significant areas to review, and explanations of important moments of the race that you might want to remember for future reference.

Pacing: The Skill We Never Talk About

Pacing in cycling is probably one of the most overlooked areas for improvement. We are much too concerned with that latest carbon-fiber widget or the newest aero helmet to consider that if we don't have our pacing strategy dialed in, and an ability to "meter" out power smoothly, then that new aero helmet isn't going to do any good. Pacing your effort is definitely a learned skill. Yes, some people are going to be able to do it naturally, but they are the minority. In cycling, many races are lost because of poor pacing skills—and not just time trials either! Pacing plays such a large role in the sport that every racer needs to make it a priority. If you have not practiced your pacing skills, or if you do not think pacing is that big of a deal, think again. In this section we'll give you some examples of how important pacing is to success in cycling and how you can use your power meter to improve in this area.

Pacing your effort is definitely a learned skill.

How many times have you been out on a long group ride with your friends and felt great in the beginning, and as a consequence hammered out the first 40 miles, only to fall to pieces in the last 20 miles, while another rider in the group (whom you consider not as strong as you) comes on stronger and stronger? All of a sudden, you are struggling, this other rider is driving the pace, and you are desperately hanging on. Is this rider really fitter than you? Or did he just pace himself better?

The importance of pacing may be most obvious in a century ride. Many "newbies" drive their pace high in the first 40–50 miles only to finish in 10 hours, after stopping at each rest stop in the last 50 miles and being reduced to 10 miles an hour. They used up all their energy in the first part of the ride.

The stakes are higher in stage races like the Tour de France, but the importance of pacing is the same. Are riders rewarded significantly for going off the front at the beginning of a stage? No—a rider taking this strategy would be more likely to get caught with 40 km to go and lose by 10 minutes. In fact, the winner of the Tour de France never undertakes that strategy. What about the Tour as a whole? Have you ever noticed that the guys who rip through the first five to eight stages are not the same ones who are in the top ten after Stage 8? Usually these riders have expended too much energy in the first third of the overall race, and in the latter third they are in jeopardy of not finishing.

Good pacing is also essential in triathlons. If you overdo your effort on the bike leg, then you'll be walking the run.

But pacing is important for racers at all levels, not just for the ones who make it to the Tour de France. And it is important for short events as well as long events. If you push yourself too hard in the beginning of a breakaway, for example, then you'll either "drop yourself" or the break will be caught because you and your companions cannot maintain your initial speedy pace. What about pacing for a pursuit on the track? Or even for an event lasting less than 4 minutes? Surely, you may think, pacing becomes less important in the shorter events. However, pacing may be even more critical in shorter events than in long stage races. In the pursuit, if you start out too hard, and expend all your energy on the second lap, then your power will drop off too quickly and your time will suffer. Pacing in the pursuit and even in short track events can be very critical to the outcome of the event. So critical, in fact, that we would dare to say that track racers should spend the most time of all on learning correct pacing strategies.

Good pacing is also essential in triathlons. If you overdo your effort on the bike leg, then you'll be walking the "run," and that will definitely hurt your overall time. All you have to do is go to one triathlon and see the participants who started too hard on the bike. They are the ones walking the run in the last 5 miles. In a triathlon, pacing is so critical that even a 10-watt difference—for example, riding at 240 watts instead of 250 watts over an ironman distance—can make the difference between a steady run and a walk in the final leg.

Pacing in a Criterium

Figure 10.1 shows the "story" of a criterium race and provides an example of how to use a power meter effectively in this type of event. This is a Category II racer with a very strong sprint and a solid fitness level. His threshold power is 350 watts, he weighs 175 pounds, and his Power Profile slopes downward to the right, the classic shape for a sprinter.

In the first part of the race, this rider's heart rate was relatively low, but you can see a major spike in power at 2 hours into the ride file (time includes the warm-up). It was at this point that the bell for a preme was rung. This rider attacked out of the field and sprinted for the preme, and he was successful. At this point, he found himself off the front solo by 20 seconds, as the field really sat up after the preme sprint. Not wanting to

FIGURE 10.1: POWER METER DATA FROM A CRITERIUM, FIRST PREME

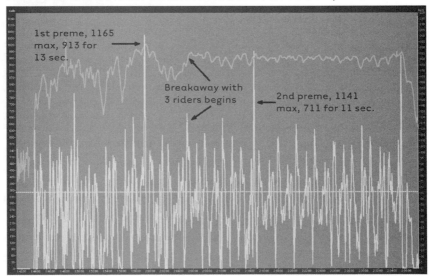

ride solo for the rest of the race, but at the same time recognizing the opportunity presented by this nice 20-second "leash," he pedaled just below his threshold power.

Less than a lap later, three riders bridged up to him and were really drilling it. He jumped on the back of the train and instantly started to work in the rotation. However, after a couple of pulls, he realized that he was pulling at over 500 watts; when he was in the "recovery line," he was still having to put out 400 watts. Just doing some quick math, and drawing on a keen understanding of his FTP, he realized that he was going to get dropped very quickly from this trio. He reasoned (and rightly so!) that if he was just sitting on the break and over his FTP, then his time in the break was very limited. So he did what every good rider should do at a point like this: Sit on! It would make no sense to continue to pull in a breakaway that was over your head, and if you did, you would only succeed at spitting yourself out of the back of the breakaway. This rider also had a hunch that the three riders were riding above their personal FTPs and were in imminent danger of blowing up.

Though he took some flak from the other riders for sitting on, he knew that was better than getting dropped from the breakaway at this point. The bell rang for the second preme, and like any good sprinter who has been sitting on, he blasted from the back of the trio and easily

FIGURE 10.2: POWER METER DATA FROM A CRITERIUM, SECOND PREME

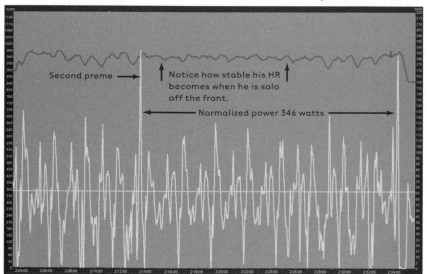

won the second preme (see Figure 10.2). After the preme, he looked around and the trio was nowhere to be found. They were rapidly going backward to the peloton. Now he was in quite a predicament: He was more than 45 seconds off the front of the field, solo, and a sprinter! He reasoned that the best he could do was to drill it on 350 watts for the rest of the race; if the field caught him, they caught him, and there was not much else he could do. He knew that if he tried to hold 360+ watts, he would only succeed in blowing himself up, and then the field would catch him for sure. In Figure 10.2, notice how much smoother his power became once he was solo off the front; his heart rate was also steady at this point.

This was really his only viable strategy at this point. By using the information on his power meter, he paced himself correctly and prevented himself from blowing up and being caught by the peloton. Luckily for him, he was able to hold off the charging field by about 10 seconds at the finish. Note his increase in power in the last 4–5 minutes. He knew he could hold his power output a little higher than his threshold for the last push and inched it up to the 360–370 range for the finish. This proved to be a crucial pacing move for his success. He was able to create a successful outcome because he used his power meter in almost every lap of the race to pace himself correctly for the phase that he was in.

Pacing in an Ironman®

Ironman Lake Placid is one of the toughest of the Ironman races because it is done on a very hilly course (see Figure 10.3). It also contains one serious climb and finishes on a solid steady uphill in the last 10 miles. Pacing plays a massive role in this triathlon, as in others; in fact, it's the crux of the entire game. Sure, you need to know how to swim efficiently, ride your bike solidly, and run fast, but once you have those skills down, the event itself is about "metering" out your energy for the entire event so that you finish strong. If you go too fast on your bike leg, you are going to be in serious trouble on the run, and if you hold back too much on the bike, it does not always translate into a faster run leg.

One of the biggest questions in training for a triathlon with a power meter is: What exact percentage of your FTP should you try to maintain for an Olympic distance, a half iron, or a full iron? Should you hold 50 percent of your FTP for a full iron, 75 percent for half, and 95 percent

FIGURE 10.3: LAKE PLACID IRONMAN ELEVATION PROFILE

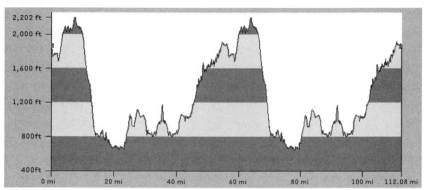

for an Olympic? Maybe you should shoot for 80 percent for a full, 90 percent for a half, and 100 percent for an Olympic. Who knows? Well, the answer to the question is that no one really knows for sure, and most likely the answer depends on the fitness level of the athlete as well. A pro triathlete might be able to hold a slightly higher percentage of his or her FTP than a weekend warrior, if only because they will have likely trained more in preparation for the event. Until some definitive studies are done on a wide variety of fitness levels in triathletes, there will not be any concrete answers to this question. In the meantime, we have estimated the Intensity Factors, FTP percentages, and training levels required by different types of triathlon events (see Table 10.1). These numbers are based on actual power meter downloads from a variety of triathletes over the various distances.

TABLE 10.1	GENERAL GUIDELINES FOR TRIATHLON EVENTS			
Type of Triathlon	Distance	Intensity Factor (fraction of NP)	Average Power as a Percentage of FTP	Training Level
Sprint	10k (6.2 mi)	1.03–1.07	100–103%	4
Olympic	40k (24.8 mi)	0.95–1.00	95–100%	4
Half Ironman	90k (56 mi)	0.83–0.87	80–85%	3
Ironman	180k (112 mi)	0.70–0.76	68–78%	2/3
Double Ironman	361k (224 mi)	0.55–0.67	56–70%	2

In pacing for a triathlon, it would be best to use Normalized Power because it would account for the differences in terrain and allow you to focus on pedaling smoothly and steadily. Currently, however, the ergomo Pro is the only power meter with this ability. SRM, PowerTap, and Polar users will need to pace themselves based on average power as a percentage of FTP.

Bear in mind that the levels provided in the table may not be exactly right for you. It is important to do some rehearsal rides in which you try to hold particular levels of intensity for the entire length of the event that you are planning to enter. If your event is longer than Olympic distance, try to hold to this pace for half the race distance, followed by a half-distance run, for a nice solid BRICK (bike-run) workout. Pacing at this distance will provide a good indication of exactly how much energy you will have left at the beginning of the run and at the end of the run.

Figure 10.4 shows data from 2005. This athlete is strong in her age group, 40–44. Her FTP is 215 watts, and her Power Profile slopes upward to the right, which is typical of most triathletes, who are often very fit aerobically but do not train their anaerobic system. This does not mean that she could not be a great sprinter; it's just that, since triathletes never have to sprint in their events, they do not usually train their anaerobic and neuromuscular capacities, and as a result they do not usually reach their full potential across all the different levels.

FIGURE 10.4: POWER DATA FROM LAKE PLACID IRONMAN

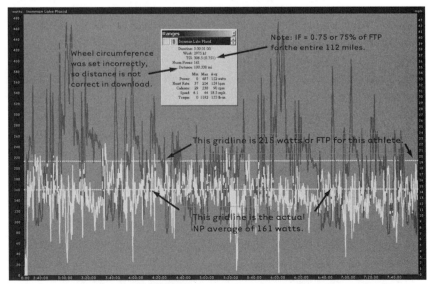

In this race, her goal was to qualify for the Hawaii Ironman World Championships. In her words, "I went all out on the bike course. My strategy was contrary to the advice of almost everyone I met. I felt that I had nothing to lose, except a slot in Hawaii. As it turned out, my body was spent and my run was about 10–15 minutes off where it should have been." Despite going "all out," she did have a strong run, and she still placed fourth and qualified for Hawaii!

Looking at her download, the first thing that you may notice is the sheer number of hills on this course. Every time the speed line goes up and down, that indicates a big speed change—an uphill or downhill. This means pacing is tougher than normal, yet it is doubly important. If you go too hard on the hills, you risk using too much muscular strength and then not having any reserve for later. Second, notice that her IF was 0.75, which indicates that she held 75 percent of her Normalized Power, which falls near the upper limit in Table 10.1 for pacing in an Ironman. Although this competitor is indeed a talented athlete, by her own admission this pace was too much, and it left her without enough in the tank on the run.

There is not one clear area in the download that we can point to that was paced incorrectly. Instead, her pace was just a touch high for the entire race. She possibly started out a little hot, as in the first 30 minutes she averaged 170 watts, which is about 80 percent of her FTP. In the longer uphill portion (the second quarter of the race), her power was higher (average NP was 170 watts), and it stayed closer to her FTP at this point than during any other extended period in the race. Others might argue that she went too hard on this section, but instead we think that she paced this section correctly. On the uphills, in almost every situation, you can afford to produce more watts than you can in other parts of a triathlon or time trial.

Why? When you are riding uphill, you have more resistance to push against, and on the downhills, there just isn't a big enough gear to allow you to produce the same level of force no matter how hard you try. This means that even with your best efforts on the downhills, your muscles are recovering. Let's say that, as in this case, your FTP is 215 watts, and on the longer uphills you ride right at your FTP, or above it on the shorter ones (106 percent, or 230 watts); on the downhills, you might be lucky to be able to produce 120 watts. That would be only 55 percent of your FTP, which is Level 1, or Active Recovery pace.

FIGURE 10.5: SAMPLE OF DOWNHILL POWER OUTPUT
IN IRONMAN LAKE PLACID

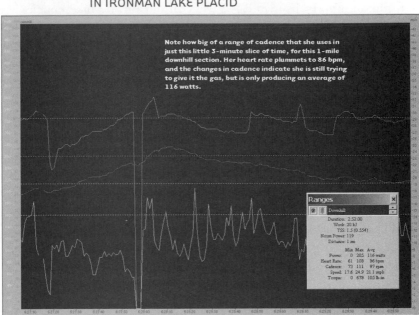

Figure 10.5 shows another interesting section of her file that provides insight into the athlete's story and outcome. It illustrates the point that no matter how hard you try, it is difficult to produce wattage on a downhill. Therefore, although your pacing may be higher than FTP on the uphills, you will be able to recover on the downhills without losing any time to your competitors. With this Ironman Lake Placid file now in hand, we can go back to the drawing board and tweak her training so that she is better prepared for the number of hills, and also their length, and develop a finer point to her wattage goals. Practicing pacing before her trip to Hawaii will be important. She also needs to improve her FTP another notch to have a chance of winning in her age group in Hawaii.

Comparing the Demands of Racing and Training

Another way to improve your racing performance is to look at the demands of the events that you want to enter and training accordingly. Defining the specific demands of your event with power meter data from the course itself is an excellent way to determine how you need to train. For example, if you know that you will have to do 20 laps of a criterium course, and that each lap has a 20-second hill on it, then you can train by doing 20 hill repeats of 20 seconds each. You can also look at the Quadrant Analysis chart of a race and compare this to a typical day of training. If you look at the number of hills or accelerations that you might have to produce, but do not take account of the neuromuscular demands, then you could be missing a very critical component.

Be sure to also think about how many kilojoules of energy you will need to produce for the event. If you are not aware of this factor during a race, you may begin to tire prematurely. The key thing here is to mark this point on your power meter with the beginning of an interval (many times you can still find this point in your data after you have downloaded the data). When you download racing data, you can see how many kilojoules of energy and TSS points you scored before you became tired, and in this way you can determine how many calories you need to consume during your next race. For example, if you did a 2.5-hour race, and consumed 500 k/cal during the race, but then downloaded your race file and found out that you expended 2,000 kJ, or roughly 2,200 k/cals, you

FIGURE 10.6: MOUNTAIN BIKER'S TRAINING FILE

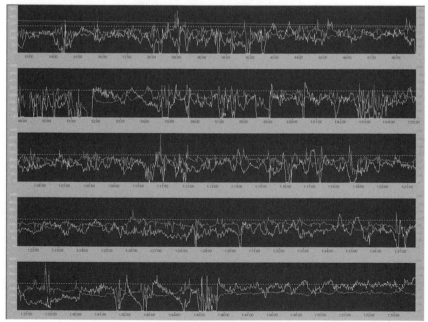

could plan to eat more for your next race. You might even try loading up on carbs in the days before the race.

In this section we will look at a typical training file from a mountain bike rider, then a race file from the same cyclist, and use the Quadrant Analysis spreadsheet in order to compare the actual neuromuscular demands of the race to the athlete's training.

Figure 10.6 shows the graph of the athlete's training ride, and it's easy to see that there is a lot of power fluctuation. He's definitely riding near his threshold for a good portion of the time, and slightly above it at other times. In the words of the athlete, "I felt good today! I was kind of dreading the workout Hunter slated for me because I was feeling tired and weary. Wow, I felt good power and excellent ability to maintain it. After the up tempo at Bob's place, we cruised over to the steepest hill you have ever seen, called Upper Springs. I ramped it up to 350 watts for the beginning 2 minutes, and then it got steep—in fact, so steep that the 32/27 I was riding was not enough gear! Ouch! The climb pitched to over 20 percent in spots and I was going over power just trying to keep the wheels turning. I really tried to focus on low cadence and high force in this workout, but I'm not sure if I got enough in."

FIGURE 10.7: MOUNTAIN BIKER'S RACE FILE

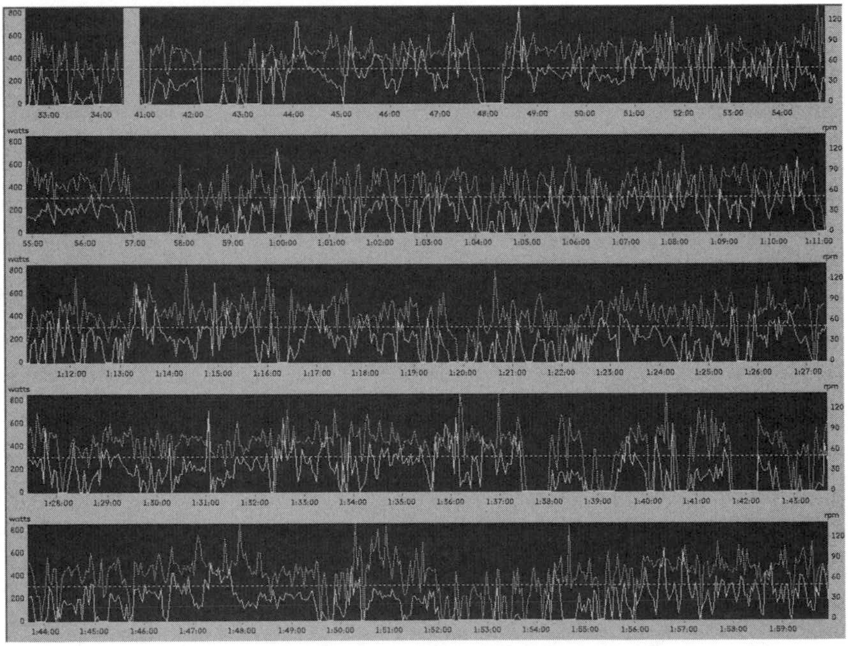

Let's compare that to his race file around the same time period (Figure 10.7). Immediately, you can see how much more "stochastic" the race was compared to the training ride. In the race, there are fluctuations in cadence and wattage; the cadence and power lines in the training file look almost smooth by comparison. The comment from the athlete was, "Awesome day! 80 degrees and clear skies at Flat Rock Ranch in Texas. Way fun race! More open Texas hill country like I had seen on TV. Hard race with lots of rocks up on top of the hills, and sweet single track. More technical than I would have thought for Texas. Good win and was still feeling strong at the end despite having drilled it for the whole race."

Now let's compare the same two power files using Quadrant Analysis and see if the athlete is training in the correct quadrants to specifically address the neuromuscular system (Figures 10.8 and 10.9). To review: Quadrant I is high force and high cadence; Quadrant II is high force and low cadence; Quadrant III is low force and low cadence; and Quadrant IV is low force and high cadence. Overall, it is easy to see that in the training ride, this mountain biker's goal was to do plenty of sub-threshold work, and from that perspective it was a great success. Almost all of the points fall just below the line representing functional threshold power. However, the majority of his time pedaling fell in Quadrants III and IV, which are relatively low force but require both fast and slow cadence. Thus, although this training ride accomplished the goal of stressing his metabolic fitness, it did not place much emphasis on the use of his Type II, or fast-twitch, muscle fibers.

FIGURE 10.8: MOUNTAIN BIKER'S TRAINING FILE QUADRANT ANALYSIS

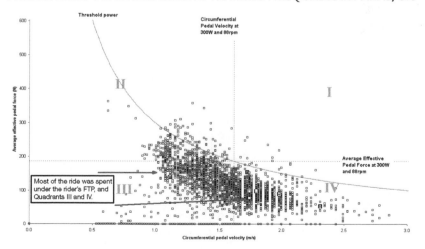

It is apparent that the race put a much larger demand on multiple neuromuscular capabilities than the training ride did. The "shotgun blast" of the race indicates a high degree of variability in the neuromuscular and cardiovascular capacities needed to win the event. Although the majority of the ride was in Quadrant III, it also contained quite a lot of effort in Quadrant II. This makes sense because in a mountain bike race, many times you have to push hard and fast in order to get over obstacles, maintain traction on steep slopes, and keep your momentum going. This distribution also shows approximately how much effort he spent over his threshold power and exactly how his muscles were working at those times. In this race, when he was riding over his threshold, it appears that he was spending a majority of his time in Quadrant II, which gives us further insight into the demands of the event.

What should this athlete do in order to train more specifically for the races that he enters? For starters, he needs to develop some workouts that will focus on Quadrant II. He needs to be better prepared, come race time, to produce a large amount of force at a low cadence and with a high degree of cardiovascular strain. Second, he should introduce more variability into his ride to be ready for the speed and force changes required by mountain biking. Perhaps the easiest and most logical way to accomplish this would be to do more race-like efforts while riding off-road—for example, he could perform time trials on a technically challenging loop. Alternatively, he could do specific

FIGURE 10.9: MOUNTAIN BIKER'S RACE FILE QUADRANT ANALYSIS

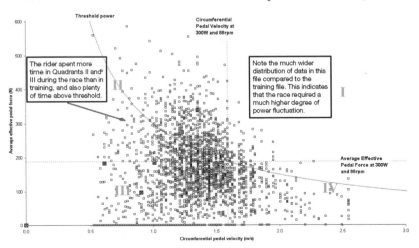

interval workouts—such as micro-bursts" using a large gear, or perhaps motorpacing—to achieve this goal.

Onsite Post-Event Performance Analysis

Using the information from your power meter for immediate onsite analysis of your performance can be very helpful because it can allow you and your coach to make quick adjustments in your pacing or racing strategy, or even in your gearing combination. At a velodrome track event, for example, you might be competing in eight different races, and in those events, you would have heats, qualifiers, and then a final. In between each event, you could have up to 30 minutes of downtime, leaving you with ample time to download your data and make changes before your next event. From training and testing with a power meter, you would know what cadence you generally use in your best performances. But you might discover when looking at your data that your cadence in the first qualifying round was faster. The track could be quicker than you anticipated, or the air density could be radically different from what you are used to in your training. With the power meter data, you would know immediately how to adjust your pace and your gearing.

A Note on BMX Racing

In bicycle motocross (BMX) racing, the events themselves are very short, much like track races. They favor athletes with quick reaction time to get out of the gate, excellent bike-handling skills to negotiate the jumps and berms, raw strength to get the bike up to speed, and excellent ability to pedal at a fast cadence. BMX racing requires many specialized skills that are developed only over years of practice. Since most participants in BMX events are under the age of 17, and power meters are expensive, not too many people have power meters on their BMX bikes—maybe only a handful around the world. However, power meters could provide some very valuable information to BMX racers and coaches. As more and more BMX riders begin to recognize the value of power meter data for proper gear selection and for defining the demands of the event, we should see more widespread usage of power meters in the sport, especially among the pros.

FIGURE 10.10: POWERTAP HUB, STRONG ENOUGH FOR AGGRESSIVE BMX RACING AND JUMPING

Power meter data from a BMX race are shown in Figures 10.11 and 10.12 and Tables 10.2 and 10.3. In this case, immediate post-race analysis of the data helped the athlete determine the correct gearing for success. In BMX racing, the start out of the gate is critical: If you are using a gear that is too large, then you will have a slow start. On the flip side, if you are using a gear that is too small, you might get the "holeshot" (that is, take the lead), but you would be spun out by the first jump, and riders with a bigger gear would easily catch up and pass you by. You also must consider the length of the track and whether there is an elevation change from the starting gate to the finish. Generally, the longer the track, the bigger the gear you should use; the same goes for a drop in elevation from the starting hill to the finish line. In BMX, the first straight makes the race, and the rider in the lead after the first turn usually is the winner.

The data shown here were captured from two sets of three races each. The rider did three races with a larger gear (Figure 10.11; Table 10.2), and then three races with a smaller gear (Figure 10.12; Table 10.3). They were done in the span of about 20 minutes and on the same course. The first set of races was done with a 42-tooth chain-ring and a 17-tooth cog (59.3 gear inches—that is, for every complete rotation of the crank, the bike moves forward by 59.3 inches). The second set of races was done with a 43-tooth chain-ring and an 18-tooth cog (57.3 gear inches). As these data show, the impact of gearing selection on BMX racing is dramatic.

FIGURE 10.11: BMX RACE, SET 1, MOTO 1

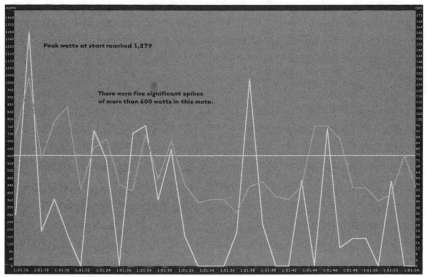

TABLE 10.2 · *BMX RACE, SET 1, MOTO 1, 59.3-INCH GEAR*

Duration	0:39
Work	12 kJ
TSS	n/a
Norm Power	315
Distance	0.202 mi

	Min	Max	Avg
Power	0	1279	315 watts
Heart Rate	153	153	153 bpm
Cadence	36	128	67 rpm
Speed	3.2	23.1	18.1 mph
Torque	0	495	110 lb in

In the first race of the first set (Set 1, Moto 1, with the bigger, 59.3-inch gear), the time was 2 seconds slower than in the second race of the second set (Set 2, Moto 2, with the smaller, 57.3-inch gear). As expected, cadence and max wattage were higher in Set 2, Moto 2. The max speed was faster in Set 1, Moto 1, which would be consistent with the use of the larger 59.3-inch gear in the first straightaway, but overall average speed was very close. Note the difference in average watts from Set 1, Moto 1 (315 watts), to Set 2, Moto 2 (397 watts), and also notice that the average heart rate was a little higher in Set 2, Moto 2.

For this track and rider, the smaller 57.3-inch gear was superior for a faster time, all other things being equal. It gave the rider a faster start at the

FIGURE 10.12: BMX RACE, SET 2, MOTO 2

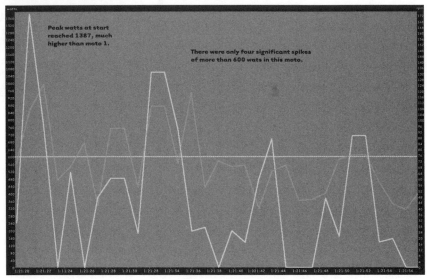

gate as well as acceleration in the first straightaway; having a smaller gear also allowed for quicker acceleration between obstacles and, ultimately, a faster time at the finish line.

Race with Your Power Meter

When you begin to race with your power meter, you will be taking full advantage of all it has to offer. The information

TABLE 10.3	BMX RACE, SET 2, MOTO 2, 57.3-INCH GEAR		
Duration	0:37		
Work	15 kJ		
TSS	n/a		
Norm Power	379		
Distance	0.202		
	Min	Max	Avg
Power	0	1387	397 watts
Heart Rate	157	157	157 bpm
Cadence	40	134	78 rpm
Speed	2.2	21.7	17.9 mph
Torque	0	616	142 lb in

that you will collect while you are on the bike in a race will help you with many aspects of creating a peak performance. It will help you learn how to pace yourself efficiently whether you are in a 40 km time trial, off the front of a criterium soloing to the line, or simply drafting in the peloton. In shorter events, such as track racing and BMX, it is easy to make adjustments to your pacing and/or racing strategy, along with your gearing, based on your power meter data, so that in your next heat, you'll have the advantage you need to perform your best. Using your power meter to guide your energy expenditure in a race can make the difference between standing on the podium as a champion or being just another rider in the field. As you learn more about the demands of your events and the requirements for success, you will be able to train more specifically and efficiently for each event. From knowing how to coordinate your nutrition for optimal energy conservation to understanding the neuromuscular demands of your discipline, defining the demands of your event can also make a big impact on your ability to make the winning move.

The Individual Pursuit: Aerobic and Anaerobic Energy Production

The individual pursuit is one of track cycling's classic races. At first glance, it may seem to be a fairly straightforward event, as it is "just" a short time trial contested on a banked velodrome (4 km for men, 3 km for women). In reality, however, this appearance of simplicity is deceptive, as the margin of victory in such races is often very small, and there are numerous physical and physiological factors that can have a significant influence on a rider's performance. This also means that there are numerous opportunities for a rider to use data from a power meter to, quite simply, go faster than ever before.

Although it is possible for a rider to learn how to pace himself or herself correctly using only lap times for feedback, post-race analysis of power meter files can speed up the feedback process by providing the rider with objective data regarding the distribution of his or her effort throughout the race. A power meter can also be used to optimize the rider's position from an aerodynamic perspective, which is crucial, since approximately 85 percent of a pursuiter's power output is used to overcome wind resistance (see sidebar, "Aerodynamic Testing with a Power Meter"). (The other sources of resistance—inertia, rolling resistance, and drivetrain and bearing friction, account for approximately 8 percent, 5 percent, and 2 percent, respectively.) Of course, data from a *(continues)*

(continued)

power meter can also be used to determine whether the rider's training program is having the desired effect—that is, whether his or her ability to produce power for various periods of time, especially over the 3.5–5 minute duration of a pursuit, is indeed increasing. Just as important, however, is that power meter data can be used to determine how a particular rider produces his or her power—the individual's relative reliance on aerobic and anaerobic energy metabolism during this predominantly, but by no means exclusively, aerobic event. In turn, this information can be used to fine tune the rider's training program by consolidating strengths while improving on weaknesses.

Consider the two riders whose data are shown in Figure 10.13. Rider A, on the one hand, is a male masters racer who excels in road races and longer time trials but has a very poor sprint and a limited anaerobic capacity. Rider B, on the other hand, is an elite female track cyclist whose specialty is the pursuit. As shown in the figure, their average powers during a pursuit are quite comparable, as are their personal best performances—3 km times on the same outdoor concrete 333.3-meter velodrome. (Although Rider A does not produce quite as much power as Rider B, Rider A is a bit

FIGURE 10.13: ROLE OF VO_2MAX ANAEROBIC CAPACITY (MAOD) AND AERODYNAMIC DRAG CHARACTERISTICS (C_dA) IN DETERMINING 3 KM PURSUIT PERFORMANCE

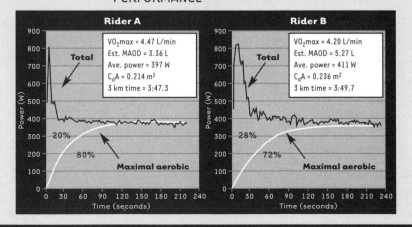

more aerodynamic and thus goes slightly faster.) However, *how* they go about generating their power and thus achieving their performances is significantly different. Specifically, Rider A apparently produces more of his power via aerobic metabolism, whereas Rider B relies more on her superior anaerobic capacity.

These differences in power can be determined by comparing the areas under the lines shown in the figure: The lower, smoother lines in the two graphs represent the riders' theoretical maximal aerobic power output, as calculated from laboratory-determined VO_2max and efficiency, whereas the more jagged lines represent their total power output as directly measured using an SRM crank during their pursuit. For Rider A, the area under the power meter line represents 80 percent of the total area (i.e., 80 percent of the work was performed aerobically), which leaves only 20 percent unaccounted for, meaning that it must have come from anaerobic sources (i.e., phosphorylated creatine/Adenosine triphosphate, or PCr/ATP, and lactate production). Expressed in terms of the amount of additional oxygen that would have to be taken up to generate this energy aerobically, this anaerobic energy production is equivalent to 3.36 liters (L) of O_2—in other words, Rider A's maximal accumulated O_2 deficit (MAOD) can be estimated to be 3.36 L. In contrast, for Rider B the area under the maximal aerobic power output line represents only 72 percent of the total area (at most she could have generated only 72 percent of her energy aerobically). The remaining 28 percent therefore must have come from anaerobic sources, leading to an estimated MAOD of 5.27 L, which is significantly greater than that of Rider A. Or, to put it another way: Despite the fact that her VO_2max is 4 percent lower (4.20 L/min vs. 4.47 L/min), Rider B is able to produce 4 percent more power (411 watts vs. 397 watts) during a 3 km pursuit because her anaerobic capacity is much larger. (This difference is even more striking when you consider that, on average, anaerobic capacity is generally lower in women than in men, even when expressed relative to muscle mass.) If Rider B were as aerodynamic as Rider A, the additional power that she could generate anaerobically would enable her to complete the 3 km in *(continues)*

(continued)

approximately 3 minutes 43 seconds, or approximately 4 seconds faster than Rider A.

Given the differences between Riders A and B in how they generate their power during a pursuit, it logically follows that, even though they might be training for the same event, their training programs should be different. Specifically, since Rider A's weakness as a pursuiter is his anaerobic capacity, his performance would likely be improved the most if he focused on very high-intensity (i.e., Level 6) intervals, especially during the "run up" to his goal event (for example, district championships). Rider B, in contrast, has a tremendous anaerobic capacity that seems unlikely to improve dramatically with additional high-intensity training. Thus, she should place a greater emphasis on improving her VO_2max (and also her functional threshold power, since this is an important determinant of muscle fatigue resistance, even during maximal/supra-maximal exercise) via training at Levels 3, 4, and 5 (especially in the off-season and pre-season periods). Indeed, after making precisely this change in her training program, Rider B improved her personal best time by more than 4 seconds and won the national championship in the pursuit.

Although in this example laboratory-based measurements of VO_2max and efficiency were available to enable calculation of the riders' maximal aerobic power output, one could just as easily use the quasi-plateau in power that occurs after the 1.5–2.5 minute mark of a well-paced pursuit. As shown in the figure, this is essentially the rider's power at VO_2max, as would be expected, since anaerobic capacity (as measured by maximal accumulated O_2 deficit) is generally completely used up after that period of time, such that further exercise can only be performed on a "pay as you go" basis (i.e., 100 percent aerobically).

Aerodynamic Testing with a Power Meter

If you are a road time trialist, track racer (e.g., pursuiter, kilometer, or 500-meter rider), or triathlete, one of the benefits of owning a power meter is that it enables you to determine your aerodynamic drag via field testing. Indeed, with an optimal venue and careful attention to detail, it is possible to measure your effective frontal area, or C_dA (i.e., the product of the coefficient of drag, C_d, and frontal area, A, measured in square meters, or m^2), just as precisely (albeit much less conveniently) as when using a wind tunnel. Data obtained using a power meter can therefore be used to make decisions about rider positioning or possibly even choice of equipment so as to maximize performance at any given power output—in other words, it can enable you to buy "free speed." A detailed description of how to best perform such testing is beyond the scope of this book, but in general, two different approaches may be used:

1. **Constant speed or constant power method:** The simplest way to determine C_dA is to have a rider perform one or more passes, or test runs, in both directions along a section of flat, windless road (or better still, in a velodrome, especially indoors) at a constant speed while measuring the power output. The measurements should be made over a distance of at least 500 meters, and the power data should be corrected (after downloading) for any slight variations in starting and ending speed (to correct for changes in stored kinetic energy). This is most easily achieved by simply selecting as starting and ending points of each run points where the speed was the same (and if testing in a velodrome, on a straightaway and not on the banking). If an SRM, ergomo, or Polar power meter is used, the data also need to be corrected for the efficiency of the drivetrain (since the PowerTap measures power "downstream" of the chain, the power value it provides can be considered equal to that driving the bicycle forward).

   As a first approximation, the corrected power itself can be viewed as a rough indicator of the rider's *(continues)*

(continued)

aerodynamic drag (or changes in his or her aerodynamic drag), provided that air density and rolling resistance are constant across trials. When testing outdoors, however, the environmental conditions—that is, barometric pressure, temperature, humidity, and wind—are subject to considerable change, which in turn will influence the air density and hence the power requirement. Thus, unless all desired measurements can be completed in a rather short period of time, it is necessary to record the precise environmental conditions to determine the air density, and then calculate the rider's actual C_dA using, for example, the free calculators available at Tom Compton's Web site, www.analyticcycling.com. Perhaps more important, when using this approach it is necessary to assume a value for the coefficient of rolling resistance (and accurately weigh the rider and his or her equipment) in order to account for the power required to overcome rolling drag. This complicates interpretating of the results should different tires or wheels be used in different tests, or if the temperature should vary dramatically (since rolling resistance can vary significantly with variations in temperature).

2. **Regression method:** A somewhat more complicated approach for determining C_dA is to have a rider make multiple passes (e.g., six to nine) along the same type of course at a variety of speeds, ranging from perhaps 20 to 50 km per hour (or the highest that the rider can sustain and reproduce for the required distance and duration). When plotted on the Y axis of a graph against speed (in meters per second, or m/s) on the X axis, the steady-state power (in watts, or W) from such trials is well described by a curvilinear equation of the form:

$$y = aX + bX^3$$

where "a" is a constant representing the rolling resistance (in newtons, N), and "b" is proportional to one-half times the air density (in grams per liter, or g/L) times C_dA.

Alternatively, this equation can be transformed into a linear equivalent by dividing the power (in W) during each trial by the speed (in m/s), and plotting this result on the Y axis against the square of the speed on the X axis. The resultant data will (should) form a straight line, the intercept of which will be the rolling resistance, and the slope of which will again be proportional to one-half times the air density (in g/L) times C_dA. Based on the environmental conditions at the time of the testing, it is therefore possible to calculate the air density, and thus in turn derive the C_dA.

Compared to the constant speed (or constant power) approach, there are two advantages to using the regression method. First, it distinguishes between changes in rolling resistance and changes in aerodynamic drag, which can be useful in equipment selection. If you seem to be faster using a particular set of wheels, for example, using the regression method will enable you to determine whether it is because they are more aerodynamic or because the tires roll better. Second, the regression method may provide a more precise estimate of C_dA, since the value derived is automatically based on multiple measurements.

Regardless of which approach is used, under ideal conditions it is possible to quantify C_dA via such field testing with a coefficient of variation (i.e., reproducibility) of around 2 percent. This is comparable to that obtained in wind-tunnel testing and approaches the limits of resolution of power meters themselves. To obtain this degree of precision, however, requires that testing be performed on an almost perfectly flat road and in the absence of any significant wind or automobile traffic (which can disturb the air enough to affect measurements for several minutes after the car has passed). Thus, assuming that a suitable location can be found, field tests to determine C_dA must generally be performed very early in the morning, immediately after the sun has risen but before the wind starts to pick up or traffic begins to develop. Many days of testing may therefore be required to obtain the data necessary to, for example, determine the optimal *(continues)*

(continued)

aerobar height, as some datasets may prove unusable owing to uncooperative weather. (Comparing the reproducibility of trials within a given session—for example, outbound versus inbound—and/or across sessions provides a good check on the accuracy of the data being obtained.)

Moreover, since it is necessary to perform such testing only when there is minimal wind, the value for C_dA that is obtained reflects only that for when the wind is from straight ahead, that is, at zero degrees of yaw. This is in contrast to measurements made in a wind tunnel, where it is possible to measure C_dA quickly and conveniently across multiple yaw angles. This distinction is important, since the benefits of aerodynamically designed cycling equipment are usually greatest when the wind is coming from an angle, rather than from straight ahead. Nonetheless, for the dedicated racer interested in wringing out every last drop of speed, field testing to determine C_dA represents a very useful application of a power meter.

PUTTING IT ALL TOGETHER

T HE GOAL OF THIS BOOK has been to take you from being a novice at using a power meter to being a savvy user of this new technology in training and racing. If your initial feeling about your power meter was, "Oh no, now what do I do with this thing?" hopefully you are now well on your way to becoming an advanced user who is more likely to ask, "Hey, my Power Profile says that I am a sprinter and I can do 4.55 watts per kilogram at FTP, so how do I increase my VO_2max power?" Along with your power meter, this book will help you to achieve your fitness goals.

A Review of the Steps

We have covered the steps that you can take to get started with using your power meter, and we've discussed some advanced tools and techniques that you can use as you become more familiar with it. To put it all together, the main steps are as follows:

Step 1: Data Collection and Determination of Threshold Power (Chapter 3)

Testing your FTP as you begin using a power meter will be one of the most important steps you take. This will define the intensity of all your training from here out. As you gather ride data over your local routes and races, you'll learn even more about what it means when you ride at a particular wattage during particular types of rides. Remember to repeat this test every six to eight weeks, or whenever you think your fitness has changed.

Step 2: Determine Your Training Levels (Chapter 3)

Once you know your threshold power, training in the correct levels will guide you to success. By understanding what happens physiologically when you train in each level, you will be able to easily target any weaknesses that need to be addressed.

Step 3: Determine Your Strengths and Weaknesses: The Power Profile (Chapter 4)

How you define your strengths and weaknesses will also be a guiding factor in your training. When you plot your Power Profile, not only will you know how you stack up against your peers, but you will learn even more precisely the physiological systems that are needed to train.

Step 4: Create Workouts and Begin Training (Chapter 5)

The work must be done. So use your new knowledge to create workouts that address your own fitness needs and goals, and that are aimed at specific power levels, and go for it. In order to really improve, you are going to have to train, and you are going to have to train hard. It is going to hurt and you are going to want to quit. But one of Hunter's favorite sayings applies here: "Quitters never win, and winners never quit." Go ride your bike ... faster.

Step 5: Interpret Your Data (Chapter 6)

Download every ride, every race, every time you throw a leg over that bike. Your data is important, and interpreting it correctly will help you to make the right decisions about the next day's training, the next month's training, and even the next year's training. Spend the time that you need to understand what the data are telling you.

Step 6: Learn Analysis Tools (Chapter 7)

The advanced tools of Training Stress Score, Intensity Factor, Normalized Power, and Quadrant Analysis can give you even more insight into your cycling skills and help you to fine-tune your training and racing. They can help you define the demands of your events and shed light on the additional factors that are necessary for success. Cycling is an incredibly complicated sport with many unknowns, and the more unknowns you can eliminate, the better your chance of success.

Step 7: Race with Your Power Meter (Chapter 10)

Your best data will come from races, your best efforts will come in races, and you stand to learn the most from your race data. Contrary to what you might think, some of the very best data will come from your failures. You'll learn exactly why you failed, and then you'll be able to take steps to avoid making the same mistakes again. You will also learn why pacing is the most important component of success in this sport.

Step 8: Make Changes to Achieve Your Goals

Training with a power meter is about results. It is worth doing only if you have a clear understanding of what needs to be done. Now that you have a good working knowledge of what needs to be done, you must be ready and willing to change. So, based on what you've learned in taking the steps listed above, go ahead and make the needed changes, and watch your cycling improve.

Some Final Thoughts

While training and racing with your power meter, avoid the "paralysis by analysis" syndrome. Training with a power meter can be very easy to do, but it can also be very frustrating, especially if you have trouble with your unit or encounter some initial technical difficulties. Sometimes your power meter may seem to be more of a hassle than it's worth. But remember to keep an eye on the big picture. Each training day fits into an overall set of objectives. Sometimes you may want to download your ride, keep it in your database, and not even look at the actual workout file. That's fine once in a while. But keep looking at the long-term graphs to get a sense of how all your systems are improving. You may even decide that ultimately you are not all that interested in the data, or choose not to spend hours poring over your data files. And that's fine, too. You can still benefit from using the power meter on your bike as the ultimate pacing tool. You can still have fun driving a Ferrari even if you never test its limits on the racetrack!

Change is tough for all of us. Whether it involves change in a job or change in a daily routine, it is always a challenge. However, in order to grow, you have to change. Be open to making changes in your training based on new information. When you begin making these changes, you will see your fitness improve, and this will be very satisfying and rewarding. Having the ability to quantify that improvement is doubly rewarding. Training and racing with a power meter will allow you to truly know that your hard work is paying off and worth it all.

GLOSSARY

Acute Training Load (ATL) The overall quantity (i.e., combination of frequency, duration, and intensity) of training that you have performed recently (during the past week or two). See also Chronic Training Load (CTL).

Anaerobic capacity/anaerobic work capacity The overall quantity of work (not the rate of doing such work, which is power) that you can perform by relying on anaerobic metabolism. Usually trained by performing short (e.g., 30-second to 3-minute), very high-intensity intervals.

Anaerobic threshold (AT) More correctly termed "ventilatory threshold"; the exercise intensity at which there is a nonlinear increase in ventilation relative to metabolic rate—that is, the rate of oxygen uptake (VO_2). Although they are not mechanistically related (i.e., not related as cause and effect), "anaerobic" or ventilatory threshold is often used to estimate lactate threshold.

Athlete Home Page The main screen that shows the user long-term changes in your fitness in CyclingPeaks Software.

Average Effective Pedal Force (AEPF) The average force applied to the pedal that causes the crank to turn.

Big-ring sprint A maximal effort completed in the largest chain-ring of the bicycle. Usually this large chain-ring is made up of 53 teeth.

BMX (Bicycle Motocross) A form of bicycle racing in which the competitors ride bicycles with 20-inch to 24-inch wheels and jump over obstacles. They compete against a maximum of seven other riders at a time. The races are very short, usually less than 1 minute.

Cadence The revolutions per minute (rpm) of the cranks at which you pedal.

Cardiovascular fitness The capability of the cardiovascular system to transport O_2 to tissues (e.g., contracting muscles), aid thermoregulation by increasing blood flow to the skin, and so on. It is traditionally quantified by measuring a person's maximal oxygen uptake, or VO_2max.

C_dA A measure of an object's aerodynamic drag characteristics. In the context of this book, the object is the cyclist and his or her bike. C_dA is the product of the coefficient of drag, C_d, and frontal area, A. Though C_dA is best measured in a wind tunnel, it can also be estimated via field tests performed using a power meter.

Chronic Training Load (CTL) The overall quantity (i.e., combination of frequency, duration, and intensity) of training that you have been performing over a substantial period of time—for example, several months or more. See also Acute Training Load (ATL).

Circumferential Pedal Velocity (CPV) The speed at which the pedal travels around the circle. CPV determines the speed at which your muscles must contract to produce force and thus power.

CompuTrainer An indoor trainer in which you place the back wheel of your bicycle. It uses an electronic brake to modulate resistance on the wheel and can measure wattage.

Critical Power Defined in scientific literature as the slope of the work-time relationship. Critical power is an inherent characteristic of the aerobic energy supply system and as such represents a power that can be sustained for a very long time without fatigue. When measured using exercise bouts that are 3 minutes to perhaps 30 minutes in duration, critical power is essentially the same as functional threshold power. See also Mean Maximal Power.

ergomo A power meter that measures the torsion of the bottom bracket axle.

Fartlek See Tempo.

Fast Find A feature in CyclingPeaks software that allows the user to easily find specified efforts based on the starting and ending wattage of each effort.

40 kilometer TT A 40 km (24.8-mile) solo race against the clock. Time trials are often referred to as "the race of truth."

Functional threshold power (FTP) The highest power that a rider can maintain in a quasi–steady state without fatiguing for approximately one hour. When power exceeds FTP, fatigue will occur much sooner, whereas power just below FTP can be maintained considerably longer.

Intellicoach Erg+ Software designed to be used in conjunction with a CompuTrainer.

Intensity Factor (IF) For any workout or part of a workout, the ratio of the Normalized Power to the rider's functional threshold power.

Kilocalorie (k/cal) The amount of energy required to raise 1 kilogram of water by 1 degree Celsius. In common vernacular, 1 kilocalorie is typically referred to as one Calorie (note the capital C).

Kilojoule (kJ) Like the kilocalorie, the kilojoule is a measure of energy. One joule is equal to 1 watt-second, or the work done by exerting 1 watt of power for 1 second. One kilojoule is therefore equal to 1,000 joules.

Lactate Threshold (LT) The exercise intensity at which the release of lactate into the blood first begins to exceed its rate of removal, such that blood lactate levels begin to rise. From the perspective of most athletes and coaches, LT is a relatively low intensity, approximately corresponding to the transition between Levels 2 and 3.

Match A reference to expending a tremendous amount of energy in a short period of time when, for example, attacking during a race. "Burning a match" is when you actually expend the energy.

Maximal Accumulated O_2 Deficit (MOAD) The difference between the rate of oxygen uptake (VO_2) and the rate of O_2 demand at the onset of supra-maximal (i.e., requiring more than 100 percent of VO_2max) exercise continued to fatigue. MAOD is currently considered the "gold standard" for measuring a person's anaerobic capacity.

Maximal heart rate The maximal rate at which your heart can beat per minute.

Maximal Lactate Steady State (MLSS) The highest exercise intensity at which blood lactate levels remain essentially constant over time. MLSS is comparable to functional threshold power and is closer to what most coaches and athletes mistakenly call "LT."

Maximal neuromuscular power The maximal power that you can generate under optimal conditions (e.g., at the right cadence).

Mean maximal power Your highest average power for a particular duration. Referred to by Joe Friel as "critical power."

Mean Maximal Power (MMP) Curve The curve of all your average best watts over each second of time, starting from zero seconds and extending to the longest ride you have completed.

Mean Maximal Power (MMP) Periodic Chart A chart of specific average best power for a certain time period. For example, a line graph of your best 5 seconds for each ride you have completed over the entire year.

Metabolic fitness The ability of your muscles to balance aerobic energy production with energy demand, which in turns determines the rate of muscle glycogen utilization, blood lactate levels, and so on.

Micro-burst Intervals with very short work and rest periods (e.g., 15 seconds "on", 15 seconds "off"). Sometimes also referred to as "micro-intervals."

Normalized Power (NP) An estimate of the power that you could have maintained for the same physiological "cost" if your power had been perfectly constant, such as on an ergometer, instead of variable.

Onset of Blood Lactate (OBLA) The exercise intensity corresponding to a blood lactate concentration of 4 millimoles per liter. An individual's OBLA is generally close to, but may be significantly higher or lower than, his or her MLSS or FTP.

Overreached An acute state of fatigue and hence diminished performance resulting from a brief period of excessive training relative to what you normally perform. Although many times riders describe themselves as being "overtrained," in reality they have usually simply overreached and their performance will recover after just a few days of rest or reduced training.

Overtrained A chronic state of overreaching from which recovery takes a long period of time.

Periodic Chart A chart in CyclingPeaks Software that allows the user to view data over a certain period of time.

Power The rate of doing work, where work is equal to force times distance.

Power Profile table A table that categorizes the watts per kilogram needed to be successful in each category of racing.

PowerTap A power meter that measures the torsion in the rear hub of the bicycle wheel.

Preme A special prize given to the winner of a designated lap in a bike race.

Quadrant Analysis A graphical means of analyzing data from a power meter to visualize specific demands placed upon the neuromuscular system.

Rate of perceived exertion (RPE) An individual's subjective evaluation of how intense or strenuous a particular exercise intensity feels. Typically rated on either a linear 20-point or a nonlinear 10-point scale, both of which were developed by Dr. Gunnar Borg.

Repeatability The ability of an athlete to repeat a certain effort many times without a loss in power.

Scientifically Computer Aided Training Era The time that we are now in, in which we are using microcomputers to help us to scientifically apply training principles for peak performance.

Self-selected cadence The cadence range in which you naturally will pedal without consciously thinking about your cadence.

Small-ring sprint A maximal effort completed in the smallest inner chain-ring of the bicycle. Usually this small inner chain-ring is composed of 39 to 42 teeth.

Specificity An important concept of exercise physiology that takes account of the fact that the adaptations to training tend to specific, or unique, to the particular demands that are imposed.

SRM PowerControl The actual microcomputer that mounts on the bicycle handlebar that comes with the SRM power meter system.

SRM (Schoberer Rad Messtechnik) Power meter invented by Ulrich Schoberer that measures the torsion in the "spyder" of the right crank arm.

Stochastic Technically, "varying randomly." Often used to refer to the marked fluctuations in power that occur when riding a bicycle outdoors. In fact, such variations are generally not really random but occur because of the ever-changing resistances (e.g., hills, wind) that must be overcome.

Strain gauges Small foil leaflets that, when incorporated into an electronic circuit and bonded to a surface, can be used to measure the amount of strain, or deformation, occurring in the underlying material. This deformation is related to the magnitude of the force that is applied; hence, strain gauges are used to measure force (or torque).

Sweet spot A small area of intensity characterized by 88–93 percent of one's FTP.

Tempo (or "fartlek") From Swedish, meaning "speed play"; workouts performed at an intensity that is "up tempo" from what a rider normally trains at when riding at a comfortable level.

Threshold heart rate The heart rate corresponding to functional threshold power.

Training Stress Score (TSS) A composite number that takes into account the duration and intensity of a workout to arrive at a single estimate of the overall training load and physiological stress created by that session. It is conceptually modeled after the heart rate–based training impulse (TRIMP).

Variability Index (VI) The ratio of Normalized Power to average power, Variability Index provides an indicator of just how variable, or "stochastic," a rider's power output was during a particular workout.

VO$_2$max The maximal rate of whole-body oxygen uptake that can be achieved during exercise. VO$_2$max is primarily limited by the ability of the cardiovascular system to deliver O$_2$-carrying blood to exercising muscle; hence, VO$_2$max is considered the best measure of a person's cardiovascular fitness and sets the upper limit to aerobic power production.

Zero offset A task that needs to be done when using the SRM and ergomo power meters. For the SRM, it must be done before every ride. For the ergomo, it needs to be done every 600 miles.

APPENDIX A:
ADDITIONAL RESOURCES

POWER METER MANUFACTURERS

ergomo
www.ergomo.net
SG Sensortechnik GmbH & Co KG
Am Berg 32
D-64546 Mörfelden-Walldorf
Germany
(49) 6105-2731-0

Polar
www.polarusa.com
1111 Marcus Ave., Suite M15
Lake Success, NY 11042-1034
(800) 227-1314

PowerTap
Saris/CycleOps
www.cycle-ops.com
5253 Verona Rd.
Madison, WI 53711
(800) 783-7257

SRM
www.srm.de
1075 Allegheny Dr.
Colorado Springs, CO 80919
(719) 266-4127

THIRD-PARTY POWER METER SOFTWARE

CyclingPeaks
www.CyclingPeakssoftware.com

Intellicoach Erg+
www.intellicoach.ca

PowerCoach
www.powercoach.ch

BOOKS

Friel, Joe. *The Cyclist's Training Bible, 3rd ed.* Boulder: VeloPress, 2003.

Wharton, Richard. *Watts per Kilogram: Using the CompuTrainer™ Indoor Ergometer to Improve Your Performance.*
Available at www.onlinebikecoach.com.

ARTICLES

Coggan, Andrew R. "Training and Racing Using a Powermeter: An Introduction."
Available at www.cyclingpeakssoftware.com/power411.html

WEB SITES

Analytic Cycling
www.analyticcycling.com

Online Power Training Guide
http://www.pdqcleveland.org/power.htm

Power Profiling
http://www.cyclingpeakssoftware.com/profile.html

Quadrant Analysis
http://home.earthlink.net/~acoggan/quadrantanalysis/index.html

Wattage FAQ
http://midweekclub.ca/powerFAQhtm

Wattage Online Forum
http://topica.com/lists/wattage

APPENDIX B:
WORKOUT GUIDE

BELOW IS A GUIDE to the workouts from Chapter 8, weeks 1–16. Workouts that are repeated from one week to the next will only be described once; in later mentions we will refer back to the full description. Remember to figure out your own wattages for these rides. The wattages below are for a hypothetical rider with an FTP of 250 watts. See Table 3.1 for percentages to use at each level. This plan is hosted on www.trainingpeaks.com. There, it is called, "Cycling Intermediate, 250 Watts Threshold" and "Cycling Intermediate, 250 Watts Threshold, Weeks 9–16."

Key to Abbreviations:

CD	Cool-down
HR	Heart rate
MS	Main set
TT	Time trial
WU	Warm-up

Week 1

Monday: Level 1, Active Recovery
WU: 15–20 minutes.
MS: 1–2 hours, easy and cruising. Try to keep HR below 68 percent of threshold HR. Total average watts for the ride should be below 55 percent of threshold watts or under 140. Just get out there and have fun today. Keep it short if you rode hard this weekend.
CD: 15 minutes.

Tuesday: Level 7, Neuromuscular Power
WU: 15–20 minutes.
MS: 1.5–2 hours. Set your pace at lower Level 3, approximately 190–225 watts (76–90 percent of FTP), and hold this pace for the next hour. Within this hour, do a 10-second, out-of-the-saddle burst every 3 minutes, trying to reach 450 watts (180 percent). Make sure your cadence stays high (over 100 rpm). There should be no more than one or two gear changes, if any. Cruise the rest of the ride at below 200 watts (80 percent). You are working on your ability to change speeds quickly and accelerate quickly.
CD: 15 minutes.
Wednesday: Level 2, Medium Endurance Ride
WU: 15 minutes, spinning at an easy pace, watts below 120.
MS: 45 minutes, watts 190–225, nice and steady. If you have to go over hills and your watts go higher, that's okay, but generally average between 190–225 watts today.
CD: 15 minutes, easy pedaling.
Thursday: Level 4, Lactate Threshold
WU: 15 minutes.
MS: Ten fast pedaling efforts of 1 minute each, with cadence over 100 rpm. Stay seated for these. Rest for 1 minute between each effort. Follow this up with 10 minutes of pedaling with watts at 200–225, then do two 10-minute efforts with watts at 250–260. Rest for 5 minutes between the efforts. These efforts are done right at your threshold and can be done on a 10-minute hill if you want.
CD: 15 minutes, easy spinning.
Friday: Repeat Ride.
Repeat Monday ride, above, except go for only 1 hour.
Saturday: Level 3, Tempo
WU: 15–20 minutes.
MS: 2–2.5 hours with watts in 180–225 range. Keep cadence at about 90–95 rpm. Try not to spend much time over 225 watts, but if you have to increase power to go over a hill, that's fine. The goal today is to extend your mileage and build your "engine." You need to improve aerobic capacity, and getting in some solid Endurance/Tempo miles will do that.
CD: 10–15 minutes, easy riding. Stretch out after the ride.
Sunday: Level 2, Endurance
WU: 15–20 minutes under 140 watts.
MS: 1–1.5 hours of easy riding. Today is more endurance work, a touch slower than yesterday. Your average watts for the ride should be in the 160–180 range. Keep cadence at 85–95 rpm.
CD: 10–15 minutes, easy spinning.

Week 2

Monday: Rest Day
Just relax and give your legs, heart, and lungs a break today.

Tuesday: Level 3/4, Sub–Lactate Threshold

WU: 15 minutes with watts at 130–150.

MS: Start out with a "blow-out" effort to "get out the carbon." Do one 5-minute effort with watts at 250–260, pushing hard, then easy spinning with watts at 150–160 for 5 minutes. Follow this up with two 10-minute efforts at 240–250 watts. Try to stay right at threshold. It's a tough pacing job, but you'll get better the more you practice. Rest for 10 minutes of easy pedaling, with watts below 140, between the efforts. Try to keep your cadence at 90–100 rpm. Remember: You'll want to start out too fast on these efforts. Don't do it! Use the first minute to build up to speed. At the end of the first minute, you should be right at 250 watts. This workout will help you to start increasing your aerobic engine.

CD: 15 minutes.

Wednesday: Repeat Ride

Repeat Tuesday workout from Week 1.

Thursday: Repeat Ride

Repeat Monday workout from Week 1.

Friday: Level 3, Tempo

WU: 15 minutes at 90–100 rpm, with watts below 150, or at the bottom of Level 2 (Endurance).

MS: Start out with one 5-minute effort at 240–250 watts, right at threshold power, and then up the intensity in the last 30 seconds to 270 watts. Recover for 5 minutes of easy pedaling, with watts under 150. Then, every 5 minutes for the next 60 minutes, do an effort in the 53:13 gear for 20 seconds. Try to hold 400–500 watts and push this big gear. Stay seated for the entire effort; try to jump hard into it and try to get it going as fast as you can in 20 seconds. This effort is aimed at developing leg strength and force; your cadence will be low in the beginning and get faster with each second, so focus on pushing hard on the pedals and being as smooth as possible. Between each effort, ride for 5 minutes of easy pedaling with your cadence in the 90–100 rpm range, using an easy gear. Your wattage should be around 150–200.

CD: 10–20 minutes, small-ring spinning, cadence 95–100 rpm but watts below 140.

Saturday: Repeat Ride

Repeat Saturday workout from Week 1, but increase the time to 3 hours.

Sunday: Repeat Ride

Repeat Sunday workout from Week 1, but increase the time to 2 hours.

Week 3

Monday: Rest Day

Take a break—you deserve it! Rest days are key because they allow the body to recover and adapt from the stress of the workouts. Listen to your body, and if you need more than one rest day, then take it.

Tuesday:	Repeat Ride
	Repeat Monday workout from Week 1, but for only 1 hour.
Wednesday:	Repeat Ride
	Repeat Tuesday workout from Week 2.
Thursday:	Level 3, Tempo (with Some Lactate Threshold Work)
WU:	15 minutes easy.
MS:	45 minutes with watts at 190–225. Use a steady, fast pace. It shouldn't be easy, but it shouldn't be your max sustainable pace, either. Then ride for 10 minutes with watts below 120. Next, do another 10 minutes, but keep your watts at threshold or just above this time. Reach for 250–260 watts for the whole 10 minutes and pedal at a cadence 5 rpm higher than your normal cadence. This is a great workout and fast paced. Keep your effort steady and smooth. If you are feeling up to it, try for another 10-minute effort.
CD:	15 minutes, easy spinning.
Friday:	Repeat Ride
	Repeat Monday workout from Week 1.
Saturday:	Level 2, Endurance
WU:	15 minutes with watts at 140–160 and cadence at 90–100 rpm.
MS:	2.5 hours of riding at a steady pace with watts at 150–210 (especially 160–190). This is a great endurance pace and will allow you to finish strong and also get some solid aerobic benefit. Within these 2.5 hours, do ten little bursts. A burst is an 8-second effort, out of the saddle, and at 80 percent of what you would do for a full sprint. The goal is to get your cadence high (over 105 rpm), create a hard, sharp effort in the muscles, and begin to improve your neuromuscular capacity. Do these bursts randomly throughout the ride.
CD:	10–15 minutes.
Sunday:	Level 2, Endurance
WU:	15 minutes.
MS:	2–2.25 hours. Just ride easy and don't push it. No watts over 215 today. Just "noodle" along and continue to build endurance. This is almost like a Level 1 (Active Recovery) day, but the ride is just a touch longer.
CD:	10–15 minutes, easy pedaling.

Week 4

This is a rest week. Allow your body to recover, rest, and adapt to the past three weeks of stress. The goal is to have your muscles, heart, and mind fresh at the beginning of next week so you can really do a great week of training. So, go easy this week. You need to be ready for next week! However, having a rest week does not mean that you never get on your bike that week. Rather, you can have some complete rest days but also do some easy rides, as explained below.

Monday:	Rest Day
	This is a complete rest day.
Tuesday:	Repeat Ride
	Repeat Monday workout from Week 1.

Wednesday:	Repeat Ride
	Repeat Monday workout from Week 1.
Thursday:	Repeat Ride
	Repeat Monday workout from Week 1.
Friday:	Rest Day
	Okay, you know the drill now. Let the legs unwind. Rest and take it easy.
Saturday:	Repeat Ride
	Repeat Saturday workout from Week 1, but go for only 2 hours.
Sunday:	Rest Day
	Catch up on stuff around the house, or just relax in front of the TV or a good book. Cleaning your bike is fine too.

Week 5

Monday:	Level 6, Anaerobic Capacity
WU:	15 minutes with watts at 140–160.
MS:	45 minutes. For the first 5 minutes, try to stay at 260–270 watts, then do 5 minutes at below 140 watts. If possible, set your power meter so you can see the average power in "interval" mode. This will allow you to also review each interval after it is completed, so that you can have a goal for the next one or know when to stop. Do six 2-minute intervals pedaling as hard as you can go, using your average watts as a "carrot" to push all the way to the end. The goal is to average more than 325 watts (130 percent of your threshold power). Stop when you can no longer reach 300 watts (118 percent) in your average. Recover for at least 3 minutes, more if needed. Just choose your normal cadence on these, whatever feels right to you.
CD:	15 minutes, easy riding with watts below 120.
Tuesday:	Level 4, Lactate Threshold
WU:	15 minutes, pedaling steadily, just getting the legs going.
MS:	Start out with five fast pedaling intervals of 1 minute each. Your cadence should be over 100 rpm, but your high watts should not be high. Work on your fast pedaling more than on achieving higher watts, resting for 1 minute between each effort. After this, ride for 10 minutes at an easy pace, then do two 15-minute efforts with your watts at 250–265. Rest for 5 minutes between each effort. These efforts are done right at and just a touch above your threshold in order to stimulate it to move higher.
CD:	10–15 minutes.
Wednesday:	Level 1, Active Recovery
WU:	15 minutes.
MS:	1–1.5 hours at an easy pace. Keep your watts below 150 if you can.
CD:	15 minutes.
Thursday:	Repeat Ride
	Repeat Tuesday workout from Week 1.
Friday:	Repeat Ride
	Repeat Wednesday workout from this week (Week 5).

Saturday: Level 2, Endurance

WU: 15 minutes.

MS: 3–3.5 hours. The goal today is to push it up another notch in your distance. Keep the watts at 150–210 for a majority of the ride, but in the second hour of riding, do two 15-minute efforts at your threshold power, 250–265 watts. Rest for 10 minutes between each effort with some easy pedaling below 120 watts. In the last hour, try for 40 minutes or so at a Level 3 (Tempo) pace, 190–225 watts. This is a breakthrough ride: Be sure to eat enough to provide the right level of energy and drink lots of water.

CD: 15 minutes.

Sunday: Repeat Ride

Repeat Sunday workout from Week 3.

Week 6

Monday: Rest Day

Take a break from your bike today.

Tuesday: Level 3, Tempo

WU: 15 minutes at a high cadence, 95–105 rpm.

MS: 45 minutes with watts from 190–235. Keep the pressure on and have fun; it's a fast pace, but it should be achievable. Keep your cadence in the 90–95 rpm range and make sure you get into a nice breathing rhythm. If you feel like it, you can do three 2-minute efforts with your watts at 300–375. Rest for 3 minutes between each. During the recovery period, keep your watts at 200. Work on smooth pedaling today. Pretend that when your foot is at the bottom of the pedal stroke, you have mud stuck on the bottom of your shoe and you are scraping it off. At the top of the pedal stroke, see if you can contract your quadriceps muscles and drive your knee forward toward the handlebar. Driving the knee forward, instead of just pushing down through the foot, will enhance your pedaling efficiency.

CD: 15 minutes, easy spinning, watts below 120.

Wednesday: Level 7, Neuromuscular Power

WU: 15 minutes.

MS: 1 hour. Get in six small-ring sprints to start—50 yards, no gear changes. Wind the gears out. You should be spinning at 120 rpm at the end of each sprint. Rest for 2–3 minutes between each effort. Then do three big-ring sprints with one gear change. Jump in the 53:17 from 20 mph and then wind out the gear and shift. Wind out that gear (110–120 rpm), and then you are done. Rest for 3–5 minutes between each big-ring sprint. Then complete three more big-ring sprints from 53:16 at 23 mph, with two gear changes, again winding out each gear. Finish with one big-ring sprint from 53:15 at 26–28 mph. Jump hard and sprint until you wind out that 53:13 gear. (This last one can be on a slight downhill grade to help you get up to speed.) One of the goals of this workout is to show that you do not need to "dump" the chain into the hardest gear for a sprint.

CD: 15 minutes, easy spinning.

Thursday: Level 5, VO$_2$max

WU: 15 minutes at Level 2 (Endurance) pace, with watts from 150–190, pedaling smoothly at a self-selected cadence.

MS: 1.5 hours. Complete six mock time trials. Each is 6 minutes long, but at only 96–102 percent of your TT pace. This should be around 240–255 watts. Start out strong, but not too fast—you need to pace yourself in these efforts—and then hold like glue to your wattage goal of 240–255. These will help you to learn pacing better, get in some solid work at threshold power, and give you enough time while at threshold power to get into a powerful rhythm. These intervals are about going fast, but not hammering at max pace. Rest for at least 6–8 minutes between each interval with your watts below 120.

CD: 15 minutes, easy pedaling, watts below 150.

Friday: Rest Day

Just stretch and relax today. Eat smart, and make sure you get enough complex carbs.

Saturday: Levels 2 and 3, Endurance and Tempo

WU: 15 minutes.

MS: 3.5 hours. Make this a hilly ride today. If you have lots of rolling hills, then do everything you can to get in plenty of them. If you have some longer climbs (20 minutes or greater), then get at least one climb in. Include at least 30 minutes of work at your threshold wattage, 250–260. This work can be done all on one climb, or it can be done in three blocks of 10 minutes each or even ten blocks of 3 minutes each (if you have lots of shorter hills). If you don't have any hills, try to simulate hills by riding into the wind. For most of this ride, keep your watts at 160–235.

CD: 15 minutes, easy pedaling. Don't forget to stretch out at the end of the ride.

Sunday: Levels 1 and 2, Active Recovery and Endurance

WU: 15 minutes.

MS: 1.75 hours, keeping it steady and smooth. Make sure to keep your watts in the 135–170 range. Do ten little 8-second bursts, however, throughout your ride.

CD: 15 minutes.

Week 7

Monday: Rest Day

Take the day off the bike, but include some stretching.

Tuesday: Level 4, Lactate Threshold

WU: 15 minutes.

MS: Start out with five fast pedaling intervals of 1 minute each. Keep your cadence over 100 rpm, but do not aim for high watts. Rest for 1 minute between each interval. After the fifth interval, do an easy 10 minutes of riding, then two 15-minute efforts with your watts at 250–260. Rest for 5 minutes between the two intervals. These efforts are done right at or just a touch above your threshold in order to stimulate that threshold to move higher. If you are feeling good after the second effort and you have time, then see if you can complete a third one. Compare the three different intervals when you get home and download your power meter data. What was the percentage of drop-off in the wattage from interval 1 to interval 2? From interval 1 to interval 3? The answers will indicate whether you are overtrained or ready for more work.

CD: 10–15 minutes.

Wednesday: Repeat Ride
Repeat Thursday workout from Week 3.

Thursday: Repeat Ride
Repeat Monday workout from Week 1, but only for 1 hour.

Friday: Repeat Ride
Repeat Tuesday workout from Week 1.

Saturday: Level 2, Endurance

WU: 15 minutes.

MS: 3.5 hours. Today, just ride and have fun. Complete the work, and make sure to stay hydrated and strong throughout. Keep your watts under 225 in the first hour, and then try to stay within 160–200 for the next 2 hours. In the last hour, go back to 225–235 watts and keep a nice strong pace.

CD: 15 minutes.

Sunday: Repeat Ride
Repeat Sunday workout from Week 6, but extend it to 2.5 hours.

Week 8

This is a rest week.

Monday: Rest Day
Take the day off the bike. This is the second rest week in this 16-week plan. Again, it is very important that you take it easy this week. The goal is to have your muscles, heart, and mind fresh at the beginning of the next week so you can do a great week of training. Go easy this week to prepare yourself for a higher level of work. Your threshold will increase this week as a result of the rest.

Tuesday: Repeat Ride
Repeat Monday workout from Week 1, but for only 1 hour.

Wednesday: Rest Day
Take the day off the bike. Stretch for at least 30–40 minutes and relax. Eat smart, and don't overdo the portions this week. You'll be hungry, as if you are training hard, but since you are resting you'll want to watch your food intake.

Thursday: Repeat Ride
Repeat Monday workout from Week 1, but for only 1 hour.

Friday: Rest Day
Take the day off the bike for another complete rest day.

Saturday: Repeat Ride
Repeat Saturday workout from Week 1.
Sunday: Rest Day
Take the day off from riding.

Week 9

Monday: Testing Protocol
WU: 20 minutes.
MS: Do three fast pedaling efforts at 100 rpm for 1 minute each, with 1 minute between each effort, then ride for 3 minutes at an easy pace. Next, do one 5-minute all-out effort. Punch it and hold it! After this, ride at an easy pace for 10 minutes, then do two 1-minute efforts with 5 minutes between them. Follow this up with 5 minutes easy, then do three 20-second super jumps. Jump as hard as you can and sprint for 20 seconds, giving it all you've got. You'll only be taking the data for the first 15 seconds of each sprint, but do the full 20 seconds of effort and make sure you push it all the way through. Rest for 3 minutes between each sprint, and after the final sprint pedal easy for 10 minutes. Finally, complete a 20-minute time trial.
CD: 15 minutes.
Tuesday: Level 6, Anaerobic Capacity
WU: 15 minutes.
MS: 1.5 hours. Set your power meter so you can see the average power in interval mode, then do eight 2-minute efforts as hard as you can go, using your average watts as a "carrot" to push all the way to the end. The goal is to average over 130 percent (325 watts) of your threshold power. Stop when you can no longer reach 118 percent (295 watts) in your average. Recover for at least 2 minutes, more if needed, and finish with three 1-minute efforts, trying to average over 140 percent (350 watts). Do all three efforts unless you can no longer reach 120 percent (300 watts).
CD: 15 minutes.
Wednesday: Levels 2 and 3, Endurance and Tempo
WU: 15 minutes at Level 2 wattage, 90–100 rpm.
MS: Do one 5-minute effort at Level 4 (Lactate Threshold) wattage, pushing to Level 5 (VO$_2$max) wattage in the last 30 seconds. Recover for 5 minutes with easy pedaling. Then, every 5 minutes for the next 60 minutes, do a 53:13 effort for 20 seconds. Push this big gear, staying seated for the entire effort; try to jump hard into it and to get it going as fast as you can in 20 seconds. Don't worry about wattage goals for this. The effort is more about developing leg strength and force. Your cadence will be low in the beginning, but it will be getting faster with each second. Between each effort, ride for 5 minutes easy, with your cadence in the 90–100 rpm range, using an easy gear.
CD: 10–20 minutes, small-ring spinning, cadence 95–100 rpm, watts in Level 2.

Thursday: Levels 1 and 2, Active Recovery and Endurance
Do a very easy ride—nothing harder than 68 percent of FTP.
Friday: Race Tune-Up
WU: 15 minutes.
MS: 1.5 hours. Include three 1-minute hard efforts, with at least 5 minutes of easy riding between each one. Also do three 30-second hard sprints, with 5 minutes between each. The rest of the ride is just easy and cruising.
CD: 15 minutes.
Saturday: Levels 2 and 3, Endurance and Lactate Threshold
You might schedule a race for today. However, if you are not racing, do the following workout.
WU: 15 minutes.
MS: 5 hours. Most of this ride is just getting in the miles and having fun. But also include two 30-minute efforts, both done at threshold, and at least ten solid hill jams (hills can be 30 seconds to 2 minutes) with watts at 300 or greater. If you don't have any long climbs, use the wind for resistance.
CD: 15 minutes.
Sunday: Level 3, Tempo
If you are not racing today, do the following workout.
WU: 15 minutes, solid and steady.
MS: 2 hours of good riding, keeping it steady and smooth. Be sure to keep your watts in the 180–220 range today and just get in a nice tempo ride. Do ten little 8-second bursts throughout the ride, bringing your cadence to 120 rpm in each effort.
CD: 15 minutes.

Week 10

Monday: Rest Day
Relax and rest after a great weekend.
Tuesday: Level 1, Active Recovery
Go for an easy ride, 1.0 hour.
Wednesday: Level 7, Neuromuscular Power
WU: 15 minutes.
MS: 1 hour. Get in six small-ring sprints to start (50 yards, no gear changes). Wind the gears out. You should be spinning at 120 rpm at the finish of each sprint. Rest for 2–3 minutes between each effort. Then do three big–ring sprints (one gear change). Jump in the 53:17 from 20 mph, and then wind out the gear and shift. Wind out that gear (110–120 rpm), and then you are done. Rest for 3–5 minutes between each big-ring sprint. Next, do three more big-ring sprints from 53:16 at 23 mph (two gear changes, again winding out each gear). Finish with one big-ring sprint from 53:15; jump hard and sprint until you wind out that gear. This last one can be done on a slight downhill grade to help you get up to speed. This workout will again demonstrate that you do not need to "dump" the chain into the hardest gear for a sprint.

CD:	15 minutes.
Thursday:	Level 6, Anaerobic Capacity
WU:	20 minutes.
MS:	1.5–2 hours. Do three 2-minute efforts, striving for 135 percent of your threshold, with 1 minute of rest between each effort, then pedal for 5 minutes at an easy pace. Next, do three 1-minute efforts, striving for 150 percent, with 1 minute of rest, then 5 minutes easy. Finish with three 30-second efforts, going all-out, with 1 minute of rest between each effort. For this final set of sprints, try to reach at least 200 percent of your threshold watts as an average. Shoot for 350 percent of threshold watts as your maximum wattage in the last six sprints.
CD:	15 minutes.
Friday:	Level 1, Active Recovery
	Go for an easy Level 1 ride.
Saturday:	Levels 2 and 3, Endurance and Tempo
	Today there are two options. Option 1 is to participate in a race. If you do this, have fun and race smart! Option 2 is to do a Level 2/3 ride with some Level 4 work—on mountain climbs if possible—as described below.
WU:	15 minutes.
MS:	4 hours. Try for a solid ride in the mountains (if you have them). Be sure to maintain your cadence on those steeper sections. The goal is to get in the time, to do at least three major climbs, and to ride at your threshold over two of them. The other climb should be done at a steady Tempo pace. Watch cadence and power, and maximize your efficiency. Also, do six fast pedaling efforts on the downhills for 3 minutes each. That means keeping your cadence above 120 and using brakes if necessary to keep pressure on the pedals. If the descent is long enough, do two of these efforts on the descent of each climb. If not, then do one on each descent and then one on some flatter sections. In the third hour, work on doing eight efforts of 2 minutes each, with your watts at 300–350. These efforts should be done on flat to rolling terrain; give it whatever you have left. Be sure to stop at a store with 20 miles to go and get a soda for a sugar and caffeine boost, and have a recovery shake as soon as you get back to the car.
CD:	15 minutes.
Sunday:	Level 2, Endurance
	Again, there are two options: Race, or do the workout described below.
WU:	15 minutes.
MS:	3–4 hours. Just focus on maintaining a Level 2 (Endurance) pace and getting in the time. No intervals: Just ride and enjoy the bike.
CD:	15 minutes.

Week 11

Monday: Rest Day

Tuesday: Levels 2 and 3, Endurance and Tempo

WU: 20 minutes.

MS: 1.5 hours. First, on a flat road do six big-ring power efforts. Do each effort just until you reach 80 rpm. Start out in 53:14 at 12 mph. Stay seated for the entire effort, and for all six efforts. Take off seated, get on that gear, bring your rpm up to 80, and then the effort is done. Recover with 3 minutes of easy spinning between each effort. Then do 15 minutes of normal spinning with your watts at 100 or less. Next, ride to a 2-minute hill and, in 53:19 or 17, and standing on the bike, go for 2 minutes, taking off at the bottom of the hill and muscling that gear over all the way to the top. Do six to eight repeats. Your cadence should be 50–60 rpm, but go careful on the knees. Rest for 3 minutes after each 2-minute effort. Your watts should be in the 250–300 range for all of these.

CD: 15 minutes, easy spinning.

Wednesday: Level 5, VO_2max

WU: 15 minutes.

MS: 1.5 hours. Do four 1-minute fast pedaling intervals with your cadence over 100 rpm. Don't worry too much about your wattage; focus more on your cadence and pedaling smoothly. Then ride for 5 minutes at an easy pace. Next, do six 2-minute time trials with your cadence 5 rpm below your normal cadence, trying to build a little more muscle strength. Start from 23–25 mph and then hammer it for 2 minutes. Shoot for 135 percent (338 watts) of your threshold power. Blow right at the end. Rest for 2 minutes between each interval. Then ride at an easy pace for 10 minutes and finish with one 6-minute time trial. Really go, pushing it at your normal self-selected cadence.

CD: 15 minutes.

Thursday: Level 1, Active Recovery

Go for an easy Level 1 ride today.

Friday: Repeat Ride

Repeat tune up from Week 9, Friday workout.

Saturday: Levels 2, 3, and 4: Endurance, Tempo, and Lactate Threshold

There are two options: Race, or go for this ride:

WU: 15 minutes.

MS: 5 hours. Try to go over two mountain passes, or do two 30-minute efforts, both at threshold power. Also get in at least ten solid hill jams (the hills can take from 30 seconds to 2 minutes to complete), with your watts reaching at least 300. For the rest of ride, just get in the miles and have fun. (This ride can be done into the wind if you don't have any long climbs in your area.)

CD: 15 minutes.

Sunday: Repeat Ride

There are two options today: Race, or repeat the Sunday workout from Week 9.

Week 12

This is a rest week. Follow the plan below.

Monday: Rest Day

Take the day off the bike.

Tuesday: Level 1, Active Recovery

Go for an easy ride for about 1.25 hours.

Wednesday: Repeat Ride

Again, go for an easy 1.25-hour ride, as you did yesterday.

Thursday: Repeat Ride

Do the same type of easy 1.25-hour ride as you did on Tuesday and Wednesday.

Friday: Rest Day

Take the day off the bike.

Saturday: Level 2, Endurance

WU: 15 minutes, just getting the legs moving.

MS: The goal today is to extend your mileage a bit and build your "engine." Getting in some solid Endurance/Tempo miles will help to improve your aerobic capacity. Ride for about 1.5 hours with your watts in the 190–225 range. Try not to spend much time over 225 watts, but if you have to go over on a hill or something, that's fine. Keep your cadence in the 90–95 rpm range.

CD: 10–15 minutes of easy riding Stretch out after the ride.

Sunday: Rest Day

No riding today.

Week 13

Monday: Level 6, Anaerobic Capacity

WU: 15 minutes.

MS: 1.5 hours. This is a hill repeat day. Find a 2–3 minute hill to simulate that hill in the upcoming races. Try to hold 120 percent of your threshold power, or around 300 watts, for the entire hill. Get 20 miles in your legs before you do the repeats, however. Do ten repeats, hammering it all the way, and explode at the top. Rest between each one hill repeat. Make these hurt!

CD: 15 minutes.

Tuesday: Level 7, Neuromuscular Power

WU: 15–20 minutes.

MS: 1.5–2 hours. Set your pace at lower Level 3, approximately 190–220 watts (76–90 percent of FTP), and hold this pace for the next hour. Within this hour, do a 10-second, out-of-the-saddle burst every 3 minutes, trying to reach 450 watts (180 percent of FTP), and hold it there for the full 10 seconds. Make sure your cadence stays high— over 100 rpm. You should have no more than one or two gear changes, if any. Return to your previous pace after each burst. Cruise for the rest of the ride at below 140 watts (80 percent).

CD: 10 minutes, watts below 120.

Wednesday: Level 4, Lactate Threshold

WU: 15 minutes.

MS: 1.75 hours. Do one 10-minute time trial effort at 310–340 watts, then ride for 10 minutes at an easy pace. Next, do one 20-minute time trial at 250–260 watts, with ten bursts within the TT. This TT can be done either on the flats or on a slight climb. For the bursts, get your watts to 350 (135 percent of threshold) for 20 seconds, then recover to 250–260 watts (not less). Then ride for 15 minutes at an easy pace, and finish with a short but very steep hill. Do four repeats on this hill with your cadence in the 55–65 range, HR maxed. Rest for 2 minutes between each effort. Each hill should take about 30–50 seconds to climb. Go hard, but select a gear that will make you push.

CD: 10–15 minutes, easy riding.

Thursday: Levels 1 and 2, Active Recovery and Endurance

Go for an easy 1.5-hour ride.

Friday: Repeat Ride

Repeat Friday workout from Week 1.

Saturday: Level 4, Lactate Threshold

This ride is a good race rehearsal for a 20 km time trial.

WU: 1 hour. This is a long warm-up that is great for getting ready for time trials. Start with 15 minutes at Level 2 (Endurance). Then begin a 10-minute "ramp" where you gradually take your wattage from Level 2 to Level 4. You should be flat out at your time trial pace in that last minute. Then ride at an easy pace for 5 minutes. Next, do four 1-minute fast pedaling efforts. For each effort, keep your cadence over 100 rpm. Don't worry about wattage but focus on fast, smooth pedaling and getting the muscles to "open up" and the blood pumping. Rest for 1 minute of easy pedaling between each effort. Then ride for 5 minutes at Level 2. Follow this up with one 5-minute effort at Level 5 (VO_2max) watts. Pedal at an easy pace for 5–10 minutes, and then start your time trial.

MS: 1.5 hours. Do a 20 km time trial, starting your timer from about 3 mph. Don't start too hard: Use the first 4–5 minutes to build up your heart rate and get right at your threshold wattage. Get up to speed, but once there, throttle back to your threshold power. It's key to your pacing that you hold back in the first 4–5 minutes of the TT. Your perceived exertion will be low, so you will want to just hammer as hard as you can, but at 5 minutes everything will catch up with you and it will hurt if you start out too fast. If you start too hard, then you'll finish slow. On the way into the turnaround, get a sip of water, and then get back up to speed, making sure you apply power all the way through the turnaround. Get right back into your rhythm and keep focused on the way home. Feel all of your muscles contributing to the forward movement of the bike. In the last 5 kilometers, start bringing up the pace and pushing a little harder. In the last kilometer, take it to the max and push to the finish.

CD: 30 minutes, easy riding with a solid stretching session.
Sunday: Levels 3 and 6, Tempo and Anaerobic Capacity
WU: 15 minutes.
MS: 3 hours. Start out at a nice endurance pace for 60 minutes . Pedal at a smooth and steady pace. In the second hour, pick up the intensity to 200–240 watts. Then do 15 bursts within this hour, reaching 350 watts for 30 seconds each, and then come back to 220–240 watts (not lower). Finish the last hour by attacking eight hills and sprinting over the top. Don't just make the crest the top: The real top is 15 meters over the crest.
CD: 20 minutes.

Week 14

Monday: Rest Day
Take the day off.
Tuesday: Level 4, Lactate Threshold
WU: 15 minutes.
MS: Do two 20-minute efforts with your watts below threshold, right around 230–245 watts, with 10 minutes of rest between the efforts. Also do twenty little bursts for 10 seconds each that reach 350 watts. You should be out of the saddle with your cadence at about 110, and there should be only one gear shift, if any. Rest for about a minute between each effort. Finish with three 5-minute all-out efforts, setting a goal to hold 280–300 watts for the entire effort, with 5 minutes of rest between each effort.
CD: 15 minutes.
Wednesday: Level 6, Anaerobic Capacity
WU: 15 minutes.
MS: 1.5 hours: Do six two-minute efforts, striving for 135 percent of FTP, with a 1-minute rest between each, then ride for 5 minutes at an easy pace. Next, do six 1-minute efforts, striving for 150 percent of FTP, with 1 minute of rest between each, followed by 5 minutes at an easy pace, and finish with six 30-second, all-out efforts, with 1 minute of rest between each. Try for at least 200 percent of your threshold watts on each sprint as an average. Shoot for 350 percent of threshold watts as your max in the last six sprints.
CD: 15 minutes, easy spinning.
Thursday: Levels 1 and 2, Active Recovery and Endurance
Go for an easy 1.25-hour ride.
Friday: Repeat Ride
Repeat Friday workout from Week 1. Or if racing the next day, repeat Friday workout from Week 9.
Saturday: Levels 2, 3, and 5: Endurance, Tempo, and VO_2max
If you are not racing today, you can do the following workout.
WU: 15 minutes.
MS: 4 hours. Start with 1 hour at Level 2 (Endurance), then in the

second hour, try for two 20-minute efforts at threshold (250–260 watts). In the third hour, add in six 3-minute efforts at Level 5 (VO$_2$max, 270–285), resting for 3–5 minutes between each effort. Generally ride in the Endurance/Tempo pace and have fun.

CD: 10 minutes.

Sunday: Repeat Ride
Today there is an option. Option 1 is to race. If you do, go for it: Set a goal to make three attacks off the front. For Option 2, repeat the Sunday workout from Week 13.

Week 15

This week you will repeat workouts from previous weeks.

Monday: Rest Day
Take the day off from the bike and relax.

Tuesday: Repeat Ride
Repeat Wednesday workout from Week 13.

Wednesday: Repeat Ride
Repeat Monday workout from Week 13.

Thursday: Level 1, Active Recovery
Go for an easy ride for 1.25 hours.

Friday: Repeat Ride
Repeat Friday workout from Week 1.

Saturday: Race
You should definitely be ready to race now. Go for it, and try at least three attacks off the front.

Sunday: Race
Go for it! You will be flying this weekend!

Week 16

This is a rest week. Follow this plan for a good recovery.

Monday: Rest Day
Take the day off from your bike completely.

Tuesday: Levels 1 and 2, Active Recovery and Endurance
Go for an easy 1.25-hour ride.

Wednesday: Repeat Ride
Repeat yesterday's ride.

Thursday: Repeat Ride
Repeat Tuesday's again.

Friday: Repeat Ride
Repeat Friday workout from Week 1.

Saturday: Race
This is your weekend! Go for it!

Sunday: Race
Make this day a great one! The work is done and you are stronger than ever.

INDEX

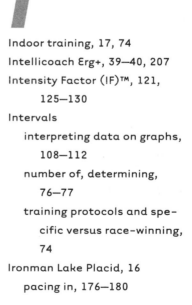